A LIFE UNIMAGINED

A LIFE UNIMAGINED

*The Rewards of Mission-Driven Service
in the Peace Corps and Beyond*

Aaron S. Williams
with Deb Childs

UNIVERSITY OF WISCONSIN–MADISON,
INTERNATIONAL DIVISION

The University of Wisconsin–Madison, International Division
261 Bascom Hall
500 Lincoln Drive
Madison, Wisconsin 53706

Copyright © 2021 by Aaron S. Williams

Printed in the United States of America
This book may be available in a digital edition.

ISBN 978-1-7374046-0-6 (cloth)

To the women who inspired me—

my mother, Blanche Theresa Green-Williams,
my greatest and most ardent champion,

my maternal grandmother, Edna Mae,
who loved, fed, and encouraged me,

my sister, Hilda Theresa Jones, who I love and admire
and who is the living spirit of our dear mother,

and my wife, Rosa Mustafa Williams,
my love and partner in our journey.

≈

For my brother, Philip, and our sons, Michael and Steven,
who have made all of this worthwhile,

and our grandsons Gabriel, Joseph, Ronin, Lucas, and Eliot,
who give us great hope for the future.

Twenty years from now, you will be more disappointed
by the things that you didn't do than by the ones you did do.
Sail away from the safe harbor. Catch the trade winds
in your sails. Explore. Dream. Discover.

—RALPH WALDO EMERSON

Contents

Foreword

I first met Aaron Williams at the US Agency for International Development (USAID) in 1992, when he was serving as the agency's executive secretary, managing the front office for the head of USAID, Brian Atwood. I arrived at USAID on an interagency loan from the Centers for Disease Control and Prevention (CDC) to head the fledgling AIDS programs. I was coming from an organization that had been my professional home for almost a decade to join a large, complex bureaucracy and lead a high-visibility program as an organizational newcomer.

Aaron must have intuited my feelings, for he laid out the welcome mat soon after my arrival. We became trusted colleagues and good friends, and our friendship continued over the decades as our paths continued to cross throughout our careers. I recruited him to serve on my board when I was the CEO of CARE, the legendary global humanitarian and development organization. Little did I know that my career path would lead me to my current role in Chicago—the very city that contributed to Aaron's foundation and early beginnings.

Throughout his multifaceted career in government service, global business, and the nonprofit world, Aaron's dedication reflected a life and career well lived in pursuit of improving the human condition. His family life—raising two outstanding sons, Michael and Steven, with his wife, Rosa, during their fifty years of marriage and Foreign Service life—approach to his work, and his interactions with those around him all embody his high level of personal integrity and concern for the well-being of others.

Readers will experience his remarkable journey from growing up in a working-class family on the South Side of Chicago to leading an iconic

American organization, the United States Peace Corps, under President
Obama.

Both hands-on experience and policy work in Latin America, the Caribbean, Africa, Asia, and the Middle East characterized Aaron's US Foreign
Service career. As the head of USAID in South Africa, he played a key role
in supporting Nelson Mandela's government by directing the US government's assistance in the country's historic democratic transformation. Further, Aaron was one of USAID's pioneers in creating the first successful
public-private partnership that contributed to the economic growth of the
Caribbean and Central American nations.

As one of the very few African Americans who attained high-ranking
positions within USAID, he successfully forged a path through the often-
elitist corps of the US foreign policy establishment and rose to the top,
achieving the rank of career minister. Aaron's story illustrates the promise
of America and what can be realized through hard work, determination,
and courage. He has been a role model and a mentor wherever he has
served, and he continues to contribute to the professional growth of the
current generation of international development professionals.

As an international development professional, diplomat, corporate executive, and leader of the Peace Corps, he has been a worthy role model for
young professionals who seek to serve our country. His life story gives us a
window into the complex world of international development and American foreign policy that he experienced on the front lines.

I hope that the life and career of Aaron Williams, as portrayed in this
book, will inspire future generations of underrepresented groups in our
society, both men and women, who seek to make a difference by serving
America and the world at large.

Helene Gayle, MD,
president and CEO, Chicago Community Trust

Preface

A Global Perspective for Twenty-First Century Leadership

The best way to find yourself is to lose yourself in the service of others.

—MAHATMA GANDHI

In May 2017, I had the distinct honor to be the commencement speaker at the University of North Carolina's Gillings School of Global Public Health. As I sat on the stage in Carmichael Arena, my thoughts flashed back across my multisector career, including my time as the director of the US Peace Corps. Writing my remarks required an introspective glance in the rearview mirror of my long career in international development, both as a Foreign Service Officer and a global executive. I had traveled a long way from my working-class neighborhood on the South Side of Chicago, the first in my family to graduate from college. The advantage of a back-glancing view helped me put into perspective how my journey could be of benefit to rising leaders in global public health—Gillings' graduates. It was a day I would remember going forward, and I hope the graduates did as well.

That same month I had retired as an executive vice president from Research Triangle Institute, or RTI International, where I had held three different senior-level positions for over ten years. In the future, I would maintain my ties with RTI in retirement as a senior adviser emeritus. However, although I love the freedom to travel as I please that retirement has made possible, I have come to realize that retiring is not in my DNA. I had enjoyed a highly rewarding career at RTI, an independent nonprofit organization committed to providing research, development, and technical services to government and commercial clients worldwide.

I have always viewed the RTI mission statement—"improving the human condition by turning knowledge into practice"—as succinctly stating a valuable lesson for leadership and life. Learning for the sake of acquiring knowledge is noble, but knowledge alone serves no purpose unless put to good use in practice. RTI, its staff, and the Gillings School of Global Public Health have shared missions and a long history of partnership. Many UNC graduates have taken a path similar to mine by serving as Peace Corps volunteers. The success of each organization requires *looking outward and upward to empower others*, an essential trait of twenty-first-century leadership.

The first director of the Peace Corps appointed by President Kennedy, Sargent Shriver, once said, "Today, no nation belongs solely to its citizens, or its ideology, or to its art, science, or its vision for the future; in the new world, recognition of our common existence is the precondition of a secure existence." His words are just as relevant and in need of recognition today as they have been at any point in history. Shriver further noted the importance of "creat[ing] leaders who champion international understanding and respect, with the ability to communicate, empathize, and see the world from diverse perspectives, which are indispensable for building shared progress."

As I take on the arduous task of writing about my life in book form, I aspire to impress on all who may benefit from reading it the value of making decisions with a global perspective in mind, especially our young, up-and-coming leaders. From the vantage point of the rearview mirror of my life, I believe it's not only a necessary but rewarding and worthwhile endeavor. That's what I did early on in my career when I set aside the safe, conventional career choice and instead chose to take an adventuresome leap into the unknown.

Many questioned my sanity or judgment at that time as a young man. To them, I might now ask, "Would I have otherwise met the legendary Nelson Mandela without a reason to be in South Africa or found myself as director of the Peace Corps working for President Obama?" I can state with certainty that the opportunity to walk in the shadow of such leadership giants would not have presented itself to me had I not taken that leap.

My decision to join the Peace Corps was clearly the turning point in my life. I met the love of my life, Rosa, and we had the great fortune to live a blessed life and raise our sons, Michael and Steven, in a world of exploration and rich experiences. I was able to launch a highly rewarding career that encompassed business, government, and nonprofit sectors, and I gained incredible lifelong friendships and reaped the benefit of invaluable experiences I would never have been able to imagine had I taken the easy, obvious path before me and played safe with my life.

I sincerely hope that my story will also provide useful insights for young people of color who may be considering the pursuit of a career in international development and more broadly in the Foreign Service. We need to be sure that the face of America around the world reflects the diversity and strength of our country, and I hope that this book will contribute to this important cause.

A LIFE UNIMAGINED

1

Life on the South Side of Chicago

My Family and the Early Years

I have a dream that . . . children will one day live in a nation where they will not be judged by the color of their skin but by the content of their character.

—MARTIN LUTHER KING JR.

Segregated housing was the reality for all black families in Chicago in the 1950s and 1960s. Doctors, lawyers, blue-collar workers, service workers, and government employees all faced the same limitations in our neighborhoods across the South Side and West Side of Chicago, where most black people lived in those years in that city. As I recall, there were only one or two suburbs where black families could find adequate housing.

I grew up in an average working-class neighborhood on the South Side. Interestingly, our community was similar to those where other leaders-to-be grew up during that era, such as Deval Patrick, future governor of Massachusetts, and First Lady Michelle Obama. But who could have imagined these possibilities during that point in our ordinary lives? Whether you were rich or poor, if you were black, your housing choices were restricted, and there was little hope for change on that horizon.

Even Martin Luther King Jr. couldn't crack Chicago. He conceded that the city was one of his biggest failures. He characterized the resistance to his efforts for open housing, economic equity, and quality education for blacks to be more hostile and hate-filled than anything he ever encountered in the Deep South, including Mississippi and Alabama.[1]

A famous dermatologist lived in a marble mansion next to our building. Our three-story brownstone housed six families at 4325 South Parkway (now Martin Luther King Drive). A liquor store was on a nearby corner. Housing and commercial businesses often coexisted in the black community. Still, a strong middle-class sense of community prevailed; everyone looked after each other, and parents sought a good education for their children. Some of the first black police and fire department senior officers in Chicago lived on the South Side, and it was always a source of pride for members of our community that folks just like us could rise to such exalted jobs.

However, the individual circumstances of each family unit would often determine their living situation. Our family lived in a two-bedroom apartment, but I never saw us as poor, and I never went without. I grew up feeling happy and loved. Food was plentiful, and my mother came from a line of terrific cooks. My maternal grandmother, Edna Mae (Terrell) Wills, a fantastic cook from Baton Rouge, Louisiana, passed her skills down to her daughters, but my mother ranked as the top chef in the family to me.

My mother, Blanche Wills, married my father, Spencer Williams, when she was twenty, and one year later, in 1947, I was born. Three more children followed: my two sisters, Ellen (1949) and Hilda (1955), and a brother, Philip (1958). The saddest moment of my young life came with the loss of my sister, Ellen, at six years old, when I was eight. Her illness began with strep throat—a common condition in children. But it advanced to rheumatic fever—also common in the 1950s. At that time there was no cure for it. Children could not visit hospitals during that era, so the last time I saw my sister, she was looking out of a small window on the eighth floor of the Cook County Hospital. I could barely make her out from the street where I stood staring up at the building.

A week later, I came home from school one day to find all of my extended family gathered together; it felt like a hundred people or more, lined up and down the long hall that led to the back of my grandmother's brownstone apartment. I remember the sinking feeling I had walking down that hall past my relatives, most of them crying. A sense of dread came over me, and I was afraid of what I would find at the end of that long walk. There, my mother, grandmother, and other relatives told me through tears that my sister had died.

That same month, my sister Hilda was born—an absolute twin to my sister Ellen. The joy and responsibilities associated with her birth probably saved us all from what would have surely been lasting and debilitating grief. Since that time, I have never taken my loved ones and dear friends for granted.

> Losing my sister during my early childhood taught me the bitter lesson that life can come to a sudden end. I consider every day and every person I love as blessings for which I am grateful.

Being older than my sister by eight years and older than my brother by eleven years resulted in a somewhat solitary life for me. I was surrounded by adults, and with the help of my mother, I found ways to stay occupied and off the streets. I spent a lot of time at the Boys Club (now the Boys & Girls Club) in my neighborhood and with the Boy Scouts at a nearby church. Under the auspices of those organizations, I made a few friends, learned to play chess, became a pinsetter in the church bowling alley, and took part in scouting activities. I also visited Chicago's great museums, went to an occasional White Sox game, played a lot of softball and baseball, and spent a fair amount of time reading. At this point in my life, I could never have imagined that some fifty years later, in 2011, I would be honored as an inductee into the Boys & Girls Club Alumni Hall of Fame, whose membership includes Denzel Washington, Jennifer Lopez, and General Wesley Clark, among others.

Though the struggles encountered by many of my black colleagues and heroes from Chicago seem far greater than mine, nothing about my early life—*absolutely nothing*—could have predicted my future career. My hard-working parents were admirable role models who offered my siblings and me a stable home environment in which to grow up and succeed. My mother was always my greatest champion. She made sure I understood that I would be successful in life, regardless of the hatred and discrimination black people faced in America.

My mother never had the opportunity to go to college despite graduating at the top of her high school class in Chicago. She, of course, insisted that her children and grandchildren attend college, which we all did. It was such a monumental moment for Rosa and me when our son Michael gave his grandmother a tour of Harvard Medical School. Sadly, my dear mother passed away in February 2002, so she did not live to see him graduate and become a doctor, but she would have been so proud to see her grandson's achievement.

But as a smart and quick learner and a resourceful and hard-working person, my mother was able to succeed even without a college degree. She was able to find work that made it possible for her to contribute to our family's financial health. She held various well-respected positions, including dental assistant, dietitian, secretary, and manager of her sister's dry-cleaning business. She also was a crackerjack typist who could type at least a hundred words a minute, which was probably why she became the first black stenographer for R. R. Donnelley and Sons, the company that printed the nation's white- and yellow-page telephone books, which became a staple in practically every home in America. But because of her race, she never had a desk assigned to her at the company's offices; instead, she worked from home. I often went with her to Donnelly's loading docks in the evenings to deliver her work.

My maternal grandmother and the matriarch of our family, Edna Mae (Wills) Terrell, lived three blocks from us. I spent weekends with her, enjoying the delicious meals she made and doing chores, which earned me my first allowance. I always looked forward to Saturdays, when she'd reward me with two dollars for the week. I'd splurge on a solo trip to see a movie and buy a hamburger at one of the grand golden-age movie theaters on the South Side. I rotated my visits among the Southtown Theater, known for its swan pool and goldfish; the Regal, where for fifty cents you could see famous Motown music artists; and the classic Tivoli. I developed my passion for the cinema during those memorable years, a passion I'd inherited from my mother and later shared with my wife, Rosa, and our sons over the years.

Edna Mae always hosted our holiday gatherings at her house, where we'd feast on her creole and southern-style cooking. My grandmother was an extraordinarily strong woman who had a significant influence on our entire extended family and me. No doubt, much of her strength came from the adversity she had overcome in her life. She married her first husband, William Wills, at a very young age. They moved from Louisiana to Chicago with their three children and had six more after that. So my mother had eight siblings—five sisters and three brothers. Her father owned a grocery store that the family lived above, and during the depression years, they survived as best they could. Sadly, William died of acute appendicitis when the children were quite young. His death left my grandmother, who had never worked outside of their home-based grocery store, to raise nine children on her own.

Fortunately, a few years later, my grandmother met a special man, Fordie Terrell, who fell in love with her. He married her, despite her having nine children—a special man indeed! Fordie was the only grandfather I ever knew. He was a cab driver when my grandmother met him, and he became one of the first black men in Chicago to get a taxi medallion—a special permit that allowed him to earn a good living owning and operating his one-man cab company, until he became a deliveryman for Coca-Cola. My grandmother and grandfather were never wealthy, but they made ends meet. When I was born, they lived in an apartment on the top floor of a beautiful red brick three-story building that they shared with a doctor's office and four other families at 4213 South Parkway. It was a grand apartment on the third floor with a sun parlor, three bedrooms, and two bathrooms.

I spent a lot of time at my grandmother's apartment because there I could enjoy her cooking and also see numerous uncles, aunts, and cousins coming and going on any given day. It was my sanctuary, where I would share with her on many mornings a forbidden but delicious cup of coffee, rich with cream. My mom believed that caffeine was bad for my growth.

The apartment also doubled as a social center for the neighborhood because my grandmother ran bingo and card games for the ladies. We also lived there during those occasional periods when my father fell ill with a chronic thyroid condition, which required hospitalization at the VA hospital. During this time we shared wonderful moments with my lovely cousins, Stephanie and Nelda, who lived with my grandmother. I remained close to my grandmother throughout her long and relatively healthy life. Born in the nineteenth century, she lived until the age of ninety-seven, long enough to see her twenty-one grandchildren and thirty-three great-grandchildren become adults before she died in 1995.

My uncles Edward and Harry both lived lives forever scarred by their army service in Europe during World War II. In retrospect, I can see that they suffered from what we now know as post-traumatic stress disorder. But in those days, the condition was not understood. Although Uncle Ed never went to college, he was a voracious reader and became a self-taught scholar. He suffered throughout his life and could never hold down a steady job to support his family. Uncle Harry never overcame depression and alcoholism, which was unfortunate because, behind his erratic façade, I could see that he was a lovely person.

I spent many happy summers with Uncle Ed and his five children, my beloved cousins, especially Jacqueline, who was my age. They lived in Altgeld Gardens, a neighborhood on the far South Side of Chicago, which later became famous as the housing project where a young man named Barack Obama carried out community organizing.[2] Uncle Ed took us on field trips all over Chicago so that we might escape the confines of that poor neighborhood. He taught me about black history, covering African people's odyssey from Egypt into Africa, Latin America, and North America. He helped me to imagine and understand that there was a big, wide world outside of Chicago. I will always be grateful to Uncle Ed for his wisdom and love for me.

William, my mother's youngest sibling, had movie-star handsomeness and a great sense of humor. I spent much of my youth around Uncle Billy because he, his wife Alma, and son Brian lived with my grandmother. Always an impressive figure in the household, he pushed me to temper my obsession with books with athletics. Because Uncle Billy saw himself as an independent man and not beholden to anyone, he spent his career as an insurance salesman, which gave him more of the freedom and control he wanted over his life.

But my six aunts were the real leaders in our family, led by the grand dame, Edna Mae. The matriarchal world I lived in thrived on my grandmother's personality and her influence over her daughters. Without question, my mother was the dominant figure in this female army. As the middle daughter, she assumed responsibility for addressing issues that typically surface in such a large extended family. She was deeply respected by all of her siblings and beloved by her many nieces and nephews.

I was the grateful beneficiary of the love of my aunts, receiving help with my schoolwork and many special birthday gifts. Each of them played a pivotal role in my upbringing, and I will always be thankful for the privilege of having them in my life, both during and after my mother's passing. What amazing ladies they were: Juanita, a nurse; Willa Rae, the head cashier at a prominent supermarket; Myrtle, an entrepreneur who co-owned a small dry cleaning business at one time and a restaurant at another with her husband, Luther; Earline, who owned a supermarket with her husband, Franklin, which was a big deal for black people in those days, and who helped me understand the syntax of the English language, along with its mystery and beauty, at an early age; and Marion, my last living aunt who died at the age of ninety-six and struggled with emotional challenges throughout her life due to severe postpartum depression, an undiagnosed condition in this era, and who taught us all to have a greater appreciation for the love and kindness required by the "village" to help a loved one.

Born in Hattiesburg, Mississippi, my father, Spencer Williams, answered the call to serve in the US Army in the Pacific theater during World War II, during which time he traveled to India, Burma, and Australia. When he returned from duty, he was eligible for the benefits offered to returning World

War II veterans through the Servicemen's Readjustment Act of 1944, also known as the GI Bill.

Although he took advantage of the GI Bill and enrolled at Dillard University in Louisiana for a couple of years, my father found studying and living in the South to be unbearable owing to racist discrimination and hate. He never received his degree. Instead, he traveled north to Chicago, and like so many black people of that era, became part of the "Great Migration."[3] He met my mother and found a job with the United States Postal Service, where he remained employed for thirty-six years, rising through the ranks of middle management and ultimately earning the position of section supervisor. Typical of the "greatest generation," as referred to by journalist and author Tom Brokaw in his book by the same title, my father never spoke much about his experience in WWII.

My father lived and breathed jazz; there's no other way to describe it. The sound of this style of music filled our house, and he collected a lot of the best of it. He resisted the change from vinyl to CDs. To this day, when I hear a classic jazz song by Duke Ellington, Count Basie, or Miles Davis, I think of my father and the time when I first heard this music.

I will always remember the long, hard battles he fought for many years with his severe health problems. He lived with a chronic thyroid condition, beat cancer twice, and survived a successful heart-bypass surgery. He was indeed a fighter. But I remember my father best for the pride he felt in the accomplishments of his daughter and sons and the achievements of his grandchildren—those are the things that made him smile and gave him the most joy.

I am the son who went away to build a career overseas, and Dad would be surprised to know he had a hand in that. When I was a young boy, he told me a few stories about Burma and India; surprisingly, this excited me and planted a seed of embarking on distant adventures in my mind. My dad served his time in the army, did his job, and returned home in one piece. He then left the South for a new life in Chicago. He died in August 2000 at the age of eighty-one, after enjoying a good retirement surrounded by his beloved grandchildren, his rose garden, and his jazz.

I never really knew my paternal grandparents, who lived in Mississippi. My Chicago-born mother hated everything about the South and refused to travel there to visit my father's relatives. I certainly understand her reasoning, based on reality and the ugly things that black people endured daily in the segregated South. She relented only once when one of my father's favorite uncles died, and I still have vivid memories of my one trip to that state as a child in 1956.

We took this trip just a year after Emmett Till, a fourteen-year-old black boy from Chicago who was visiting Money, Mississippi, had been lynched for allegedly offending a white woman in her family's grocery store. An all-white jury acquitted the accused murderers of the teen. This horrified black people across America and became another stark example of what the South represented to all Negroes.

Horrific is the only way to describe our trip, except that I had the chance to meet my paternal grandmother, Janie Williams, for the first time; my paternal grandfather, Henry, had died several years before. Our traveling group included my father, my uncle Wilson (married to my father's sister, Mary), my mother, my one-year-old sister, Hilda, and me, then nine years old. My father made a huge mistake by driving his brand-new Chrysler with Illinois tags to Mississippi.

We only stopped overnight once, spending the night with relatives in Memphis, Tennessee. Black people didn't have access to hotels or restaurants in those days, and even gas stations were problematic, except for buying gas. A movie titled *The Green Book* recently portrayed how "colored folk" who were traveling relied on a guidebook that listed places to eat and stay that were more welcoming to African Americans. I don't recall any "green book" at the time of our trip, but I was very young. Every time we stopped for gas, my father would warn me not to drink from the "whites-only" water fountain; I'd never seen anything like that before. My mother, on the other hand, forbade me to drink water from the usually dirty or rusty water taps or buckets designated for "colored people." I was only a child, and this was all very confusing to me.

The worst part of the trip occurred during a terrible incident in northern rural Mississippi, near the village of Pope, population 250, when the local sheriff stopped my uncle and accused him of speeding. The interstate highway system had not yet been built, and I distinctly remember that we had followed the sheriff's car slowly for nearly an hour down a two-lane highway at thirty miles an hour in a forty-five-mile-per-hour speed zone. After an hour of this, my uncle very slowly pulled around the deputy sheriff's car to pass him, going about forty miles per hour. That's when the sheriff turned on his siren and pulled us over.

He forced us to follow his vehicle down a dirt road through nearby woods to a small building for a meeting with the local justice of the peace. Many ugly things happened in the two long hours we spent in the woods. The entire episode is not worth describing in detail. The main events in this frightening and humiliating experience included the deputy sheriff trying, unsuccessfully, to intimidate my mother, who waited with us children in the car, while the sheriff pressured my father and uncle to pay two $50 speeding tickets—an equivalent of $500 each in 2019. The fear that we experienced during that two hours in the woods would stay with us.

We continued our trip and attended the funeral, where I met many of my Mississippi and Louisiana relatives for the first time. However, during the rest of the trip, my mother worried incessantly about the possibility of a repeat of the terrifying experience on the way home. We never drove to Mississippi again.

2 A Fork in the Road

Choosing the Peace Corps

May your choices reflect your hopes, not your fears.

—NELSON MANDELA

My parents had sufficient income to send their children to Catholic schools, which was not an unusual choice for black families on the South Side of Chicago. Catholic education from kindergarten through sixth grade was considered superior to the public schools for families, even if they weren't Catholic. So Catholicism, either born into or acquired along the way, often became the primary religion among black families in many large cities all over the country. In Chicago numerous Catholic elementary and high schools were open to black families. Without question, I benefited from my years at St. Elizabeth Elementary School. For example, I started to study German there, and I continued studying the language through college and became very proficient in its use, although I did not travel to Germany until I was an adult.

There's an interesting story as to why the German language became part of my school curriculum. One day, Sister Agnes walked into our class and made an announcement. "We are now going to study languages at this school, and *we* will learn German." We just stared back at our teacher blankly, having no real understanding of what she was saying, as if to affirm, "Ok, Sister Agnes, whatever you say." I now realize that this curriculum change occurred during the era of Sputnik and the space race against the USSR. The new national education policy, launched by President Eisenhower, focused on the expansion of curriculum in science, math, and languages. The nuns at St. Elizabeth were from Alsace-Lorraine along the German-French border. And that's the reason I became proficient in German, rather than in a language that would have proven far more beneficial in my life, such as Spanish.

Thanks mainly to my mother's initiative in directing my Catholic school education, I almost always came in at the top of my class after I transferred to public school. Even then, if my mother didn't believe a school was integrated enough or provided a well-rounded curriculum for me, she became very creative in getting me into the best schools on the South Side. As a result, I attended four different elementary schools as a child. She had to manage this on her own, because in the 1950s she did not have access to information about schools and their policies that today help parents selecting schools for their children. Since the school locations were often far flung, she either drove me or arranged for my aunts to take me to the school I attended at the time.

I didn't particularly like leaving the friends I'd made or being the new kid at so many schools. But my dear mother was laser-focused on getting me the best education possible, and she succeeded. I was reading fluently at four years old, received two double promotions in elementary school, and attended summer school every year in my elementary and high school years. These achievements enabled me to graduate from elementary school in six years and from high school in three. It may have appeared that I was in a rush to get through school, but in reality I just loved learning as many new things as fast as possible.

Because I attended schools in so many different neighborhoods, I got to know the librarians in many public libraries around Chicago's South Side, and they got to know me. I lived for a couple of years with my Great-Aunt Pansy—another significant influence in my life. She lived in a nice neighborhood with a quality school, so naturally I transferred to that school, and thus began my love affair with my favorite library—the Chatham Branch Library (now the Whitney Young Branch Library). The librarians there saved all the new science fiction books for me to read first. The only catch was that I had to read them in the library and only on Saturdays. But since I loved to read, especially science fiction, biographies, and history, I spent much of my free time happily reading in libraries.

People like teachers or librarians we encounter during our formative years often end up becoming significant influencers in our lives. Someone who stands out in my memory as one of those special people is Wally Smith. Wally was a fortyish-year-old white man and the Hi-Y Leader at the Southtown YMCA. He saw potential in me and my best friend, Harry Simmons, and took an interest in finding opportunities that would benefit us. In the summer of 1962, Wally coached our team to a Hi-Y basketball city championship and took us to our first big college campus—St. Olaf College in Northfield, Minnesota. That was the catalyst of an exciting and expansive change in the worldview of kids from the South Side of Chicago.

Harry and I grew up three blocks apart. We became friends during our freshman year in high school and made the one-hour commute together to the all-boys Tilden Technical High School, a place that today would be a magnet school with strict admission requirements. We were inseparable whether we were playing basketball, studying, or working. We shared some "crazy" times together (e.g., shoveling snow off the local school's basketball court so that we could play in the winter). Thinking of ourselves as the princes of the city during our summer vacations, we embarked on strenuous workouts in the public parks each morning. Entertaining a faint dream of playing college basketball, we traveled all over the South Side to play pickup basketball, looking for the best competition we could find. And sandwiched between all of that was summer school; beyond the goal of boosting our education, we also had the distinct goal of dating girls in the coed high schools we selected to attend.

I have been blessed with Harry's lifelong friendship, sharing the joys, successes, and occasional tough times at every phase of our different careers and lives. Our wives, Rosa and Carrie, our children, and grandchildren remain connected in the "Harry-Aaron family." We have shared nearly every major event, both personal and professional, in our collective lives. I have found that it's crucial to have such a close friend and confidant in life. I have always regarded Harry as my spiritual rock during our shared life's journey.

The incredibly talented Lin-Manuel Miranda, best known for his Broadway hit *Hamilton*, gives credit to his fifth-grade teacher, who first recognized his talent for drama and encouraged him to pursue it. I believe that schoolteachers and other mentors deserve to hear more often about the impact they have had on their students. Two significant teachers come to mind in my life. My high school geometry teacher, Mr. Caldwell, once told me that I had an aptitude for math and science. He encouraged me to take advanced math in high school, which became essential to my future college studies. My favorite college professor and adviser, Irving Cutler, a renowned geographer who wrote the definitive history of Chicago, influenced how I thought about the soils, crops, and climates of different geographical regions. An excellent professor, he brought the subject matter to life for me. I loved studying geography under his guidance and took several of his courses. This knowledge came to bear fruit in my career with the US Foreign Service.

In 2018, I used the internet to locate Dr. Cutler. I ultimately found him with the help of the Jewish Historical Society and went to Chicago to visit him. Very active at the age of ninety-five, he was occasionally still leading architectural tours for the Chicago river cruises. I told him I wanted him to know how much of an influence he had on my career. I took a walk down a delightful memory lane with Dr. Cutler and his daughter, Susan, over lunch in Chicago. Making an effort to find him and deliver that message was important for me, and he appreciated it.

> I have learned that when someone pays me a kindness and cares for me in some way, it's important to stay in touch with them to let them know how much they mean to me. I believe my intention to build and maintain valued relationships can be considered a hallmark of my career success, which has resulted in my ability to lead a purpose-filled life.

Thanks to observing my parent's hard work, I developed a strong work ethic early on. When I was only eleven years old, I convinced my mother, with a big assist from my grandmother, to allow me to work at a small neighborhood store owned by a Jewish man named Joe. He was always kind to me when I was in his store picking up items for my grandmother, and I repeatedly asked him to hire me. But he just laughed and said I was too young and not strong enough.

Finally, after many months of continuous attempts to convince Joe, he agreed to let me deliver groceries in the neighborhood with my little red Radio Flyer wagon. When I turned sixteen, my Aunt Earline and Uncle Franklin got me a job at D&S Supermarket. I worked there part-time all through my high school and college years; my plan was to spend as little money as possible on college tuition by graduating as quickly as possible. The eight years I worked for D&S Supermarket on the corner of Eighty-Third and Cottage Grove, one of four supermarkets owned by four Jewish brothers, was a valuable life experience. There, I quickly learned what hard work was and the importance of a college education because I saw fifty- and sixty-year-old men doing the same job I was doing.

I started at $1 an hour as a grocery bagger, and after a few years I moved up to assistant produce manager at $2.50 an hour. I worked all day unpacking and preparing produce for display and then joined the floor crew to mop floors at night with big industrial mops that were difficult to maneuver. It snowed a lot in Chicago, and snow days called for double-duty mopping. We put sawdust down on the floors inside the store during the daytime, so customers wouldn't slip and fall on the snow and slush that got tracked in. At night, we had to get the sawdust, dirt, and slush up before we could mop. It was a dirty, nail-breaking, and body-aching job. I learned that hard work doesn't hurt you; it creates an opportunity to appreciate personal discipline.

I'll never forget how hard my mother tried to stop me from taking that job, but I insisted on having my independence. I'm proud to say that I managed to save enough money in those eight years to pay my way through college. I also supplemented my D&S wages with two other part-time jobs during my college years, one as a library aide at the school and the other as a camp counselor at a public housing project during the summers. Fortunately, I lived at home, and the tuition was reasonable, so my parents never had to pay a dime for my college expenses. I completed my college studies in three years at Chicago Teachers College, now Chicago State University, and became the first person in my family to graduate from college.

My friend Harry and I both graduated from Chicago Teachers College, then regarded as an innovative teacher's college with a reputation for being the gold standard in teacher training. The school's mission was to train K–12 grade school teachers for the Chicago Public School System, and graduates of the college were recognized as highly qualified candidates for a teaching position anywhere in Chicago. Chicago State University has played a critical role in my family's life, as it has in many minority families. My sister Hilda and her two daughters, Ellen and Anita, are also graduates. I'm extremely proud of my sister's academic success. Not only was she an excellent scholar there but she also earned her bachelor's and two master's degrees while pursuing a teaching-counseling career and being a wife and mother. She's now enjoying a golden retirement from the Chicago Public School System, after nearly thirty years as a master guidance counselor, dedicated to assisting the students and parents in her schools in whatever way possible.

I'm so proud of our superstar sister Hilda; she is the rock of our extended family, following in the illustrious footsteps of our mother and grandmother. She and her husband, Michael Jones, who had a terrific career in the US

Air Force, have been an inspiration to everyone in our family. We are fortunate to have their love and support in all that we do. My brother, Philip, and I often wondered how Hilda did all that she did so effortlessly; we remain her great admirers. Philip enjoyed the good fortune of living in Chicago for most of his life and so was able to see our sister frequently. He worked as an insurance underwriter for a number of years in California, but the 2008 recession cost him his job and career. Fortunately, thanks to Hilda's guidance and wisdom, he was able to become a teacher in the Chicago Public School System, completing the circle.

I decided to study geography in college because there was a shortage of teachers in that subject area. Little did I know how that decision would play out in my life. When I made it, it was merely a wise choice that offered me the best job opportunity as a teacher. In studying the geography of places around the world, however, the seeds once planted by my father of distant travels began to take root.

After completing my one year of student teaching at Hearst Upper Grade Center located on Chicago's South Side, I proceeded to line up my first teaching position. From a wide range of options, I literally could have selected any high school in the city, given the shortage of geography teachers. Life looked like it was following the plan initiated early on in the mind of my mother, and from all accounts I had aced the plan. But that was before serendipity intervened.

I heard about an organization that would allow a person to live in a foreign country and learn a foreign language under the auspices of the United States government. With it came the added benefit of participating in a worthwhile global endeavor. The Peace Corps, itself, was foreign to me; I didn't know anyone who had served in it, yet I saw it as a fascinating idea. Majoring in geography in college had afforded me the opportunity to learn about countries all over the world, but it had not allowed me to travel to any of them. I could even speak German, thanks to Sister Agnes. Understandably, given the working-class frame of mind of my circle of friends and family at that time, everyone I consulted thought this *fascinating idea* was a bad one. They were cautious folks by nature; life had taught them to be so. Besides, the foundations of my road to success had been laid out as planned. I graduated from college and had my choice of teaching at any high school in Chicago. I could settle down, get married, have a lovely apartment, and a great job. Why then, many people around me wondered, would I out of nowhere all of a sudden consider a trip into the unknown?

The only two people who could see the Peace Corps as a good idea were my mother and, of course, my best friend, Harry Simmons. My mother surprised me the most. From all appearances, I had arrived at the successful career she helped orchestrate for me my whole life. Perhaps the opportunity for travel offered by the Peace Corps had her dreaming even bigger. My mother had only traveled to a couple of states outside of Illinois and nowhere outside of the country. I believe she could imagine her unrealized dreams of seeing the world come true through me. But, for whatever reason, my mother found the Peace Corps to be an excellent idea, and she championed my desire to volunteer.

Harry had the kind of rational mind I could always count on for help with a big decision. After college, he became a well-respected educator and went on to have an outstanding career as a teacher, administrator, and school-system executive. Harry has remained my confidant and sounding board throughout my life; I consider myself fortunate to have a person of such high integrity and wisdom with me on my lifelong journey. The support and encouragement I received from two people I loved and respected and whose judgment I could trust were invaluable in my decision-making process—my choice to join the Peace Corps changed everything and put me squarely on a path to an incredible future. Looking back, I wouldn't change a thing, and I can't thank them enough for their perspective and wise advice.

Happily, my mother's dreams of travel did come true through me. She visited every foreign post I served, except South Africa, due to a severe illness she had at the time I was there. During my years as a Peace Corps volunteer (PCV) and a Foreign Service Officer (FSO) with the US Agency for International Development (USAID), she traveled to the Dominican Republic, Honduras, Haiti, Barbados, and Costa Rica. The Peace Corps put me on the road to a life unimagined.

Don't let fear hold you prisoner from taking well-thought-out chances. When I faced the grand decision to abruptly change career paths from public school teacher to Peace Corps volunteer, I had no idea it would become the most transformative decision of my entire life.

---

3 How I Met Your Mother

Teaching Teachers in the Dominican Republic

Life presents many choices, the choices we make determine our future.

—CATHERINE PULSIFER

I accepted an invitation from the US Peace Corps to become a trainee in a teacher-training program for Honduran and Salvadoran teachers at San Diego College in California. I later found out that all Peace Corps training took place at American universities and colleges in those days. So I left Chicago on the first airplane trip in my life, not realizing that this was the beginning of the transformation of my life. As part of an outstanding group of sixty-two trainees with whom I bonded immediately, I quickly learned how fortunate I was. Our group was almost entirely white, except for two Japanese Americans, a Puerto Rican, a Mexican American, and me. My training group, like all other groups worldwide, received three-plus months of training, which consisted of the following components: intensive Spanish language training; extensive cross-cultural training in the country's history, its people, politics, economy, traditions, and culture; and student teaching for our specific program in San Diego County and in Tijuana and Ensenada, Mexico.

We came together as a group with tremendous "esprit de corps," so to speak, united by our ideals, which we explored in great depth over our weeks of training and socializing. We fully epitomized the 1960s, later recognized by history as the decade when meaningful social change and protest swept across America. We were part of the baby boomer generation that assumed an active role in the Vietnam War protests, the civil rights movement, the women's movement, and the war on poverty. We wanted to change the world and make it a better place; the Peace Corps represented a vehicle through which one could do so.

Overall, I did well in the cross-cultural and teaching components of the training program. I did not fare well in the language training, however, despite the best efforts of our excellent teachers from El Salvador and Honduras. My typically excellent study skills took a backseat to my interest in enjoying the California lifestyle. As a result, I had, without a doubt, one of the lowest Spanish scores of anybody in my group when we completed our training in San Diego. Of course, my German didn't help me at all!

The toughest part of the program was the survival training we had to complete in northern Mexico, close to Tijuana, which in those days was not a dangerous drug-trafficking region. Paired with a partner and given ten dollars for the week, we set out to find our host family and explain why we were there. Fortunately, my partner, Craig Wanke, was bilingual. Our host family had ten kids who slept in the same bed, which they wet all night long. Unfortunately, that's also where we had to sleep until we got cots and could sleep out on the porch in frigid temperatures, which beat waking up wet and reeking of urine in the morning. During our time there, the final phase of our preparation for Peace Corps service, we taught in local Mexican schools in Ensenada. I left Mexico very worried about my weak Spanish skills, and upon our return to campus I was grateful when I passed my final language test.

After PCV training in San Diego, 15 percent of the group chose not to serve in the Peace Corps, about 60 percent of the trainees went to Honduras, 10 percent went to El Salvador, and 15 percent went to the Dominican Republic. I had developed a special connection and friendship with my roommate, Dennis Kroeger, and considered it serendipitous luck to have met him. Dennis was from Hayward, California, a graduate of the University of California at Santa Barbara, and we just clicked. He was very accomplished and wide open to the world of different cultures and ideas—an attitude I was not used to seeing in white people. I felt a unique acceptance from him; he genuinely seemed to see me as an equal and a brother of like mind, though different in color. That experience meant a lot to me; it opened my eyes to a hopeful vision of more promising relations between the races.

The Peace Corps attracts a wide variety of people from all economic backgrounds and areas of the country. Some of my cohort had attended Ivy League colleges and had influential parents, some were middle class and graduates from some of the largest state schools in America, and others, like me, had working-class roots. The good thing was that where you came from didn't matter in the Peace Corps. Your road to success depended on you and how well you could thrive in an environment foreign to you. The clock reset on day one.

Dennis and I were both assigned to go to Honduras, but in the end, I became one of ten who volunteered to go to the Dominican Republic instead. A convincing appeal for ten certified high school teachers by the country's visiting deputy minister of education, Victoria Sanchez, made me feel that I would be most effective there. That decision proved to have a long-lasting and positive impact on my life and career, though I was sad to part with my new friend at the time. We agreed to remain in contact during the year and planned to catch up with each other afterward.

I can still vividly recall flying on a Pan American World Airways Boeing 707 (the airline and airplane that created the global airline industry), one of the earliest passenger jets, to Santo Domingo, in December 1967. Our group of ten newly minted PCVs flew from Miami to Montego Bay and Kingston in Jamaica to Port-au-Prince, Haiti. We finally arrived in the evening at the dimly lit terminal in the old Santo Domingo airport. We were exhausted and filled with both anxiety and excitement about this new life and job.

We were greeted by Henry Reynolds and Kyra Eberle, the Peace Corps associate directors. Henry was a laid-back black man with an eclectic professional background—in many ways he was a "renaissance man," although at the time I didn't know what that was. He was an educator, a scuba diving instructor, a social worker, a jazz aficionado, and then an amazing Peace Corps executive. Kyra was an impressive leader, a determined and knowledgeable blonde woman, and a returned PCV who immediately mesmerized us all with her knowledge, discipline, and enthusiasm.

Henry, my boss and mentor, played a key role in my success in the Peace Corps. Ten years my senior, he saw something in me that I did not see in myself. He was my go-to guy, my lifeline, always providing the advice and encouragement I needed to get me through the tough times. He reminded me that success often comes from what we see at the time as our biggest failure. What doesn't kill you makes you stronger, as the saying goes. Henry remained a treasured friend and USAID colleague long after my Peace Corps days, and in later years we ended up living about fifteen minutes apart in northern Virginia.

I still vividly recall the long ride in the Peace Corps van from the airport to the city and the drive into the old colonial section where we would be housed during the orientation, prior to being assigned to our villages, towns, and cities across the country. Not only were we worn out from our trip by this point but we were also overcome by the heat of Santo Domingo, whose weather starkly contrasted with the frigid winter of the United States we had just left. So we hit our bunk beds and tried to sleep. I recall lying awake under my mosquito net (which I didn't secure well; I paid a price for that first night and hoped my antimalaria pills would protect me). I was think- ing about what this new adventure would entail, but I was determined to stay the course no matter what. Santo Domingo, the first colonial capital of the Spanish Empire in the New World, was founded in 1496 by Bar- tholomew Columbus, Christopher Columbus's brother, four years after the historic voyage of discovery by Christopher Columbus (Cristobal Colon in Spanish). Its colonial zone (the old city sector) offers one of the most beau- tiful examples of Spanish colonial architecture during the height of the Spanish conquest and control in the Americas. We stayed in the colonial zone, at the PCV "hotel" called the Hotel Colon. In true Peace Corps fash- ion, it was a one-star boarding house with spartan furnishings and ade- quate food, the only grand thing about it being its name. It was located in a poor neighborhood, and I was surprised to be awakened that first morning by a loud rooster outside my window.

I barely remember the first week. It was a total blur of activity— orientation for Peace Corps programs and operational policies, trying hard to speak as much Spanish as I could in my daily interactions on the street, finding where to bank our $150 a month salary (the Royal Bank of Canada to my surprise), and learning about the ins and outs of the public transpor- tation between my assigned town and the capital city of Santo Domingo. I was overwhelmed but also elated.

I was pleased that I had graduated from a respected teacher's college in Chicago and then landed in the Dominican Republic as a Peace Corps volunteer where I was assigned to provide a high school education to rural schoolteachers. In 1967, rural Dominican schoolteachers had, on average, an eighth-grade education, which was barely above the level of the students they taught.

Funding for the program came from USAID, which was heavily in- volved in education in the Dominican Republic. USAID funding allowed the Dominican government to provide incentives for this particular train- ing program over two years. Teachers in the program could obtain a high school degree, a salary increase, and the opportunity to bid on jobs in urban schools. In return, they sacrificed their weekends during the fall semester and their summer vacations to participate in the program.

Peace Corps volunteers were assigned to teach at ten in-service training centers around the country, and each center had an estimated eighty Dominican teachers enrolled in the program. We taught language arts, math, and multiple science courses to these teachers in Spanish. It was a fantastic way to develop my Spanish language skills. I was determined to excel in Spanish, so every day, I would read the entire daily newspaper, the *Listin Diario*, which contained an average of twenty-five pages. I would have to stop and look up just about every third word in a dictionary. Becoming fluent in Spanish required a lot of blood, sweat, and tears on my part, but my determination to succeed won out over the pain.

I joined a team of four other PCVs—Judy Johnson, Victoria "Vicky" Taylor, and a couple, Frank and Jackie Murphy—for an assignment in the small town of Monte Plata, with a population of two thousand, located about fifty miles from the capital of Santo Domingo. The team provided my orientation to this new world, and we became fast friends and colleagues. Plus, we relied on each other for both programmatic and moral support, as we shared a common bond in our determination to work on behalf of our teachers.

On Saturdays during the school year and in the summer vacation period, our team of PCVs taught the courses offered in the program. However, we operated independently during the week, visiting the five to eight teachers assigned to each of us for the entire year, traveling around like circuit riders, getting to them either by horseback, motorcycle, or hiking. As part of my routine, I spent a week with each of the teachers to observe and coach them on the subjects and to ensure they were applying the lessons I had taught them.

A very close-knit relationship often developed between the teachers I served and me. I came to appreciate that this opportunity brought with it tough personal sacrifices for these poorly paid, rural schoolteachers. My empathy for their situation helped foster a great friendship between us. They would give me the food off their table when I visited them. I slept in their homes, played with their children, and learned about their hamlets. They also helped me improve my Spanish skills. Children and young people displayed far more patience than older people with me as I practiced integrating their language into my everyday use. Being in these teachers' homes with their families gave me not only tremendous life experiences; it played a crucial part in my success as a PCV in the Dominican Republic.

The first six months in the Peace Corps comes with a massive period of adjustment for every volunteer. You immediately realize you're "not in Kansas anymore"—or anyplace you may have called home in the United States. Your first thought is "Do I have what it takes to be a good PCV, to be of service to the people I am assigned?" You could exercise the right to resign anytime you wanted. But I had never allowed surrender to be an option in my life, and I wasn't about to begin now in what I believed could be the opportunity of a lifetime. Even though volunteering in the Peace Corps could be extremely challenging at times and definitely was not for the faint of heart, I found the rewards to far exceed the struggles.

The overwhelming feelings of homesickness were compounded by the frustrating language barrier that separated the PCVs from the people they wanted and needed to get to know in what would be their home for the next two years. Soon enough, the poor living environment resulted in bouts of illness, and some volunteers would typically feel physically sick half the time. Many of the places where Peace Corps volunteers get assigned do not have running water, so unless you are careful this could lead to dysentery or severe diarrhea caused by bacterial infections in the intestines. I had a latrine behind my house, and my neighbor's pig lived next to it . . . so my frequent forays were often exciting and odorous encounters, especially at night!

Perhaps the unrelenting tropical heat contributed to the migraines and seizures that some experienced, or perhaps the cause was one among a whole host of strange viruses they'd never encountered before. With them can come severe illnesses like dengue fever—a kissing cousin of malaria. This mosquito-borne infection causes severe flu-like symptoms that can be very painful. Not only is there no treatment for it but very little can be done to reduce the bone pain or relieve the itching it causes underneath the skin. The effects of the dengue fever can last a couple of weeks, and it can reinfect over and over. Fortunately, it only *got me* twice!

In that era, most parents did not visit their sons and daughters serving in the Peace Corps, but my mother couldn't wait to visit me. Nine months into my new world, she decided to make the trip. I was immediately worried about her coming. The environment was like nothing she'd ever experienced before. The thoughts of her sleeping under mosquito netting and riding on the back of my motorcycle to get around town overwhelmed me with concern. When I got her letter that she would be arriving in the capital city of Santo Domingo, I told her to meet me at the Peace Corps office there. It never occurred to me that she might find it hard to locate, given that she didn't speak Spanish! How would she find her way from the airport to the office?

When the taxi pulled up, and my mother got out, all I could say with overwhelming relief was, "Oh my God, you're here! How did you make it without knowing the language?"

She explained that she just gestured with her hands and kept repeating "the Peace Corps" over and over to everyone she met. I had a wonderful time with her, and she acclimated much better than I expected. She loved Henry and his wife, Grace, and she had a great time going with me everywhere I went on my motorcycle. She cooked me delicious meals on a kerosene-fueled stove. I knew how much I would miss her when she left, and of course, I did.

In the Peace Corps, once you arrive at your destination, you must learn to integrate with the people you serve in towns and villages that can be miles away from the camaraderie of other volunteers; this requires you to become very resilient. To be successful, you had to become resilient; and to become resilient, you had to be confident.

There were ten teacher training centers in the Dominican Republic, all staffed by PCVs and Dominican counterparts. I remain good friends with some of the people I served with to this day—fifty-some years later! The Peace Corps was an incredible but challenging experience that I will always be glad I had for many reasons but especially for the friendships I made and carried with me afterward.

After our first year was up, my training roommate, Dennis, and I met in Honduras as planned. We decided to embark on an adventure to the Caribbean coast of Honduras. We knew that the location was mostly jungle and uninhabited, but in hindsight, it could be more aptly described as a spot "at the end of the world." Two decades later, it would be the site for a movie by Harrison Ford called *The Mosquito Coast*, about an idealist who moves his family to a remote Caribbean region to escape the consumerism of America. That paints an accurately vivid picture.

We were flying out of Tegucigalpa to the Mosquitia region on the national air carrier SAHSA (aka Stay at Home, Stay Alive) in a WWII–era, twin-engine DC-3. We were surprised when we saw the pilot unloading goats and chickens from the plane to make seating room for us! The plane did not have the standard modern technology to normalize air pressure on takeoff, and my eardrum immediately burst, an incredibly painful experience. We landed in the territorial capital of Puerto Lempira on a Monday at an airport marked by a windsock. Between us we had enough money to stay two days as planned. We didn't think anything could top the strangeness of everything that had already happened; however, we were soon proven wrong.

Upon arrival, we met a teacher from the community named Francisco Flores, who had a PhD in ornithology from UC Berkeley. An ornithologist studies birds, and our destination happened to be the world's best migration route for rare species of birds. Excited to get on with our adventure, we told Francisco that we'd see him on Wednesday when we'd be leaving.

"No, you're not," he said, looking directly at us.

We looked at each other and then showed him our tickets specifying a Wednesday departure.

"That's the old schedule. The plane only flies on Mondays now," Francisco said.

Too shocked to be angry, we commented that each of us had brought only twenty dollars apiece for a two-day stay based on SAHSA's advertised three flights a week. Francisco went on to inform us that there were no hotels where we were going—only a boarding house over the bar in town. Luckily, it only charged two dollars a night for the two of us, meaning we each had thirteen dollars to eat on for a week.

Francisco was sympathetic to our plight and was a great host. He took us to his village of Tasbarraya on the island of Tancin, whose local flora, fauna, and customs he was studying, and he fed us several meals from his modest home at the edge of the jungle. As it turned out, there were Mennonites, Southern Baptists, and Catholic priests in the region, all seeking to convert the local people. They invited us to dinner a couple of times, during which they also served up their version of Christianity. Our two-day vacation had quickly turned into another survival-training exercise, but Dennis and I enjoyed catching up. Dennis reminded me that we had been told in training in San Diego that no PCVs would be sent to the Mosquitia because it was deemed too rugged, isolating, and primitive! We endured several three-hour cayuco (canoe) rides across lagoons and mangrove swamps. It was a time neither of us would ever forget—or wish to repeat. We felt confident that we would have no issue on our flight to Tegucigalpa a week later because the wife of the general who ran the province planned to be on the plane with us.

During the early part of 1968, my second year in the Peace Corps, Martin Luther King, Jr. and Robert F. Kennedy—both champions of the civil rights movement—were assassinated within months of each other in the United States. The devastating news made me beyond angry. For the first time in my life, I was ready to quit something—the Peace Corps. I wrote to my parents and told them I couldn't continue to represent the US given these tragedies, and that I was coming home to join the civil rights movement. And I wasn't the only PCV who felt that way. In response to these events, my father wrote a letter to me, for the first time in my life: "Don't leave," he said. "You're angry, and I fear for your life. You need to finish what you started, and people are counting on you." Because Dad had never written to me before, his words carried more weight than the usual letter from a parent. I took his advice, and I'm so grateful that I did. Seeing into the future was impossible for me at the time, but looking back now, I can see that my dad had provided wise advice, and I remained in the D.R. I couldn't change the hatred that followed the civil rights movement in the United States during that era, but the future would show that I could represent a positive step forward for minorities in the Peace Corps. I would later also realize the value of the opportunity given to me to improve education for the people of the Dominican Republic in more ways than one. Equally important, my career path and personal life, which has meant so much to me, would have not been the same if I had not decided to stay. I have my dad to thank for that; in many ways, he kept me on the right path.

My second year of teaching in the Dominican Republic would have farther-reaching implications going forward than I realized at the time. I met Rosa Mustafa, my future wife, the first week I arrived in town. Some of my new young friends told me about the beautiful high school science teacher and then introduced us. About a month later, I tried to recruit her to work with the Peace Corps as a teaching counterpart or Dominican master teacher. Rosa spoke very little English, and my Spanish was still pretty basic, so communication between us was understandably limited. Unfortunately, my arrival in her home country came on the heels of the US invasion of it in 1965 and the ensuing occupation by our military, which effectively ended a democratic revolution. So there was a reasonable amount of anti-American sentiment in connection with these actions, but fortunately the reputation of the Peace Corps was not tarnished. During the revolution, PCVs and PCV nurses had crossed rebel lines to help injured and wounded Dominican rebels. Exacerbating tensions, some PCVs had openly condemned the invasion in the US media and local press. At considerable personal risk, volunteers openly challenged the Johnson administration. As a result, Peace Corps senior leaders traveled to the Dominican Republic to suppress the PCV uprising.

The Dominicans never forgot the support they received from the PCVs. Those of us who came later benefited from their legendary reputation. But that reputation was not enough to convince Rosa to work for the Peace Corps. She had been a third-year medical student at the National University of the Dominican Republic when her homeland was invaded. She had already become a skilled midwife as part of her medical training and, in the process, had delivered hundreds of babies by that time. She taught science classes in the night high school in Monte Plata; her students and others considered her a scholar and were in awe of her.

As I learned more about Rosa, I found out about her fascinating family history. Rosa's paternal grandfather, Ali Mustafa, was Lebanese, and he immigrated to the Dominican Republic in the 1880s from Lebanon, then part of the Ottoman Empire. Her paternal grandmother, Ana Rosa Medina Portes, was Dominican, and her family was from the city of Moca, located in the northern agricultural valley of the country. Her father, Alido Mustafa, was born in the Dominican Republic. In 1930, Ali found himself in difficult financial shape; nearly broke, he decided to return to his native land. His plan was to sell his property in Lebanon and then return to the Dominican Republic with resources to rebuild his life and solve his family problems. Because of the devastation to the port of Santo Domingo caused that year by Hurricane San Zenon (one of the deadliest in history), he had to catch a ship in Port-au-Prince, Haiti. The plan was that young Alido, then fifteen years old, would travel with him to Lebanon. The Haitian port authorities would not permit Alido to leave, however, because they didn't have documents proving that he had his mother's permission to leave the country, a rather surprising requirement for those times. Faced with a dilemma, his father left him with a friend in Port-au-Prince and departed on his voyage to the Middle East.

For reasons that have never been determined, Rosa's paternal grandfather never returned, and young Alido became the sole supporter of his family. He worked hard, learned surveying, and became a surveyor and public works expert. He was very successful and rose through the ranks to become the superintendent of public works for the northern region of the country, responsible for the construction and maintenance of the highways and roads across the region to the Haitian border. Rosa's mother, Encarnacion Mejia, was fifteen years old when she met Alido, during a period when he was building the road through her small town near the city of La Vega. She worked in her mother's kitchen cafeteria, and they sold food to the workers in the area. Rosa's maternal grandmother was Benedicta Mejia Quesada and her grandfather was Cirilo Mejia. Her maternal grandfather had been a member of the infamous (or patriotic, depending on your perspective) Pata Blanca ("the white feet," meaning barefoot) rebel army that fought for Dominican independence against the US Marines during the first US occupation of the Dominican Republic that lasted from 1916 to 1924. He was killed in the civil wars of that era. A few years later the future dictator Rafael Trujillo took over the country, crushed all opposition, and launched a thirty-plus-year reign that lasted until he was assassinated in 1961.

The turmoil caused by the 1965 revolution and the US invasion destroyed the Dominican economy and negatively impacted Rosa's family. Her father had created a good and secure life for his family. Following the revolution, however, he lost everything—his government position and his personal businesses. In the midst of this family calamity, her mother, Encarnacion, became ill, and her parents found it nearly impossible to care for their twelve children. In the face of this familial tragedy, Rosa discontinued her medical education and found a job as a high school science teacher in Monte Plata in order to take care of her siblings. She was solely focused on her family, so she didn't want to have anything to do with the Peace Corps, America, or me, and my first meeting with her went poorly.

"No, I'm not interested in working with the PCVs! Your people invaded my country and helped support a new dictator. No!" she said adamantly.

Clearly, I would need to find another way of recruiting Rosa—one that had nothing to do with the Peace Corps. After two years of working on her sisters and milking my story about Dennis and our trip to the Mosquito Coast, I finally wrangled myself into Rosa's inner circle with an invitation to a birthday party for her boss, and her attitude toward me began to soften. Because Rosa was not fluent in English, we conversed mostly in Spanish, which helped improve my use of the language, and so I credit Rosa with my crowning achievement, becoming fluent in Spanish. After three years of service, I was fully conversant with a respectable Dominican accent! I consider my mastery of Spanish to be one of my outstanding achievements in life. Mastering the Spanish language led to a magnificent opportunity that set the stage for my third year in the Peace Corps.

My highest lifetime achievement, however, came in winning over the heart of Rosa. It took a focused campaign and a lot of confidence building on my part to eventually win that battle. I believe my heart knew long before I consciously realized it that she was the one for me. Rosa had all the strong characteristics of the accomplished matriarchs I had grown up around in my family. I so admired her because of her vast knowledge of science, obvious success in medical school, the courage she demonstrated in leaving medical school, and her determination to take care of her family and the strength she showed in undertaking that arduous job. She and I shared the same dream of exploring a world outside of our limited experience. I was certain that we could build a good life together, and I decided to ask her to marry me. Fortunately for me, she said yes!

However, we had to meet three standard US government conditions before we could be married. Rosa had to complete the required background checks with the Dominican Police Department and the US Embassy. She had to be employed, and I had to obtain approval from the Peace Corps to marry a Dominican citizen. We quickly wrapped up this "clearance" process and planned a small wedding in town. But Rosa was so well known and respected that the whole town showed up to our wedding! What a challenge that was, because we then had to serve food and refreshments to all comers! My boss and mentor, Henry Reynolds, was my best man, contributing to the cementing of what would be a long friendship. Our honeymoon consisted of a weekend trip to Santo Domingo.

Rosa's quiet strength has been the rock of our family and a source of loving support to me in my various career decisions that we embraced together. Our story is not unique, but we do often reflect on the good fortune and serendipity that led to our paths crossing. We were individuals from two distinct cultures, living in two separate nations, thousands of miles apart, and speaking different languages for most of our youth. Now, we have been married for more than fifty years and have been blessed with two phenomenal sons and five amazing grandsons! I can't imagine how different my life would have been if I had not volunteered to serve in the Dominican Republic instead of Honduras at the last minute or if I had quit the Peace Corps in 1968 instead of taking Dad's advice to stay.

After working for two wonderful years in the Dominican Republic, I had compiled a vast knowledge of the education system there, from top to bottom, and I knew many officials in the Ministry of Education. In the 1960s, following the Dominican revolution and the US intervention, USAID formed a partnership with a group of progressive Dominican businessmen. This group's mission was to improve the lives of people in the Dominican Republic by creating key financial and social organizations that could effect positive change through new programs.

In 1962, the idea to create a brand-new university in the Dominican Republic modeled after the same type of liberal arts universities in the United States became a reality. The Madre y Maestra Catholic University, created by a group of Catholic priests and businessmen in Santiago, the second largest city in the Dominican Republic, became one of the institutions that USAID decided to fund at a crucial time in the university's development.

Just as my two years in the Peace Corps neared its end in 1969, I heard about a new program that offered Dominican professors at the Madre y Maestra full scholarships to study for graduate degrees (MAs and PhDs) in the US. That program presented a challenge for the university that opened up a rare opportunity for me.

Instructors would be needed to temporarily replace the Dominican professors who headed to the United States to participate in the program. The university therefore requested a few PCVs to serve as instructors during the absences of the professors. Fortunately, by that time, I spoke Spanish fluently, and I was well acquainted with the Dominican education system. So when the Peace Corps asked me to consider staying on for a third year to take a job teaching at the College of Education at Madre y Maestra, I agreed to take advantage of the unique opportunity.

I traveled to Santiago for an interview with Father Felipe Arroyo, the dean of the College of Education as well as a dynamic leader and Jesuit priest. Interestingly, Arroyo had been the headmaster of the high school that Fidel Castro had attended in Cuba. He was one of the last Jesuits forced out of Cuba; his relationship with Castro and the degree of protection that that offered him had enabled him to stay after other Catholic priests had been expelled. But he would not bend to the policies of the Communist regime, and eventually he had no choice but to leave. Cuba's loss would become the Dominican Republic's fortunate gain, as Father Arroyo would become the one to build a relationship with St. Louis University—a Jesuit school and

USAID contractor—and who initiated the graduate education program. Due to Father Arroyo's efforts and USAID funding, Madre y Maestra received ten to twenty scholarships every year to send faculty participants to the United States.

Six PCVs replaced the participating professors. Besides me, Bill Miller, Dan Mizroch, Sally and Norm Miller, and Gary Orso were offered the fantastic opportunity to teach at Madre y Maestra. Bill and Dan became my lifelong friends, and we take annual family vacations together. I still consider this extraordinary serendipity beyond the realm of probability. To this day, I vividly recall my interview with Father Arroyo. He was so relieved that I was fluent in Spanish because he needed instructors who could teach at the university level. We discussed philosophy and education and everything in between that day. I felt honored that he agreed to have me join his department as a teacher!

Suddenly, I had advanced from teaching rural grade school teachers to teaching seniors in their fourth year at a prestigious private college in the second largest city of the Dominican Republic. Not only was this a terrific professional opportunity for me, but it was the beginning of a fruitful relationship with Father Arroyo, a brilliant person to work with and an incredible mentor for me during that year. The experience also took my Spanish skills to a whole new level. I used more sophisticated vocabulary and expressions than ever before.

But before this new assignment could become a reality, Rosa and I once again had a few obstacles to overcome. The Peace Corps' policy at that time required my wife to have an independent source of income. Rosa had a teaching position in Monte Plata, but she would have to become gainfully employed in the new city of Santiago. Through Father Arroyo's connections, he arranged a teaching job for Rosa at one of the leading high schools in Santiago. So off we went as a newly wedded couple with exciting new teaching opportunities—a dream unimagined.

We are often blind to opportunities on the horizon.
So always put forth your best effort.

Father Arroyo's focus was on capacity development, and developing the best teaching faculty in the Americas became his primary goal. Most college professors in Latin America in those days worked part-time. Doctors, lawyers, nurses, and engineers all taught part-time at the universities, and they were not well compensated. The Madre y Maestra aspired to the same model used by St. Louis University and USAID (that is, to offer well-paid, permanent jobs for academic experts in their fields that also gave faculty the chance to pursue an advanced degree). The vision was that the Madre y Maestra would develop a faculty in the true sense of an American liberal arts university, and that vision was realized.

Today, the Madre y Maestra Catholic University is one of the most prestigious universities in the Dominican Republic and all of Latin America. Many future leaders of the Dominican Republic were either educated there or became members of the faculty. Many of those leaders, across all sectors for the last three generations, are my friends and former colleagues from those years, including a former president of the Dominican Republic, the former president of the university, several former cabinet ministers, and prominent business leaders.

The Madre y Maestra remains one of USAID's greatest success stories. Several other Dominican institutions, including a new private development bank and a technical agricultural institute, were also created in a partnership between USAID and this group of progressive business leaders at a critical juncture in Dominican history. Those were the most amazing times, and I had a front-row seat. As the first of my many experiences with USAID to come, I had no idea how much this particular introduction to the organization would impact my future life and career.

4

Returning Home to a New Unknown

Corporate America

If somebody offers you an amazing opportunity but you are not sure
you can do it, say yes—then learn how to do it later.

—RICHARD BRANSON

In many respects, serving in the Peace Corps in the Dominican Republic had
been a transformative experience, a journey of self-discovery and growth. I
lived through many events and learned many lessons in a global arena, and
I made new connections and memories I would carry with me forever. Now
that my "tour of duty" was ending after three years, it felt like I was traveling down the yellow brick road in reverse, leaving behind the land of adventure for life in the new unknown—home. I experienced the same anxious
excitement I had when I first arrived, but this feeling was accompanied
by a whole new set of other feelings and challenges. Heading back to the
States in 1970 as a married man, I was far different from the college graduate that had left there just three short years earlier. I was returning with my
beautiful wife, both of us newly unemployed, and leaving behind me the
support team I had enjoyed over those years. We were on our own to a place
I still called home but where we faced unchartered territory.

Foremost on my mind were my next steps in terms of a job and career—
not just for me but for Rosa as well, who was leaving her country of origin.
I could always return to teaching in the Chicago Public School System, but
I was a different person now. My view of the world had been altered by my
Peace Corps experience, with my exposure to other cultures, new friends
and colleagues, an exciting lifestyle, and a sense of global purpose.

My first decision was to redirect my career trajectory. I set my sights
on a master's degree in business administration (MBA). I saw that as the

means to expand my options of working in either business or government. But before that could happen, I would need to find funding for graduate study through a fellowship or a scholarship opportunity, since neither Rosa nor I had an income or savings. Fortunately, during my exit interview with the Peace Corps, I paid attention to an essential piece of advice. The recommendation to stop by the Peace Corps headquarters in Washington, DC, to check on potential job openings led to the perfect next step for me.

I arrived in Washington on a Monday and headed straight for the Peace Corps headquarters. During this period, Joe Blatchford had been appointed Peace Corps director by President Nixon. I met with Bill Inglis, who had been a Wall Street investment banker before being appointed as the director of Peace Corps recruitment. Right away, Bill wanted to know if I would be interested in becoming a recruiter. It sounded like a terrific opportunity, considering my recent experience. When Bill asked what my preferred location would be, I said Chicago, and so he told me to go there and meet with the head of the regional office. As fortune would have it, at that time my former Peace Corps director in the Dominican Republic, Tom Gittens, happened to be a senior executive at the organization's headquarters in Washington, DC, and he wrote a letter of recommendation for me to carry to Chicago.

Two days and three interviews later, I had a job. The formation of a new office was under way that aimed to increase the number of minority PCVs, consistent with the great philosophy of Sargent Shriver, who firmly believed that the Peace Corps should reflect the makeup of the people of America. As the coordinator of minority recruitment in Chicago, I covered the vast Midwest region—from Pennsylvania to Nebraska and from Minnesota to Missouri. There were ten minority coordinators across the country, based in all the major cities. We reported to Leonard Robinson, a black Republican, which was a rarity in those days. Lenny was a terrific boss who gave his team substantial autonomy and encouraged creative thinking and operational flexibility. An outstanding leader, he was a risk taker and admirably served many future GOP administrations. The other minority recruiter in the Midwest was Eldridge "Skip" Gilbert, and we formed a strong partnership in carrying the "gospel" of the Peace Corps across the region; we traveled to scores of universities and colleges, especially focusing on historically black universities and colleges.

The job would turn out to be one of the most enjoyable and fulfilling of my life. The Chicago office recruiters were a great team of former PCVs who had a remarkable esprit de corps and enthusiasm for our work, and a number of them became lasting friends, including Jim Feaster, Paul Mack, and Nancy Nollau. Jim also went to graduate school at the University of Wisconsin–Madison, where he met Cynthia Davis, then pursuing her PhD in English literature; they were married and we now consider her to be an honorary PCV! Paul and Nancy also got married, and we all remain close friends to this day. Once a year the three couples take a group vacation.

Thanks to this job, I visited just about every major university in the entire Midwest region and developed excellent working relationships with faculty and admissions office staff. Because of this, I received three or four offers from various universities, including a special fellowship from the Consortium for Graduate Study in Management, a minority recruitment organization representing some of the leading graduate management schools in the country. I accepted the joint offer from the Consortium and the University of Wisconsin–Madison, where I would study to receive my MBA.

Professor Isadore Fine was my MBA adviser at the university, a warm and insightful human being whose expertise was in marketing, which was my primary area of concentration, along with international business. We developed a terrific relationship, and he provided excellent advice concerning my academic progress and future job opportunities. I also greatly enjoyed my marketing classes with Professor William Peters, who also provided excellent career advice on opportunities with the leading Fortune 500 corporations in the consumer products marketing arena.

One course became my Achilles heel in the MBA program: production scheduling, which required the ability to perform linear programming. This subject represented a never-ending mystery to me, no matter the amount of homework I did or the number of consultations I had with the professor. I needed an intervention! I noticed that one of my fellow students always had the answers to the professor's questions and often pressed for a deeper understanding of the subject. His name was Harbhajan Grewal. He was a Sikh, and he went by Bill. Bill's family was from Kenya, and his father had been the director of the Kenyan national railroad.

The family had decided to immigrate to Canada due to the widespread racism that Indians faced in East Africa during the era in which the mad despot Idi Amin controlled Uganda and the fear that this could spread to Kenya. Bill, a brilliant student, later received a scholarship to study at the University of Wisconsin. I didn't know this back story at the time, but because he was such a smart guy, I decided to ask him if he would tutor me in production scheduling. Luckily for me, he said yes. Bill turned out to be an excellent tutor who opened my eyes to the subject matter, and as a result, I received a B in that demanding course.

> Although challenges will always rise up in life, I came to realize that things have a way of working out when you keep moving forward.

It was during our time at Wisconsin that my mother made a momentous decision to change her life. After nearly thirty years of marriage, my parents divorced. She would later marry a long-time family friend, Louis "Sonny" Green Jr., a career noncommissioned officer in the US Air Force who served for thirty-five years and participated in both the Korean and Vietnam wars. Before he retired, he had achieved the top rank for a noncommissioned officer in the air force of chief master sergeant. My mother's dream of world travel came true during her marriage to Sonny. They lived at air force bases all over the world, including Korea, Germany, and around the United States. I'd never seen my mother as happy as she was during those years, and we will always be grateful for this.

As they prepared to leave for Okinawa, Japan, my teenaged brother, Philip, surprised us all with his decision to remain behind with Rosa and me to finish high school in the United States. He moved into our graduate-student apartment, and for the first time in years, I had the good fortune to spend some quality time with my brother. My mother was finally able to focus on her own life and dreams. On every base where Sonny served, he was the senior noncommissioned officer, and this prestigious position came with the traditional perks of excellent housing and a vehicle with a driver. It was a life of luxury that my mother had never experienced before. I could not have been happier for the two of them, especially for my mother, who was getting the life she deserved.

When we arrived in Madison, it was apparent that the fellowship would not be adequate to cover our expenses. I set out to get a part-time job and amazingly ended up with three part-time jobs and three separate offices! The key to my luck was Les Ritcherson, the assistant provost at University of Wisconsin. Les had come to Wisconsin as the first black assistant football coach in the Big Ten Conference after a legendary career as a high school and college football coach in Texas. This pioneer and highly respected university leader came to my rescue when we faced the usual grad student problem of earning supplemental income. Rosa and I became good friends with both him and his lovely wife, Velma. He was an important mentor for me and a role model in my life. Sadly, Les passed away in 2019, a significant loss for all of us who were blessed to cross paths with this great leader. Because of Les's efforts on my behalf as a grad student, I secured jobs as an instructor for introductory Spanish courses in the College of Arts and Sciences, as an instructor of Spanish for Travelers in the university extension program, and as a research fellow in the Department of Tourism for the state of Wisconsin. No doubt, my Peace Corps travels to foreign lands and my fluency in Spanish paid off for me many times over.

Rosa had continued her intensive English language training in Chicago and then at the University of Wisconsin. In addition to this challenge, she learned that her three years of coursework from the National University of Santo Domingo's medical school would not be fully accredited by American universities—a real setback. So, in the face of these obstacles to reentering medical school, she decided that she would return to college and pursue a career as a medical technologist after I completed my MBA. Although her spoken English was still on a basic level, her medical school experience, bolstered by Les Ritcherson's recommendation, enabled her to secure a research assistantship at the University of Wisconsin Hospital in the Renal Research Department. Rosa started in the lab on the graveyard shift from 11:00 p.m. to 7:00 a.m., performing the various lab tests on the research animals. But due to her hard work and demonstrated lab expertise, she moved up to the human research lab after just a couple of months.

After I had acquired my three university jobs, along with managing the usual semester load of sixteen credit hours, the Peace Corps asked me to share an on-campus recruiter job with another returned Peace Corps volunteer who had served in Mali. So now I had four jobs, four offices, and my studies to manage! Frenetic would be the best way to describe that time in my life. While I was at the University of Wisconsin I met people I would later end up working with during my Foreign Service career. Many of them studied at the Center for International Development or the Land Tenure Center—both hotbeds of progressive thinking and activist professors.

The overall university environment could be summed up as very progressive and very liberal. Many students and professors were active in the anti-Vietnam war movement, the women's movement, and the civil rights movement. Given that I was studying in the "despised" business school, I often encountered a kind of philosophical hostility, despite my visibly progressive social viewpoints in favor of the movements. However, among my circle of friends and acquaintances, most of whom had been PCVs, our common ground made for warm friendship and rapport. With them, I received "forgiveness" for studying to become a budding capitalist. It was the perfect place for Rosa and me—great days and times. Graduate school is tough, even without four jobs to manage, but in the end, it all worked out.

In 1973, I became the proud recipient of an MBA degree from the highly respected University of Wisconsin–Madison. With that milestone accomplished, I found the familiar question waiting for me. "What's next?" I thought briefly about going on to law school, but I felt it was time I got out into the world and earned a living.

Having decided to enter the business world, I thought my adventures in foreign affairs had come to an end. I began the job search once again; my plan was to stay in the United States and get a job with a large corporation. With an MBA in tow, I wanted to secure a career opportunity with a Fortune 500 company. The Twin Cities of Minnesota was attractive to us because the location was a mecca of corporate headquarters and progressive communities.

I secured several offers from companies in New York, Chicago, and Atlanta, but I was very interested in a position at a low-profile Fortune 500 corporation called International Multifoods. I found myself intrigued by the man who had offered me a job—a corporate vice president on the executive management team named Ted Rugland. A fascinating guy with an interesting background, Rugland was a WWII vet deeply connected to his Norwegian heritage. He was known to have a no-nonsense personality, matched only by his wicked sense of humor. I learned much later that Ted belonged to the famous Harvard Business School class of 1949. Known as the "49ers," the class would become Harvard's most successful MBA class in the history of the business school.[1] Ted was straightforward in our interview and wasted no time telling me that he was the only MBA at the company.

"I'm not even sure we should hire MBAs because young professionals have such unrealistic expectations," he told me. He went on to say that if I took the job as his special assistant, I would have six months to prove myself. The way he challenged me—as if he didn't expect me to accept such a bold offer—was appealing to me. I liked his direct approach to this new position. I figured I could learn a lot about executive management from such a savvy executive. So even though IM's salary offer came in slightly lower than other job offers I received, I accepted it and took on the challenge. It proved to be precisely the correct decision and a great start for my corporate career.

Ted was generous in showing me the planning, strategy, and operations across his division and throughout the company. I gained exposure to senior management in every business group and learned how to delve into the functional activities of our regional offices and plants across the country. I traveled with him to meetings with our major clients and suppliers and assisted him in every aspect of the business. It was a terrific launching pad for me, and I learned a lot from him. I found him to be an outstanding boss and mentor—direct, firm, and open to discussion about the gray areas of the business. He opened doors for me in the company, which enabled me to gain in-depth knowledge about a company's management style and procedures that I would not likely have received in this early stage of my career in a larger corporation. I met other superb leaders at International Multifoods, like Richard Vessels, who also mentored me.

I learned a few months ago that after Ted Rugland retired from International Multifoods, he went to law school, earned his degree at the age of eighty, and dedicated the rest of his working life representing the Blackfeet Indian Tribe in Montana. I'm not surprised that he took on such challenges because Ted set as high a bar for himself as he did for others, and he always wanted to make a difference. I feel fortunate to have had the opportunity to learn from such a unique leader.

Sometimes what you think you're looking for is not what you find to be most important. Never ignore your intuition or gut instinct when it comes to critical leadership and life decisions.

After two years at International Multifoods, an executive search firm recruited me with a generous offer from General Mills, also based in Minneapolis. After this first encounter with a recruiter, often called headhunters in those days, I learned to master the search process. In the future, I would effectively engage with search firms during my career, both as a client and a candidate.

General Mills presented me with an opportunity to work as an assistant brand manager in the fast-paced world of consumer product marketing, and it was one I couldn't resist. Further, I was proud to join a group of the first wave of black MBAs at this corporation; we represented the vanguard of diversity at the company. There were five of us in 1975, and we were fully aware that we had to succeed as "pioneers" in this corporation and that we were part of a nationwide trend across corporate America.

General Mills' food brands group were well-known staples in households across America. Wheaties, Cheerios, Betty Crocker, and Hamburger Helper could be found on the shelves of most kitchen pantries. It was an exciting place to work, and more importantly, it offered me a chance to learn about high-profile marketing in the big leagues. Product diversity was seen as a critical strategy for increased revenue and profitability by many corporations.

General Mills also owned Red Lobster restaurants, Gorton's, FootJoy, and Parker Bros. A company managing such a diverse range of product categories became somewhat commonplace in that era of conglomerates. General Mills was a fertile training ground for young managers, but it was very demanding and quite military-like in terms of the workplace hierarchy. I worked every Sunday, except Super Bowl Sunday, during my entire time there, which was not exceptional if you intended to compete with your peers for promotions and career advancement.

I worked with potato products in my category of brand management. I learned everything there was to know about Idaho potatoes, taking in all aspects of the food chain from the farm to the Betty Crocker kitchens to product production and marketing to the consumer. And I worked with all types of potato products, including instant mashed potatoes, au gratin, and scalloped potatoes.

At the same time, I learned essential aspects of value chain management and new product development, such as meat substitutes. I worked on one of the first teams that created beef and chicken substitute foods using soy protein, marketed as a healthy alternative to meat. We formulated imitation ham and chicken that tasted like the real thing. However, the American consumer did not buy into the concept of imitation meat, and the market never became more than a specialty food sector during that time. I thoroughly enjoyed the competitive environment, the daily challenges, and the chance to learn about business systems and operations, as well as the high-profile advertising and marketing campaigns.

We settled into a comfortable life in suburban Minneapolis and bought a house. Rosa completed her medical technology studies and got an excellent job in Minneapolis working for one of the first health management organizations (HMO) in the United States. Life was good, and we bought a house. After a few promotions, I began scouting for my next big move. After a couple of years at General Mills, an executive recruiter contacted me and asked me to consider an opportunity with Frito-Lay. Recruitment of competing up-and-coming marketing managers at top corporations like General Mills by other firms was common.

Eventually, I received an attractive offer for a marketing director position with Frito-Lay in Dallas, Texas, that amounted to a significant promotion with an impressive salary increase. The company was then and is now one of the most successful marketing companies in America. The big career decision would have me either stay at General Mills or move to Texas with Frito-Lay. In the end, I decided to stay put.

Interestingly, owing to its marketing success, Frito-Lay ended up being acquired by PepsiCo, and a few years later, the Frito-Lay executive team took over the reins of the company leadership. A good friend and former General Mills colleague moved into a similar level of management at PepsiCo, and several years later he became one of the top three executives there.

One never knows about the road not traveled, and during this period of my career debate I got an unexpected call offering me a unique opportunity—one that would prove better for my family and me, a life-defining road I felt called to take.

5 My Call to Foreign Service

International Business
Development at USAID

The entrepreneur always searches for change, responds to it, and exploits it as an opportunity.

—PETER DRUCKER

"I heard you have experience in the food industry, and we need a person with business management experience to assist in the design and implementation of a new agribusiness project. The deputy director of the USAID mission wants to include an experienced businessperson working on this project."

The voice on the other end of the line was that of Tony Cauterucci, head of the multisector office for the USAID mission in Tegucigalpa, Honduras. I'm confident that my former Peace Corps program manager in the Dominican Republic, Henry Reynolds, must have told Tony that I might be interested in working at USAID. The time was 1976, an era when the USAID mission in Tegucigalpa was very highly regarded and responsible for designing and managing the US government's foreign aid program in Honduras. USAID/Honduras had a dynamic leadership team, led by Frank Kimball, a highly regarded mission director and a reputation for being an excellent place to work.

The surprising conversation with Tony happened on an unusually cold, wintry day in Minneapolis, and it immediately stirred my imagination. *Wow—Aid . . . Honduras.* Instantly, I knew this idea deserved serious consideration. I immediately called Rosa for her opinion.

"Let's leave this frigid tundra and move back to Latin America!" she said, without hesitation.

With Rosa onboard, I agreed it was an offer worth pursuing. Soon, we headed to Honduras for my new opportunity as a contractor on a USAID agribusiness project.

I started as a personal services contractor in the multisector office, and Tony Cauterucci was the office director. There were several such contractors in the mission, and most of us were returned Peace Corps volunteers. One could say that I started my new career on the bottom rung of the ladder, according to the Honduras mission's organizational chart; it was a perfect starting place to learn international business development.[1] At General Mills, I had been surrounded by smart, demanding people, all engaged in pursuing our business goals in terms of sales, profits, and market share. I found the same qualities in the driven executives at USAID/Honduras, which further added to my ease of entry into international development.

Nor would any effort be required to reacclimate to the Latin American lifestyle. Rosa and I were happy to be in Honduras. Working with farmers in the central valley of Honduras and with the Honduran Ministry of Commerce enabled me to use my Spanish again. I had great respect and admiration for my new colleagues, and I found an outstanding boss in Tony, who became my mentor and lifelong friend. With Tony and his experienced deputy, Dick Apodaca, a savvy senior manager and a great source of support, I recognized that I had landed in the perfect place to enter into a Foreign Service career. The key lessons that I learned from working with Tony have guided my leadership approach throughout my career. He was an exceptional leader, and I consider myself fortunate to have started my USAID career in his office.

I was hired to design and implement the new agribusiness project in Honduras, and I soon learned that I was one of four young professionals tapped to carry out similar assignments on different projects in the Mission. Each of us worked on high-profile projects that would serve as launching pads for our bright futures in ways unimagined. But that day was yet to come. For the time being, we were all grateful and thrilled to be able to share our new experiences with people with whom we had so much in common. Two of my colleagues had also been Peace Corps volunteers, Rob Thurston and Paul Hartenberger. Juanita Thurston had also served in the Peace Corps, and she and Rosa became dear friends. Rob and I hit it off right away. We bonded well as colleagues and (eventually) young fathers, and this evolved in a special lifelong family friendship. The young wives in this group of contractors also formed a tight community in Tegucigalpa.

Newly married, most of us didn't have children yet. Rosa was an amazing partner in our first venture in the Foreign Service. She managed this new life effortlessly and with amazing flexibility, and it was clear that we had made the right family and career decision to move to Honduras.

Designing the agribusiness project was a fairly complex process, and over the next several months I worked with a mix of players in an uncertain and somewhat precarious situation. To carry out a national land reform program, the Honduran government decided to expropriate some large estates in the central valley of the Comayagua region and give the land to local peasant farmers, most of whom were tenants and squatters from local towns. So, there was a mix of experienced farmers and quasi-farmers who had been city dwellers, all desiring land. Under the new agriculture program these farmers received twenty hectares of land from the Honduran government's agrarian reform program. We worked with multiple government agencies, including the National Office of Agrarian Reform and the minister of agriculture, who had overlapping responsibilities. The United States Embassy leadership held Rafael Leonardo Callejas, the minister of agriculture, in high regard; clearly, he was seen as a rising political star and a potential candidate for the presidency of Honduras, which he subsequently won in 1990.

USAID provided significant resources to the agrarian reform program, contracting experts from the renowned Land Tenure Center at the University of Wisconsin to help manage land reform projects in Honduras. My assignment revolved around the design of a project that would benefit the land reform taking place and aid farmers by creating an export crop agribusiness in the Comayagua Valley.

The vision was to integrate the production, packing and shipping, and, ultimately, the marketing and sales of fresh fruits and vegetables for the US market. Several vital indicators made it immediately evident that this was going to be a very challenging project. The lack of experience on the part of the farmers with new crops, the complex postharvest operation of processing fresh produce for shipment, and the marketing challenges associated with penetrating a unique and sophisticated market were just some of my concerns. An unforeseen issue that further complicated this effort lay in wait just around the corner.

My initial review of the situation caused me to focus on the availability of refrigerated trailers and market channels for the produce. Overcoming the challenges associated with the critical tasks of growing and packing the crops was pointless if we couldn't successfully deliver them to the market. It became clear that the only reliable sources of technical expertise, refrigerated trailers, and market access were the two US banana companies that had operated and controlled the banana industry in Honduras for more than seventy-five years.

I relayed my observations to the mission leadership. I told them that the only viable solution would require a partnership with at least one of the two banana corporations operating in Honduras, United Brands (now Chiquita Brands) and Castle & Cook (now Dole Food Company). However, a political scandal between the Honduran government and United Brands, related to a $2.5 million bribe scheme, made the partnership I was proposing a challenging proposition. The objective of the bribe was to obtain a major reduction of taxes on banana exports from Honduras. A few weeks before the scandal hit the media, Eli Black, chairman and CEO of United Brands, jumped to his death from his forty-fourth-floor office in the Pan-Am Building in Manhattan.[2]

This new project launch, coming one short year after that scandal, produced an understandable reluctance on the part of the US Embassy and USAID leadership to approach the banana companies regarding any assistance or partnership. However, I realized that these companies had technical, management, marketing, and shipping assets that were critical to the success of the new project. So I appealed to USAID's leadership and Tony for approval to discuss a partnership with the banana companies. I was impressed by the willingness of management to take this risk, given the political situation.

As I anticipated, it turned out to be a perfect time to talk to the banana companies. They were more than willing to entertain some technical assistance or a partnership role that would lead to an improved image for themselves and contribute to the development of Honduras. Further, given that we would be farming new crops, the project wouldn't interfere with their banana business. I chose to call on United Brands as my first order of business. Although it was not involved in land reform, it had recently started a pilot crop diversification program focused on melons and pineapples. The in-country expertise present at its headquarters near the city of San Pedro Sula was impressive, with a staff that included some twenty-plus PhDs covering a wide range of agricultural sciences and postharvest crop management.

I led a team to meet with United's managers at its offices and found that we had common ground regarding the business and technical aspects of the proposed project. I found kindred spirits within the company's senior management, as we all desired to cut a deal; fortunately, these leaders saw the advantages of working with USAID and the Honduran government. They also had many young MBAs on board who hungered for involvement with something new and innovative.

We subsequently reached an agreement on a technical assistance contract that assigned five of their top experts to work on the project. They would assist with project design and implementation, and the company guaranteed the refrigerated shipment of our produce to the United States at a fair price. Much of the technical work these employees performed was pro bono, as money was not their motivation. They saw the value of improved public relations by contributing to Honduran agricultural development.

Following the successful negotiation with United Brands, I then pursued a partnership with Castle & Cook to assist in a new agricultural research project for another region of Honduras. The partnership model we developed with United provided valuable experience for future projects in Honduras. Even more important, our success opened the door for a new wave of private-public partnerships by USAID in Central America. If our negotiations had failed, we could not have launched the agribusiness project. United Brands provided crucial assistance in the form of agriculture experts who contributed to the high degree of success enjoyed by the project. The company's business was to grow, pack, and ship bananas in an unforgiving tropical climate. Their ships traveled daily to Miami and New Orleans, delivering this time-sensitive and low-margin product to demanding American consumers.

With such strong public sentiment against banana companies on the part of Hondurans—United Brands in particular—we recognized how important it would be that this program be successful. In hindsight, we also realized how fortunate it was that Minister Callejas assigned some impressive young Honduran agronomists and MBAs to work with me, who decades later became prominent business and government leaders. I formed strong working relationships with two very talented executives, Ramon Medina Luna at the Ministry of Economy and Norman García at the National Investment Corporation. They played key roles in the startup of our projects and in coordinating with all government agencies.

The first lesson I learned was that it's essential to develop these types of partnerships in a developing country because you had to identify willing allies to push innovative change. With counterparts in the government, in the banana companies, and in USAID prepared to support this vision and approach, I had the green light to design and implement the project.

We went on to later form an alliance with the Zamorano Pan-American Agriculture School, which had a stellar reputation for training outstanding agronomists. The school developed a partnership with United Brands to produce melons in southern Honduras, and this gave us the opportunity to work with another diversification project and gain insights into a parallel export pilot project.

The USAID mission gave me the latitude and support to make deals that led to successful agribusiness partnerships. I also received substantial assistance in my design work from Henry Reynolds and other terrific colleagues. The experience and trust afforded me by these individuals in writing USAID project papers were invaluable to me during my years in Tegucigalpa.

In that period, all major projects were approved in USAID/Washington. I traveled to DC as part of a team to present the agribusiness project to various senior officers in the Bureau for Latin America and the Caribbean. I got a close-up look at the project review process and learned what was entailed in writing a successful project paper. Fortunately, I worked under Tony's superb mentorship throughout the Washington trip, and the Development Assistance Executive Committee approved the project, giving me my first USAID victory!

With the project's design and agribusiness mission approved, my central question became "Is my short-term contract up?" Once again, the call to global service had expanded my worldview. I felt at home at the USAID/Honduras mission. I wasn't sure if I was ready to return home to corporate America. And I thought it was a pretty good bet that Rosa would be less than excited about leaving Latin America and heading back to Minnesota winters so soon.

After the project's approval, I was happy that I was asked to stay on to implement the agribusiness project. So, as it turned out, Rosa and I would not be heading back to the States after all. There was even more terrific news in that my contractor colleagues, now our good friends, had also received contract extensions for their projects' implementation phase. So, we would all remain in Honduras, the best possible outcome in terms of our jobs and our family life.

USAID's Bureau for Latin America and the Caribbean headquarters had a predictable management system. You knew you could gauge your success by the countries where you served, and the positions you were selected for at each stage of your career. It was very much like working for General Mills in the corporate world. Once you were tapped to work on the most profitable brands of the company—like Cheerios or Wheaties—this was senior management's recognition that you were a manager with great potential. I was beginning to observe that USAID also had its "brands" in terms of highly regarded country missions. The profile would be a USAID mission in a nation that was considered important to US foreign policy, with a highly regarded mission director and senior staff, talented FSOs and a substantial program budget. USAID/Honduras was clearly such a place.

In creating a new, evolved role for the private sector to engage in public-private partnerships, it was apparent that this could be a win-win for both sides. The agribusiness project was one of those examples, and I was glad to see that USAID's senior management was open to exploring such an alliance despite the political landmines.

The Hondurans were angry, and the Americans were embarrassed. But thankfully, we were able to convince all parties to agree to a suitable and mutually beneficial arrangement at the right moment. These partnerships between the government of Honduras, USAID, and the banana companies would be the beginning of larger investments in agribusiness development via public-private partnerships. Some of these executives would later rise to corporate leadership at Castle & Cook and become strong advocates for the USAID–supported diversification projects in Central America.

Our original plan for the project was to grow tomatoes and cucumbers. But before success would be ours, we had some tough lessons to learn. Losing our very first crop of cucumbers to wind scarring was one of the most devastating. I will never forget driving into the Comayagua Valley, feeling excited about our first shipment to the United States and seeing all the banquet tables set up in anticipation of a celebration. The mayor of the town had already arrived for the big event. With the trucks from the United Fruit Company standing by, everything seemed ready to ship our first harvest. It was a big deal.

Then, the lead expert from United shocked everyone, saying, "We can't ship any of these cukes; they won't be accepted as top-quality produce by the American market due to the scarring on their skin." My young agronomists from the Honduran extension services looked at me for direction.

The farmers felt thoroughly defeated; they had followed the advice of these American wizards, and it hadn't worked. "Now what?" we all were asking ourselves. Very thin plastic trellises were typically used to grow cucumbers, but because heavy winds in the valley led to the scarring of the cucumbers by the trellising, we couldn't use them. A whole new method for dealing with the wind issue had to be devised if cucumbers were to become the dominant export crop. Since we used Israeli trellising, I contracted with the Israeli Embassy in Honduras to provide technical experts to assist in this task. We also introduced drip irrigation, again with Israeli experts. In the meantime, the farmers lost that first crop. But the National Credit Bank covered the financial losses for these impoverished farmers, who could not afford to lose a crop.

We had originally planned for tomatoes to be another export product, but that crop never stood a chance because tobacco had been planted on the same land in the Comayagua Valley ten years earlier. Another lesson learned: tomatoes and tobacco come from the same family, the nightshade family. Because of that, our first and last crop of tomatoes wilted on the vine due to the "tobacco mosaic virus" that was still in the soil from previous years.

The mission's staff and I often shared our experiences of project success and failure with colleagues who visited us from other USAID missions. I saw this as an essential part of my role, and I think it was a valuable asset to the bureau because it enabled others to replicate our success and avoid the failures.

In the early phases of the project, I realized that we should study and document the activities of this new project so that we would have a written record of "lessons learned" that would help us improve our implementation and build a base for the future. For this purpose, I reached out to Dr. Ed Felton, a dynamic and innovative professor of business at Harvard Business School, who was then based in Nicaragua at the Central American Institute of Business Administration. This B-school was founded by the Harvard Business School in 1964, and its staff used the "Harvard case study method" to examine past and current business situations. Ed and I agreed that this new agribusiness model in Honduras would be an excellent case to study and document for both Honduras and the rest of Central America. This arrangement led to both a series of case studies and seminars attended by government officials and private businessmen, which showcased the project's challenges and achievements. Based on this successful venture in Honduras, Ed and I would continue to collaborate on similar projects over the years throughout our careers in academia and the Foreign Service, respectively.

Eventually, after many years, the agrarian reform farmers became successful, in that cucumbers were grown and packed in the fields and shipped directly from Honduran farms to supermarkets in the United States. The Comayagua farmers' standard of living changed dramatically with increased vegetable exports and their corresponding increase in income. They became the elite farmers in that region of Honduras. I have had the opportunity to visit the valley a couple of times over the years, and I saw the trajectory of economic changes in the farmers and their families over a five- to ten-year period. They were able to purchase pickup trucks and color TVs. They could afford to send their kids to private schools, and they had become respected members of their community.

Change can take a while, but with patience, and technical and financial support, it's possible, and clearly both USAID and our banana company partners played a significant role in this agricultural transformation. The farmers and the Honduran government counterparts we worked with became the true pioneers of that successful program and created a new export industry in Honduras that eventually became a multimillion-dollar business.

Tony left Honduras at the end of his tour in 1978, and my project was transferred to the agricultural development office under my new boss, Bill Janssen. Bill had worked with the new mission director, Jack Robinson, in the Dominican Republic. Recognized as determined leaders, they were highly respected by the Honduran government for their strategic thinking and judgment in building up the mission's portfolio.

Jack also brought in the experienced senior expert and development guru Len Kornfeld. An old-school USAID master strategist and tactician, Len spoke fluent Spanish and never took no for an answer. He usually won every argument concerning project design and implementation, and he was the architect of the new and massive agriculture-sector loan that would be the cornerstone of USAID's agricultural and rural development strategy. We "young Turks"—Rob, Paul, John Kelly, and I—were each given a project component to lead under the agriculture sector loan. I was asked by Len to design an agricultural research project to strengthen the National Agriculture University in Honduras, another important step in broadening my experience during my first tour.

By this time, Jack Robinson had pulled off a major feat by securing FSO appointments for all four of us. As personal services contractors, we were temporary employees. Our conversion to direct-hire status was a stunning accomplishment on Jack's part because he achieved this during a federal hiring freeze instituted by President Ford's administration in 1977. The stability of a permanent position was crucial to us at this age and time when we were starting families. In 1977, Rosa and I had our first child, Michael Aaron, and a few other couples in the mission also had children during that year, including to our great joy Juanita and Rob with the birth of their son Thomas, joining his lovely sister Anita.

Our entry into the Foreign Service life also illustrated another aspect of service: the recognition that spouses were clearly the unsung heroes of the Foreign Service. Rosa and I learned that the representational responsibilities of embassy life were substantial, especially for the senior officers. It was expected that one's spouse would assist the senior women (e.g., the ambassador's wife or the USAID director's wife) with the "meet and greet" tasks associated with hosting dinners and receptions for host government officials and other local groups as well as visiting US delegations. As I observed Rosy Cauterucci, Rosa, and the other wives take on the these "informal volunteer" tasks, we gained a great appreciation of the inherent unfairness of this situation. We were glad to see that these young women in Tegucigalpa started to push back against this unpaid "staff" work and demanded more employment opportunities for spouses at post. This was also a reflection of the 1970s and the fight for women's equality in America. Fortunately, the world and the Foreign Service have changed, and the new generation of Foreign Service spouses—now men and women, many of them partners in two-career marriages—would not tolerate such practices.

Honduras was an exciting place to start my USAID career. It was an impressive mission where I had outstanding mentors and superb colleagues. We managed substantial US government funding for building a broad program portfolio across various sectors (education, health, agriculture, etc.), and we were extraordinarily well connected to the Honduran government. The vast majority of our officers spoke fluent Spanish and had excellent professional relationships in that society, and it was also a tranquil and excellent place to live and raise a family. Unfortunately, the Honduras of today has a reputation as one of the most dangerous places in the world to live. It is fraught with violent crime and a very high murder rate. It is a far cry from the Honduras that I remember, a place where I could drive myself to every major city with no fear whatsoever for my safety.

The call I received from Tony on that cold day in Minnesota turned out to be the beginning of an incredible career opportunity for me. Once that decision was made and more opportunities presented themselves, I was prepared to embark on a worldwide Foreign Service career. My three amigos from the beginning—Rob Thurston, Paul Hartenberger, and John Kelly— and other outstanding FSOs on staff—including Marty Dagata, John Lovaas, Eric Zalman, Marcy Birnbaum, and Ken Scofield—all went on to have long-term, outstanding careers in USAID. We also met Mike and Cecilia Viola during our time in Honduras. Mike was a returned PCV who had served in Brazil, and at that time he was the deputy director of CARE. This was the beginning of a long friendship that would include, in my yet unimagined distant future, an important partnership in South Africa. Mike was the photographer who took the first photo of our infant son Michael, thereby cementing our friendship over the years!

Working in USAID/Honduras was an important career-building experience for me, and I have many fond memories of friends, family, and significant life events from our tour there. I turned thirty in Honduras, and that milestone birthday produced an extraordinary memory for me with my dad. One thing I can say for sure about Spencer Williams—he was not a fan of air travel! He had no appreciation for the friendly skies and would prefer to drive down any highway in his Chrysler any day of the week. The one time I did convince him to take a jet plane was for my big birthday.

We flew together from New Orleans to Tegucigalpa, and he did his best to pretend to like it. Although flying was not his thing, he could not have been prouder and happier that he got to see me on the job overseas, representing the US government. We traveled all over the country, and I, too, had reason to be proud of my dad. He overcame a great fear to celebrate my thirtieth birthday with me in a faraway place.

6 High Hopes for Haiti
A Chance for Democracy

Corruption is the enemy of development and good governance.

—PRATIBHA PATIL, former president of India

After three years in Honduras, I received an offer to transfer to USAID/ Haiti as a private sector officer in the project development office. Haiti had always held a great attraction for me, ever since my Uncle Ed first introduced its history to me when he told me about the impossible slave revolt, led by the heroic Haitian general Toussaint Louverture, which led to Haitian independence in 1804.[1]

This geographical move would work out well for my family because Haiti was only a twenty-minute flight to the Dominican Republic, where Rosa's family lived. Logistically, it ended up being an especially advantageous location because in 1981 Rosa and I welcomed our second son, Steven Joseph, into our family. He was born in the Dominican Republic, and I knew that this would give our sons the opportunity to bond regularly with at least one set of grandparents and Rosa's extended family.

In preparation for our new assignment, during the first three months of 1979, Rosa and I received intense French-language training at the Foreign Service Institute in Washington, DC. We lived in a two-bedroom apartment and spent eight hours of every day studying French. Rosa's sister, Thelma, and her son, Augustin, traveled from Santo Domingo to care for Michael during this period of grueling studies. Although French is the official language of Haiti and was essential for working with the Haitian government, all Haitians spoke Creole—a blend of several languages.[2] I often regretted that we didn't learn more Creole beyond a rudimentary level. The Haitian elite commonly spoke French and used it as a class-discriminating factor; it was almost considered more important than skin color.

In my new position, I would be a project development officer, and my responsibilities would involve designing private sector development projects. I went to work in a mission led by the highly regarded Larry Harrison. I worked directly for Scott Smith, who reported to a highly respected USAID economist, William S. "Bill" Rhoads. It was also in Haiti that I met Stacy Rhodes (a returned PCV who had worked in Bolivia), who worked in the same office; this would be the beginning of a cherished personal and professional relationship that continues to this day. A skilled writer, Stacy also was analytical, hardworking, and an outstanding officer.

Stacy formed a team with a brilliant and dynamic Haitian lawyer named Guy Malary. They created the first organization designed to provide legal assistance for the poor in Haiti, a truly pioneering effort funded by USAID. In 1993, Guy Malary agreed to leave a prominent and successful law practice to become the first minister of justice (attorney general) in the new democratic government of President Aristide. Tragically, that great man and patriot was assassinated a few months later by antigovernment forces.

Malary's murder came less than two hours after a radio broadcast sent out a warning from President Clinton that the United States would hold Haiti's military responsible for the safety of members of the transitional government.[3] Due to the heinous act, Haiti lost a courageous leader who believed in the rule of law, Florence Malary and her children lost a husband and father, and Stacy and I lost a dear friend.

Stacy and Trish Rhodes became great friends to Rosa and me, and our children attended the same schools. Our partnership, which began in Haiti, set the stage for Stacy and me to work together over the coming decades in the Washington headquarters of USAID and, ultimately, on the Peace Corps' leadership team. We have had the great pleasure of seeing our children grow into amazing adults, and our family bond has deepened as we each have welcomed grandchildren.

Despite this being an era of turmoil, United States–Haiti relations had the potential to dramatically improve. The US government had become increasingly concerned during this time about the influx of both Haitian and Cuban boat immigrants to the Miami area. Fidel Castro emptied Cuban prisons and mixed the prisoners with immigrants on boats headed to the United States. At the same time, Haitians were fleeing poverty and oppression in high numbers, braving the treacherous waters of the Gulf of Mexico in rickety boats for the shores of Florida. The Carter administration labeled Haitians and Cubans that came to the United States during the 1980 Mariel boatlift "Cuban-Haitian entrants" and relied on the discretionary authority of the attorney general to have them admitted.[4]

In 1981, the new Reagan administration responded to the mass migration of asylum seekers who arrived in boats from Haiti by establishing an agreement with then-dictator Jean-Claude Duvalier that authorized the US Coast Guard to go aboard and inspect private Haitian ships suspected of transporting undocumented Haitians on the high seas and to interrogate the passengers. At that time, the United States government considered Haitian boat people as economic migrants who were trying to escape one of the poorest countries in the world.

Governor Bob Graham of Florida decided to launch an initiative to address Haiti's myriad economic and social problems in what became known as the Florida-Haiti Program, led by Lieutenant Governor Wayne Mixson. This innovative plan aimed to encourage the Haitian people to remain in Haiti and thus halt the exodus of migrants to Florida. Governor Graham recruited leading executives from major Florida-based corporations, universities, and nongovernmental organizations, including Eastern Airlines, Disney World, SeaWorld, University of Florida, and various hotel groups. The executives participated in a mission to Haiti to meet with the Haitian government and business leaders, during which they attempted to come up with ways to increase jobs and overall economic growth in Haiti. Joe Thomas, the governor's international affairs director and senior adviser to Lieutenant Governor Mixson, accompanied the company leaders to Haiti.

I was assigned as the USAID coordinator for the delegation's visit, the details of which I worked out with our superb embassy colleagues, notably the dynamic David Weiss. David went on to have a distinguished career in the State Department and as a senior official at the US Trade Representative Office. Following his federal career, he continued in international development and is now the CEO of the highly respected development organization Global Communities.

The Florida-Haiti project evolved into a task force led by Joe Thomas and managed from Haiti under my supervision. Joe and I developed a terrific working relationship over the ensuing months, as we directed this bilateral and unique commission. Our time together working on the Florida-Haiti project resulted in a productive, professional relationship. Our mutual admiration grew into a beautiful forty-year friendship between Rosa and me and Joe and Diana "Dynee" Thomas.

Historically, Haiti had never had a decent chance at political stability, democratic government, or economic and social progress.[5] Between slave revolutions, ruthless dictatorships, and fending off wars, the country faced many challenges. All attempts to erect a democracy had failed. With the help of the military, the worst dictator in the country's history, François Duvalier, known as Papa Doc, declared himself president for life in 1964. The corrupt dictatorship marks one of the saddest chapters in Haitian history, during which tens of thousands were killed or exiled.

By 1979, Haiti was under the leadership of Francois Jean-Claude Duvalier, also known as Baby Doc, the son of Papa Doc, who had died in 1971. The United States and other donor countries wanted to see a democratic transition in Haiti, but they were not sure this would be possible with an unprepared playboy who appeared to have limited intellect.

With the collective support of major donors such as the World Bank, France, Canada, and the UN, the policy of the United States toward Haiti shifted and the significant USAID foreign assistance program was seen as an instrument to assist Jean-Claude Duvalier and a small group of progressive ministers educated in France, Canada, and the United States. These new ministers expressed their support for pursuing democratic governance and massively reforming the Haitian government, and they focused on ways to stimulate economic growth and generate hundreds of thousands of jobs.

US trade policy provided the stimulus for substantial job creation in the country.[6] These policies incorporated long-standing trade preferences for Central American countries with new ones, which triggered the growth of offshore sourcing of components and finished products (primarily apparel and electronics) for the US market. At first, Mexico was the primary offshore location for US companies, but then US companies began building plants in Central American and Caribbean countries.

The Caribbean Basin Initiative, which came into effect on January 1, 1984, was another trade program that provided several tariff and trade benefits to many Central American and Caribbean countries.[7] These trade benefits proved to be a vital opportunity for Haiti and led to rapid job growth in the assembly sector (apparel, toys, electronics) for the country. Given that Haiti was known for its hardworking, low-wage workers (i.e., cheap labor), fifty to sixty American companies moved quickly into Haiti to take advantage of this. Owing to these new policies and economic initiatives, trade between the United States and Haiti increased significantly during the Reagan administration.

Given the anticipated rapid expansion of corporate investment in the country, mission leadership decided to create an office of private enterprise development; I was selected to head up that office during my second year in Haiti. I saw this as a perfect opportunity for my former colleague, Joe Thomas, who had returned to Florida, to come back to Haiti and work on projects that we had designed in anticipation of the launch of the Caribbean Basin Initiative. Fortunately, he agreed to join my team as a senior adviser and resident director of the Florida-Haiti Program. Joe played a lead role in the design and implementation of some of USAID's most important projects. He possessed superb analytical and writing skills and provided savvy wisdom in solving complex issues. We had a very productive partnership and built strong relationships with both Haitian and American business leaders in Haiti.

Bob Burgess, the dynamic and highly respected managing director of the General Telephone & Electronics/Sylvania Corporation in Haiti, became one of our principal partners. Bob was a prominent advocate of and key player in creating public-private partnerships, often funded by USAID, with our Haitian partners in both the government and the business community that promoted and supported expanded trade with the United States. In addition to his advocacy efforts, Bob and his wife Pat were very gracious in opening their home to host various business delegations that traveled to Haiti as business opportunities became more apparent under the expanded Caribbean Basin Initiative trade policy.

A few years later, Bob was promoted to vice president of the company's Central America Lighting Group, based in San José, Costa Rica. He was the only influential African American business executive that I encountered in the Caribbean region during those early years of my Foreign Service career. Fortuitously, I would have the pleasure of collaborating with him once again, during my next posting in USAID/Costa Rica.

To help implement the trade policy changes, USAID's budget was increased significantly in all of the Caribbean Basin Initiative countries, and USAID/Haiti used these funds to support new private sector programs. We began to develop significant alliances with the top trade association run by Haitian entrepreneurs in apparel, toys, and electronics. During this same period, major American companies (GTE Corporation, Disney, MacGregor, Sara Lee, Rawlings, Gap, and Mattel) set up assembly plants in Haiti's tariff-free zones. They assembled garments, electronics, baseballs, games, toys, sporting goods, footwear, and leather products. Haitians began stitching all

Major League baseballs in plants that operated on a tax-free status as if they were in the United States or Puerto Rico. The Haitian government typically did not interfere in plant operations. Under the new free zone regulations, a new manufacturing operation could incorporate in Haiti in as few as ninety days without the typical voluminous paperwork and red tape. It was a period of amazing and rapid industrial expansion.

All raw materials, cloth, and components went to Haiti, where the final product was sewn, finished, or assembled. Under the Caribbean Basin Initiative, a twin-plant manufacturing approach became standard. Large steel arched streetlamps, for example, were manufactured in Puerto Rico by GTE Sylvania and then sent to Haiti for workers to insert the filaments. The companies saved an enormous amount of money and did not have to pay duty on those shipments.

Hundreds of thousands of Haitians found jobs in these factories. Since one Haitian often supported five or six other people, an estimated 1.2 million people benefited when two hundred thousand people were employed. There were always discussions about whether the factories provided decent working conditions. I toured a great many of them with American congressional delegations and with American and Haitian business leaders. I found some 80 percent of them operated modern, air-conditioned facilities. The work was difficult, but there were not a lot of alternatives for the average Haitian. For many of them, this was the first time they had well-paying jobs by Haitian standards.

All production shipped to the United States went through one export zone, and there were few restrictions to setting up a facility with a single export zone in an individual plant. Haiti's ability to be very competitive from a wage standpoint and having a very profitable location for the electronics and apparel industries facilitated this type of rapid export growth. Timing also played a role since it occurred before China became a low-wage destination for global corporations.

The role of USAID was to design projects and programs under the mission's overall private-sector-led strategy. We assisted the efforts of business associations to attract investment to Haiti. We also helped American companies that came to Haiti explore ways to set up businesses in the country. So we worked on both sides of the equation.

The mission leadership team, Harlan Hobgood and Phyllis Dichter, gave me great latitude to carry out my duties. They were both creative thinkers with strong personalities, and they appreciated the fast pace of our private sector portfolio and were pleased by the broad partnerships we created to support economic growth in Haiti. My superb colleagues and great friends Mike Baldwin, Linda Morse, Sylvie Kulkin, and Gene George, along with the USAID veteran Ann Fitzcharles, were a continual source of inspiration and wisdom in managing and understanding the complicated mores of Haitian society. I thoroughly enjoyed the company of Mike and Gene, both returned PCVs who had served in Nepal, who were always ready to "volunteer" for unanticipated activities. Also, we were reunited with Paul and Doris Hartenerger, who had started out on this FSO journey with us in Honduras.

During my tour in Haiti I was also introduced to the potential for career planning and the opportunity to pursue senior management positions in USAID. Judy Ross, the new headquarters' "talent scout" and a dynamic human resource executive from the private sector, came to visit us. She was building a modern management training and tracking system for the agency and wanted to ensure that she included up-and-coming young officers. She told both Stacy Rhodes and me that we should consider more senior positions and gave us guidance for pursuing such opportunities in the future. I greatly appreciated her wise advice, and we have remained friends throughout the various phases of our respective careers.

In connection with our investment and export promotion programs, we used the additional funding under the Caribbean Basin Economic Recovery Act to work with local investors to create the first private development finance corporation in Haiti in 1983. It was modeled after similar USAID projects in countries like Peru, the Dominican Republic, Panama, and others. In the project to establish the private bank, I benefited greatly from the extraordinary assistance of Humberto Esteve, a legendary Cuban American consultant and visionary who was vice president for Latin America at Arthur D. Little Management Consulting Company.

I valued Humberto's expertise, friendship, and sound advice, which he generously provided across a wide range of topics. Along with his brilliant team of young consultants, which included Robert Wagner and Eduardo Tugendhat, Humberto played a significant role in helping us create the new and innovative project that led to the creation of SOFIHDES (Société Financière Haïtienne de Développement S.A.). Haitians raised a million dollars to invest in this remarkable bank.

Most people did not believe that the cut-throat Haitian families who had historically been at war with each other in their business practices would come together to invest in one bank, but they did. Their joint-venture bank resulted in a source of lending for exporters that fueled change in Haiti. For the first time in the history of the country, Haitians were substantially investing in the equity of a private firm. The investment wasn't public because there was no public equity market in Haiti at the time, but it was a multi-owner, development financed corporation.

At the same time, we worked on promoting small business development. The Pan American Development Foundation backed several micro-enterprise development projects that sought to create lending operations throughout Latin America. We worked with the foundation to support the sector that encompassed handicrafts and artwork, for which Haitians are world renowned. One of our major initiatives was to arrange, for the first time in the history of the country, a Haitian delegation to exhibit at the annual American Craft Show in Atlanta, one of the top handicraft fairs in the United States.

Joe Thomas was the architect of this innovative undertaking. We led a Haitian delegation to Georgia, where Andrew Young, then mayor of Atlanta, presented us with a key to the city. We enjoyed a gracious and warm welcome, and the time we spent was very memorable for all of us, but especially for the Haitian artisans.

Eventually, top-name designers would produce high-fashion creations in Haiti, using raw materials of leather and silk. We brought in Italian designers to help Haitian designers create new high-value end products, which opened up world markets to them for the first time, resulting in quite an opportunity.

Overall, we designed and managed a wide array of innovative projects in Haiti over my four years there with USAID. It appeared that Jean-Claude Duvalier and his regime were on track to create a more progressive and democratic nation that would provide thousands of jobs and greatly improve the general welfare of the Haitian citizens. He seemed to be willing to promote increased economic growth in the country. His economic cabinet, talented young Haitian technocrats, had free rein to manage the Haitian economy. They led the progressive wing of the Haitian government and served as the "go-to" guys for foreign donor nations.

Young Haitian businessmen also flooded the private sector side; like their government counterparts, they returned to Haiti after completing their overseas studies in the United States and Europe. They saw the range of opportunities and sought to benefit from this evolving business environment. They became the primary contacts for American companies and

often partnered with them. The Caribbean Basin Initiative, a precursor
to the North American Free Trade Association (NAFTA), initiated under
George H. W. Bush and implemented by Bill Clinton, was the policy and
funding platform for this work by USAID.

We worked closely with the minister of finance and the minister of
planning—two cabinet ministers who were leaders of the Duvalier administration in private sector development. I felt we continued to make progress, until 1980, when President Duvalier married Michèle Bennett. The
US government was already suspicious of Baby Doc and concerned about
many of his policies and activities, and so its worries only intensified when
he married into a family of corrupt "kleptocrats."

Michèle Bennett and her father were determined to reap the benefits
of being the leaders of Haiti. One of their main areas of focus was the successful export promotion business and how they might take advantage of
the role that the Haitian government played in supporting this sector. We
began to see growing corruption and interference in private-sector-led
growth. The Haitian business community and American firms soon began
to complain about the situation.

This tragic turn of events stymied the substantial economic growth
and democratic awakening that could have led to a better future for the vast
majority of Haitians. Tourism was booming; Club Med even opened a re-
sort in Haiti during that time. For the first time in this country's history,
hundreds of thousands of Haitians were working and earning a decent
income, which was, unmistakably, the most positive development of all.
However, owing to the corruption of Duvalier and his in-laws, the country
began to unravel. He faced and could not resolve several national crises,
including the onset of the HIV/AIDS epidemic and an African swine fever
epidemic. Eventually, he was overthrown by the military in 1986, but instability persisted after that in the form of a series of coups and political crises.
Most of USAID assistance programs by this time were being implemented
by local nongovernmental organizations in the health sector.

The time I spent in Haiti with USAID, from 1979 to 1983, was probably
one of the most promising periods in the country's history—a renaissance.
It was exceptional in terms of the broad sector projects and programs that
the mission implemented in conjunction with the support of the progressive cabinet of the Duvalier government. We thought Haiti had a real
chance because of the economic drivers in that economy—both local and
foreign private investment and the number of jobs that had been created.

With the export economy becoming so big and powerful, we believed the government would not be able to interfere and thwart the momentum.

Meanwhile, with the large numbers of Haitians employed, trained, and moving up the social-economic ladder, one could see the beginnings of a broad middle-class taking shape. At least for a time in their history, a real middle-class seemed possible. But the traditional resistance of the Haitian elites to more equitable treatment of the poor majority reemerged, and unfortunately, Haiti remains a broken and tragic society today.

After I left in 1983, I continued to follow the Haitian political scene from afar. Corruption eroded the political and social environment across all sectors of Haitian society, and Jean-Claude began to lose control. The historical infighting between the Haitian oligarchs resumed in cutthroat style after the brief pause during the few years of progressive development. Not only did Haiti gradually lose its "cheap labor" advantage to China but the increasing political instability and social-economic turmoil in the country was a significant disincentive for foreign private investors. As long as the US trade incentives were in place, American investors stayed because their operations were still profitable, and the Duvalier administration didn't interfere with them. But the military coups, the chaotic elections that ensued, the continued political corruption, the devastating earthquake in 2010, and the 2021 assassination of President Moise all contributed to Haiti's continuing struggle characterized by extreme poverty and traumatic governance. Under such conditions, it's difficult to find room for hope in a society where there is a continual political crisis that cripples future social and economic development.

My mother,
Blanche Wills,
in a high school photo
from 1944.

My father,
Spencer Williams,
upon entering the
US Army in 1942.

My parents' wedding in 1946 (from left to right): my mother's sisters Earline, Myrtle, and Juanita; my parents, Blanche Wills and Spencer Williams; my mother's mother, Edna Mae, and her stepfather, Fordie Terrell; and my mother's sisters Willa Rae and Marion.

With my sister Ellen, dressed for a school play in 1954.

My college graduation photo from 1967.

My maternal grandmother, Edna Mae Terrell, at the age of 95.

Blanche and Louis Green, recently married, in 1976.

My father, Spencer (wearing the long scarf), with his brother Alvin in 1990.

Rosa on the Staten Island Ferry during our first trip as a married couple to New York City in 1969.

Peace Corps volunteers at a teachers' conference in Bayaguana, Dominican Republic, in 1967 (I'm the tall guy in the back).

This was the first USAID project that I designed and led as a Foreign Service officer in Honduras in 1977. The farmers are showing us their first crop of tomatoes, which were grown under a joint project of the Honduran government and USAID, the first phase of a new export industry for fresh fruits and vegetables.

With my childhood friend Harry Simmons and Michael (age 2) in Haiti in 1979.

Family portrait with Steven (age 2) and Michael (age 6) in Costa Rica in 1983.

At a State Department awards ceremony in 1988, after receiving my first presidential award as director of the Latin America and Caribbean bureau's private sector office. I am joined by my friend and colleague Phil Gary, Rosa, and my mother. (courtesy of Clyde McNair, USAID photographer)

As mission director of the regional Caribbean mission, frequent air travel was the norm for my staff and me in order to cover the vast region that included more than twenty island nations. For official visits—such as here, where I'm about to depart on a trip to meet with the prime ministers of St. Lucia and St. Vincent in 1991—I occasionally traveled on the regional US military attaché's plane, seen here with two US Embassy officers.

Receiving a presidential award as deputy assistant administrator at a State Department awards ceremony in 1993, presented by Secretary of State Warren Christopher and my boss, Ambassador James Michel.

As USAID executive secretary I was an electoral observer during the Haitian parliamentary and local elections in 1995. Here I am with Deputy Mission Director Sarah Clark and our US Army escort team.

7 Success Breeds Success
Lessons in Good Governance

Costa Rica believes in building bridges, in looking for solutions to problems, and not clinging to positions.

—OSCAR ARIAS, Nobel Laureate and former president of Costa Rica

With the introduction of the Caribbean Basin Initiative, I had the opportunity to consult with and present the Haitian public-private partnerships model to several other USAID missions in the region. In 1983, I was pleased to be called by the deputy director of USAID/Costa Rica, Bastian Schouten, who asked me whether I might be interested in transferring to that country. My work in Haiti was going along very well. Still, I was aware that Dan Chaij, the USAID/Costa Rica mission director, was leading the most extensive private sector development program in the Latin America and Caribbean region.

Dan and Bastian had created a new private sector office and wanted to know if I'd consider joining them as the director. After hearing their plans, it sounded like an excellent career move. I would be in charge of a portfolio that was significantly larger than the one I managed in Haiti and working alongside a strong leadership team in one of the fastest-growing programs—private sector development. The Arthur D. Little team led by Humberto Esteve was already working with the mission on similar programs that we had started in Haiti, and that was a definite plus for me.

Additionally, Costa Rica was a beautiful country with a rich history. Rosa and I knew we'd enjoy being in Spanish Latin America again and speaking the Spanish language on a daily basis, especially after the language challenges we experienced in Haiti. The schools our two sons would attend were excellent, and after being in Haiti for four years, I was open to a new career opportunity. So I agreed to go to Costa Rica for an assignment as head of the private sector office. It would be my family's home for the next three years, from 1983 to 1986.

Costa Rica and the entire Central America region was a prime target of US foreign policy at the time, and the area received massive funding under the US government's foreign aid program. USAID was designated to promote economic and political stability in areas where the United States had special strategic interests.[1] The *New York Times* described Costa Rica in 1986 as "the only fully functional democracy in Central America and the only country in the region without an army," adding that it had "Central America's highest literacy rate, the most equitable distribution of farmland, and a national budget that apportion[ed] large amounts of money to health and education."[2]

In San José, the capital of Costa Rica, I had the privilege of working with Carlos Torres, an exceptionally talented international development professional and brilliant executive. He had worked at Arthur D. Little headquarters in Boston as a protégé of Humberto Esteve, and Dan Chaij hired him as an adviser to my newly created office. Beginning in Costa Rica and later in my career, Carlos would play an important role as one of my most trusted colleagues, and both Carlos and Anita Torres would become our lifelong friends.

In addition to being a visionary thinker, Carlos was a very talented strategist, a sharp financial analyst, and a superb planner. He was without parallel in developing productive partnerships with the government and business leaders of Costa Rica. After leaving USAID/Costa Rica, he cofounded a new company with Eduardo Tugendhat—an international consulting firm called CARANA—and the company was very successful in both Latin America and the former Soviet Union after the end of the Cold War. Carlos and I received tremendous support from Bastian Schouten, and later the new deputy director, Dick Archie, and our outstanding financial controller, Frank Latham, as we built a substantial project portfolio focused on banking and investment promotion.

Dan was considered a brilliant thought leader in private-sector-led economics and policy reform. I learned a lot about sophisticated banking programs from him. He was also extraordinarily well connected to the Costa Rican leadership, including the two major political parties and the business community. He had spent some of his youth in Costa Rica, and he spoke fluent conversational Spanish. His distinctive personality exuded a high level of confidence in operating in this social environment.

Although we had several mission directors in the Latin American and Caribbean region who were very experienced Latin-American "hands" and fluent in Spanish, Dan was a recognized leader among those individuals based on his knowledge and standing, particularly in the context of Costa Rica. He led a sizable program and enjoyed a close and productive relationship with the government of Costa Rica, especially with Luis Monge Álvarez, the president of the country, and his cabinet members. I often accompanied him to meetings with the business community and occasionally with the government. Our senior mission team met routinely with the ministers of planning, finance, and ministers of the presidency and vice president.

One day, Dan called me early in the morning at home.

"I want you to get ready and come with me to an important meeting at nine o'clock," he said.

"Where are we going?" I asked. "What do I need to wear—a business suit or casual attire?"

"Dress casually; we're going out of town to the suburbs," he told me. I still had no idea where we were going or for what reason when he picked me up in his official car. I was astonished when we arrived for an impromptu meeting at the private home of the president of Costa Rica, who graciously offered us breakfast! Costa Rica is a very egalitarian society, so the president didn't live in the presidential palace but rather in his private home.

As a result of this meeting, I developed the utmost respect for President Monge as a man of the people who was explicitly concerned with the well-being of the citizens of Costa Rica. Over time, I attended a few other meetings with him, the main topics of which were how the leadership in the Costa Rican government planned to improve the lives of the average Costa Rican. They were truly enlightening discussions.

As an agency that provides comprehensive, full-scale economic growth and reform programs, USAID engaged broadly with both Costa Rican government agencies and business organizations that led export and investment promotion efforts in the country. USAID developed a wide range of programs and projects aligned with the Costa Rican government's goal of transforming the national economy. We participated in and supported the government's plan to privatize several public companies and assisted in the creation of three private finance corporations, one of which was a full-scale merchant bank—a first in Costa Rica.

The mission also helped create and strengthen a private sector organization for trade and investment promotion that became the model for similar

USAID-funded organizations throughout Latin America and the Caribbean. Named CINDE in Spanish, this organization is a private, nonprofit, nonpolitical organization created in 1982 to attract foreign direct investment into Costa Rica. Since its founding it has enabled hundreds of companies to invest in and provide significant benefits to Costa Rica.

Further, we shared our strategy and plans for these types of initiatives with all interested parties in USAID (both in the Washington office and with other missions) and with other countries' business and government leaders. Various conferences and policy forums in both the United States and the Latin American/Caribbean region often showcased our efforts, which we welcomed and believed to be an important factor in supporting the US government's trade and investment policies.

Costa Rica abolished its army in 1947 after World War II and sought to resolve conflict through peaceful negotiations rather than war. Considered a bastion of democracy in Central America, the country was undoubtedly a favored state in the eyes of the United States.[3] It's important to understand that during this period in the 1980s, the Reagan administration was determined to combat any perceived communist threat in the region.

When the bordering country of Nicaragua came under the control of the democratically elected but leftist Sandinista regime of Daniel Ortega, an insurgent group of right-wing Nicaraguan rebels known as the Contras attempted to overthrow the government. Viewing Ortega as a communist threat to democracy in Costa Rica, the Reagan administration made the decision to support covertly the rebels with arms. Once discovered, it created a political scandal known as the Iran-Contra affair in the United States.[4]

In 1986, around the time I left Costa Rica, Óscar Arias Sánchez was elected president of the country. He had a far different view about what America's role should be regarding wars in Central America, and his goal to pursue peace across the region very much dismayed the Reagan administration. President Arias received the Nobel Peace Prize in 1987 for his efforts to end the Central American crisis.[5]

It was an exciting time to be in Costa Rica, and I would rank it in the top three career-defining opportunities of my life. All the elements for success existed in this mission: excellent leadership, an experienced senior staff, a stable national government with brilliant leaders, a strategic vision for the future, and substantial program funding. The USAID mission played a considerable role in the economic transformation of the country, as Costa

Rica moved from an economy dependent on coffee and banana exports to one with a diversified export base of small consumer electronic products, apparel, flowers, and ornamental plants. Eventually, Costa Rica would turn ecotourism into a staple industry of its economy.

Probably the most relevant factor of Costa Rica's success story during that time was the extraordinary group of Costa Rican leaders, both the dynamic businessmen and cabinet ministers who worked together to stimulate rapid economic growth. It was rare to have the privilege to work shoulder to shoulder with outstanding visionaries who were honest and candid; they knew precisely the outcome they wanted for the country.

Luis Diego Escalante was one such leader. He would serve as minister of foreign trade, minister of economy, and eventually ambassador to the United States. As a former businessman of exceptional integrity and tremendous leadership, he earned the great respect he received.

Another visionary leader of that era was Muni Figueres. Muni was the daughter of José Figueres Ferrer, the president of Costa Rica who had abolished the country's military at the end of World War II. To this day, while there has been civil unrest and warring in countries nearby, peace and stability have been the rule in Costa Rica.

Muni Figueres served as both the minister of foreign trade and, subsequently, as the Costa Rican ambassador to the United States during the Obama administration. The trade delegation that we led to Chicago remains one of the highlights of my tour in Costa Rica. We were graciously welcomed by the city's government officials and business leaders and given the keys to the city in a presentation by Harold Washington, the legendary first black mayor of Chicago. As a native Chicagoan, I felt incredibly honored and proud to be a part of this event. An inspiration to many, including Barack Obama, Washington sadly died of a heart attack before he had the chance to be reelected.

Due to the mission's substantial budget, we could entertain several innovative projects that were crucial to the country's long-range development. One such initiative, the brainchild of Dan Chaij, was EARTH University (Escuela de Agricultura de la Region Tropical Humeda).

Dan recognized a pressing need for an agricultural university that focused on the subtropical zone of the central highlands, where a large percentage of farmers lived—both in Costa Rica and throughout Central America. He felt that this vast ecological zone had not been researched

enough and that such research was needed to improve agricultural practices and to train future experts to operate there. Dan lined up support from
the Costa Rican government and private agribusiness leaders and identi-
fied potential support from some significant US foundations like the W. K.
Kellogg Foundation.

Despite considerable opposition to his idea, Dan managed to play a
crucial role in the design and launch of the new university. Today, EARTH
is one of the most successful universities in Central America! Every idea
is said to be born dying, but obviously it doesn't have to end that way—
especially if you have leadership qualities and the determination of someone like Dan Chaij.

Because of my work in Costa Rica, I enjoyed working with folks in both
the Costa Rican and American expatriate business community, and I developed several significant friendships with incredible individuals through my
connection to these communities. One person, in particular, stands out—
the incomparable Jack Harris.

Harris was "an African expert, one of two dozen US anthropologists
working for the Office of Strategic Services, . . . a McCarthy witch-hunt
survivor, Costa Rican entrepreneur, [and] development pioneer." According
to an obituary feature story written about him, "With a Costa Rican business partner, Harris' first venture was a taxi fleet. He had never even read
a balance sheet, but the taxis were so successful that he used the profits
to start Costa Rica's first cement plant with a group of Costa Rican associates. Many other enterprises followed, among them Ricalit, a fiber-cement
roofing factory started with Swiss investors; COFISA, a major development
bank; the country's first mushroom farm; the Tropical brewery; INPASA,
which manufactures industrial paper bags."[6]

Accepting the position in Costa Rica was an excellent decision; the job
both advanced my career and suited our lifestyle. Rosa, Michael, Steven,
and I had wonderful times exploring the immense beauty of Costa Rica—
a small country but one with 5 percent of the world's biodiversity. We enjoyed many family beach excursions with our colleagues and friends and
their children, all former Peace Corps volunteers, like Tom and Chris
McKee, John and Michelle Swallow, and Dave and Anita Kaufman. These
outings provided much-needed rest and recreation after my many twelve-
hour workdays on the mission. Costa Rica was a great place to live, work,
and raise a family. The excellent advice we received from the Swallows also

persuaded us to buy a home in Reston, Virginia, on our return to the US, where we have continued our close family friendship for over thirty years.

What came next for me was, in large part, due to the landmark success of the Costa Rica USAID mission. The mission was able to be innovative and contribute to critical sectors of the economy owing to its substantial budget and resources. I was given a great deal of latitude to lead the private sector office, and I came away with an excellent reputation for innovative project design work and pragmatic management of private sector programs.

8 The Washington Game
Serving at USAID Headquarters

The best way to learn the rules of the game is to get in the game.

—UNKNOWN

In 1986, Costa Rica was an ideal place to live and work. I had a great job in a highly regarded mission, and I was gaining valuable experience and recognition for my efforts. Equally important, my family was happy living in Costa Rica. So, understandably, we had mixed emotions about moving back to Washington, DC. The move, however, came with an offer for me to head up a new stand-alone private sector development office in the Bureau for Latin America and the Caribbean.

I had a considerable amount of familiarity with most of the USAID private sector programs in Latin America at that time, and the new job would be an excellent opportunity to utilize that expertise. It would also offer me a chance to gain valuable exposure and experience at USAID headquarters for the first time. I decided therefore to accept the position of director of the private sector development office.

Peter Bittner, an outstanding leader and innovative thinker who had led the private sector portfolio, also created a successful HQ strategy and provided superb assistance to the field missions. I looked forward to working with the DC staff and the large cadre of private sector officers throughout the Latin American and Caribbean region. Overall, this promised to be a busy and exciting time in my career.

Malcolm Butler was the deputy assistant administrator for the Bureau for Latin America and the Caribbean and my boss. He reported to the assistant administrator of the bureau, Dwight Ink. Malcolm and his wife, Leticia "Tish" Butler, were a dynamic power couple in USAID. At one point in her career, Tish, an outstanding officer, served as the US representative to the Asian Development Bank, and she would later hold several senior positions at USAID. After the fall of the Soviet Union, Malcolm led the team that created the Newly Independent States Bureau (later known as the Eastern Europe and Eurasia Bureau.)

Malcolm was the ideal officer to manage this challenging assignment due to his vast government experience and his background as mission director in three USAID missions. He also had held senior positions on the staff of the National Security Council and in the Office of Management and Budget. He led an outstanding team of twelve mid-career officers, each of whom was in charge of either a technical office (education, agriculture, etc.) or a staff office (legal, program, and projects). Each of these officers would go on to have distinguished careers with USAID and beyond, and it was a pleasure to be their colleagues during this period.[1]

The private sector programs had typically been located in the larger Development Resources Office, but a significant expansion of these programs created a need for an independent office. Ably assisted by Lorelai Russell, my terrific executive assistant, I recruited five or six officers for the new office, and I extended an existing consulting contract to ensure we had the short-term technical assistance required to provide support services to both my office and the field missions. My new job at headquarters was to promote private sector growth throughout the entire Latin American region by helping USAID missions to develop export, investment promotion, and banking/finance projects.

My office would assist the private sector officers in individual missions to develop their strategies, projects, and programs. We had a large group of officers that met twice a year to share ideas and lessons learned. In my first year, I had the chance to engage in short-term consultative assignments with missions in El Salvador, Honduras, and Guatemala.

The Caribbean Basin Initiative remained a key trade policy of the United States government, and George H. W. Bush expanded it through the new trade initiative called the Enterprise for the Americas, which later led to the adoption of NAFTA.[2]

With the expansion of the private sector profile of the Bureau for Latin America and the Caribbean in Washington, I focused on developing a broad spectrum of interagency relationships on behalf of USAID in Latin America. The interagency work was crucial in Washington and a key part of my job. Our office worked quite a bit with Larry Theriot, an impressive official at the Department of Commerce. As director of the Caribbean Basin Initiative office and the top gun on private sector development in the region,

Theriot was very influential within the US government interagency and business community. The Department of Commerce was a lead agency in the Caribbean Basin Initiative framework, and Theriot had a large staff working on trade and investment issues in the region.

We also worked closely with the Caribbean-Central American Action (CCAA), an organization that promoted private-sector-led economic development in the Caribbean Basin and throughout the hemisphere, and that had partnerships with several USAID-supported entities in Latin America. CCAA's president, Peter B. Johnson, held an annual high-profile Caribbean and Central American business conference in Miami. Presidents, senior cabinet officials, and local corporate executives from across the region attended. The keynote speakers were usually US government cabinet secretaries, prominent Fortune 500 executives, and of course, the leaders of the region's nations. It continued for twenty years as the most prominent showcase for trade and investment promotion under the Caribbean Basin Initiative umbrella in the Western Hemisphere.

USAID played a leading role in the Caribbean-Central American Action conference every year. The State Department sent a senior spokesperson, usually the assistant secretary for the region. There were many key speaking slots for other senior US government officials from USAID, the Department of Commerce, the Department of the Treasury, the Overseas Private Investment Corporation (OPIC), and the US Trade Representative Office—the entire US government interagency was on display and fully engaged. This event was a top priority for me every year because our host country partner organizations were crucial participants under the umbrella of the association in a wide range of activities regarding export and investment promotion across the region. The event promoted economic growth along with private sector development under the Caribbean Basin Initiative and, eventually, for the Enterprise for the Americas. As one of the lead agencies, our office had a lot of influence. Our various US government interagency partners never proceeded with a private sector initiative policy or project idea without consulting us.

Latin America seemed to many observers to be an ideal region in which to pursue new private enterprise initiatives. I went on a few exploratory delegations with a few of the senior officials of the new USAID Private Enterprise Bureau, established under President Reagan, which helped shape the agency's private sector development policies and program directions. I traveled with them to Haiti and Central America to identify new opportunities for USAID support and specific projects; it was an exciting time in terms of trade and investment promotion policy—which overall received bipartisan support. As manager of USAID's broadest private sector program portfolio, I spent a lot of time presenting and negotiating our strategic approach and implementation methodology with my Private Enterprise Bureau counterparts.

The Bureau for Latin America and the Caribbean was deeply involved with trade policy discussions because USAID was a major donor agency that ran massive and innovative country programs in the region. Further, it had extraordinarily good contacts across the countries with both the political and private sector leadership, which assured it a prominent seat at the interagency policy table. During the period when Ronald Reagan was president, private sector engagement was perceived to be a useful tool in the foreign policy arena, and those of us who worked at USAID during that time had the great fortune to serve under USAID chief Peter McPherson.

As described in the Devex five-part series *USAID: A History of U.S. Foreign Aid*, "McPherson's four pillars strategy toward development was sensible and stressed policy reform, institutional development, innovation, and private sector growth. But what seemed to have truly elevated McPherson were his interpersonal skills and ability to manage the diverse constituencies with a stake in the assistance program. He was an astute leader who balanced his approach between economic reforms traditionally favored by Republicans and the basic human needs strategy favored by Democrats."[3]

Another powerful leader USAID had during that time was the masterful and legendary civil servant Dwight Ink, assistant administrator for the Bureau for Latin America and the Caribbean. Known as "Mr. Implementation," he began his career under the Eisenhower administration, and he'd held senior positions in every Republican administration since the 1960s. He had served seven presidents, and owing to that service, he was extraordinarily well connected to the White House. Dwight supported our private sector strategy, had an unmatched understanding of the federal bureaucracy, and knew how to achieve his goals accordingly. Under his direction, the Bureau for Latin America and the Caribbean gained a reputation as a respected player in the interagency process.

Dwight usually won every policy debate he engaged in, and he was particularly effective concerning budget issues. He was one of the most powerful senior executives I've ever seen in government. No one could manage the bureaucracy like him, and that's an absolute necessity for success in

Washington. He was practically clairvoyant in his awareness of the type of critical information to present to the Hill and the interagency about the results of the USAID assistance programs. Dwight was a determined leader, and at the time he was the most highly decorated civil servant in the history of the US government.

Dwight Ink's reputation stemmed from crucial roles he had played in the 1964 Alaskan earthquake reconstruction program and the navy's nuclear submarine program as a senior staffer to the famous Admiral Rickover. In 2011, *Government Executive* magazine named him one of the twenty all-time greatest federal government leaders.

Overall, I spent much of my time on interagency work and on advising American firms interested in investing in the Caribbean Basin region, where I led or co-led several business delegations. We also participated in meetings held during official visits made by the presidents of the region's nations, including the National Security Council's meetings on trade and investment policy.

> Once you learn the rules of the game and are willing to play it, then you stand a chance of winning it; that's true of work and life in general.

In developing a network of key individuals and government agencies, I was—I now see in hindsight—laying a foundation for a future leadership role. This position in Washington's USAID headquarters provided me with invaluable experience and insight. I was willing to serve on a wide range of special committees (recruitment, promotion panels, various task forces, etc.), and I reached out to the heads of each staff office to gain an understanding of their priorities and operations. I also sought out opportunities to promote diversity across USAID, including by serving as the chair of the agency's outreach program for historically black universities and colleges. I learned that the people who don't succeed in Washington are those who are uncomfortable with risk. Exercising caution in the Washington game is like getting caught in quicksand; you quickly lose your grounding and without a strong network of support to pull you out you might sink. Then, there are those who don't mind risk but hate the game—also a losing proposition. The only way to master the Washington game is to value and recognize the importance of the work and understand how to manage and *work* the game—without *hating* the game. I learned this from the many incredible leaders I was fortunate enough to get to know and work with—many of whom became my lifelong friends.

My tour at headquarters laid an excellent foundation for my move into a leadership position as head of a mission. After three years in DC, everything I learned would be put to the test, as a golden opportunity was closer than I could ever imagine.

9 Storm-Tested Leadership
Hurricane Hugo and the Historic Hearing

Leadership and learning are indispensable to each other.

—JOHN F. KENNEDY

I had worked in USAID's Washington headquarters for nearly three years by the end of 1989. The well-staffed office I then led had become a key player in the Bureau for Latin America and the Caribbean. One cold, wintry evening, Malcolm Butler asked to meet with me. I asked his assistant what the meeting was about, but she didn't know. I was both curious and surprised by his request. I found myself even more surprised when Malcolm asked if I would be willing to serve as the mission director for the Caribbean Regional Program, based in Bridgetown, Barbados.

Earlier that year, I'd gone down to Barbados as team leader for a mission management assessment, during which time I worked with two outstanding USAID officers, Patricia Buckles and Steve Wingert. So I'd been well briefed on the mission's staff, the program's strategy, and the mission's primary goals. My opportunity resulted from the reassignment of the current mission director for the region. I was pleased to be selected for the position; it would be my first opportunity to lead a mission, and a rare distinction, as I would be the youngest mission director at the age of forty-two. I would also be the first African American to hold the position.

When people learned of my appointment in Barbados, they automatically assumed it was a most idyllic assignment, given that I would be living and working in the Caribbean. But the challenging aspects of this position would prove to be substantial, as it required both traveling to ten different islands and coordinating with their governments and regional organizations. Rather than being in charge of a USAID mission in one country, in

Barbados I would be responsible for the assistance program across several governments. Of course, I was aware that it was a deceptively large region with multiple responsibilities when I accepted the job.

The US government's foreign aid program in the Caribbean region supported the island nations of Guyana, the British dependencies (Anguilla, the British Virgin Islands, the Cayman Islands, Montserrat, and the Turks and Caicos Islands), and all of the independent Leeward and Windward Islands (Antigua and Barbuda, Dominica, Grenada, St. Kitts and Nevis, St. Lucia, St. Vincent and the Grenadines). The region covered many square miles of ocean and islands but did not include the Dominican Republic, Haiti, Jamaica, or Cuba.

The island nations served by the mission in the 1990s were fiercely proud of their independence. Each had populations of fifty thousand to two hundred thousand people, and each was led by individuals who had dominated the political battles for independence from British rule for decades and remained as respected founders of their countries. I always kept in mind the cultural and political aspects that were important to the leaders of the Caribbean regions as I worked with them.

They had all trained in the UK, where most of them were barristers; they were extraordinarily eloquent, sharp, and analytical people. They were masters of their universe and could deliver a fifteen-to-twenty-minute Winston Churchill–type speech on any topic at the drop of a hat. Dialogue with them was thus always an interesting proposition. Through my experience working with the prime ministers, I learned many debating tools I used to quickly size up an individual's ability to negotiate. In my opinion, they all deserved to govern countries ten times larger than these islands, given their huge intellects and capacity.

My staff and I traveled extensively to cover this vast region, which was vital to our engagement with the Caribbean officials, and I usually averaged two business trips per week. We interacted with scores of local and regional government officials and their corresponding power structures. Whether it was a new road in St. Lucia or a proposal to promote ecotourism in St. Kitts, there were always multiple projects across the region to consider. Every island nation sought USAID's regional funding for its priority projects. The island nation of Grenada was the only exception because it was already receiving US government funds for reconstruction following the US invasion in 1983 to restore a democratic government after a Cuban-supported military coup.[1]

A US government organizational chart revealed that this mission was uniquely challenging due to both the vastness of the region and the bureaucratic relationships that were in place. Under normal conditions in any given country, a typical USAID mission would serve the ambassador accredited to that nation. In the Caribbean Regional Program mission, however, there were six embassies in the region that we worked with and four US ambassadors to serve. Excellent diplomatic skills were crucial in successfully managing this vast "empire."

Further, the mission served as the US government representative to several regional institutions, including the Caribbean Regional Development Bank, the Caribbean Epidemiology Centre, the Pan American Health Organization, the Caribbean Community, and the Organization of Eastern Caribbean States. Each of these entities zealously pursued their objective of getting their "fair share" from our mission. If I had not mastered the Washington game by this time, it would have been challenging to avoid manipulation during the constant power struggles between these organizations and their leaders. In Barbados, I faced the Washington power game on steroids!

The other members of the embassy country team faced similar challenges, depending on how their respective US government department or agency configured the Caribbean region. Probably the group most similar to the Caribbean Regional Program group was the United States Information Service, led by Dr. Katherine Lee, a senior FSO who managed a large regional staff. Katherine was highly regarded in the region, and our respective staffs worked closely together. We benefited greatly from her extensive knowledge of the region's culture and its communications executives (in both the public and private sector) as well as from her strong rapport with both the regional and island nations prime ministers. We collaborated on several joint initiatives and programs that created a synergy for US government policy across this complex region.

Fortunately, we had an outstanding staff in the mission, 70 percent of whom were Caribbean citizens and 30 percent of whom were FSOs, led by Larry Armstrong, the deputy mission director. Larry was a talented veteran FSO with two decades of experience in the Latin American and Caribbean region and at USAID headquarters in Washington. We had never worked together before, but he had a stellar reputation. We became an outstanding team, and our deep mutual trust enabled us to build on our respective strengths. Larry was a talented leader when it came to project design and project implementation, and he was an exceptional supervisor and mentor for the staff, basically operating as the chief operating officer of the mission. Along the way, Rosa and I had the good fortune that Larry and Carol Armstrong became our great friends.

The travel was key to our engagement with the Caribbean officials. The operational reality, often overlooked by the casual observer, was that each of the independent island nations' governments consisted of a prime minister, a cabinet, and a parliament—which meant that we had to interact with multiple players across the region. We were actually interacting with scores of local and regional government officials and their corresponding power structures. So my first big step into leadership required that I learn to navigate working with many people in different positions in multiple locations who needed my attention, necessitating that I spend 80 percent of my time in air travel! I would fly out on Monday and not see my family until Wednesday if everything went as planned. I flew with LIAT Air (Leeward Islands Air Transport), or "Leave Island Anytime," as the local saying went. I learned to balance the frequent travel with the rest of our life on Barbados, and we thoroughly loved living in this beautiful setting. We often joked that our most difficult decision on any given weekend was whether we'd swim in the pounding surf of the Atlantic or the tranquil waters of the Caribbean.

Tourism was the primary driver of the regional economy for jobs and the generation of foreign exchange revenues, and the mission continued to support this sector. The tourism industry was financially sound, so USAID played a supporting, but minor, funding role in the region. Consistent with this approach, we developed strong relationships with the Caribbean Tourism Association and invested in training and improving hotel management.

Economic diversification was a critical goal for the eastern Caribbean nations, and USAID's strategy focused on projects and initiatives aimed at reaching that goal. Sugar was the dominant export crop in the region until the 1950s, when a regional diversification strategy turned bananas into the primary export crop. As reported by Patrick Barkham in *The Guardian*, the "banana wars" was the culmination of a six-year trade quarrel between the US and the EU. "The US moaned that an EU scheme giving banana producers from former colonies in the Caribbean special access to European markets broke free trade rules." The US filed a complaint against the EU with the World Trade Organization (WTO) and, in 1997, won. The EU was instructed to alter its rules. This decision became a problem for the eastern Caribbean region because the crop represented a significant source of its foreign exchange, especially in St. Lucia and St. Vincent. In light of this trade war, we had to pivot to a different approach. In conjunction with the local governments, we focused on agricultural diversification programs for the entire region.

The Caribbean Basin Initiative was still in operation. But unlike the Dominican Republic or Haiti or the Central American countries, the West Indies islands with small populations didn't have the labor force necessary to benefit from special trade incentives to attract companies that could take advantage of the initiative. Owing to the low economic growth in most of the islands, the island governments received substantial aid from major donors that included USAID, the Canadian International Development Agency, the UK's Official Development Assistance, the European Economic Community, the Caribbean Development Bank, in conjunction with the World Bank, and the Inter-American Development Bank.

Donor coordination was essential, and the mission had forged excellent working relationships with all the donor agencies. I developed close professional relationships with the directors of the Canadian and British donor organizations. These friendships would become crucial in weathering all types of storms—economic and otherwise. When Hurricane Hugo blew into the Caribbean, it put the donor country support system to the ultimate test. This hurricane caused widespread damage and loss of life in Guadalupe, St. Croix, Puerto Rico, and the Southeast United States.[2]

Hugo formed over the eastern Atlantic near the Cape Verde Islands on September 9, 1989. It reached category 5 hurricane strength on its journey of destruction through the Caribbean. It restrengthened into a category 4 hurricane before making landfall just short of Charleston, South Carolina. As of 2016, Hurricane Hugo remained the most intense tropical cyclone to strike the East Coast north of Florida since 1898. Hugo caused thirty-four fatalities in the Caribbean, twenty-seven in South Carolina, and left nearly one hundred thousand people homeless. As the most damaging hurricane, it was also the costliest at $9.47 billion in 1989 US dollars.

Barbados lies just south of the central hurricane belt, yet the island hadn't experienced any significant storms since Hurricane Janet in 1955. Storms start in West Africa and come straight across the Caribbean, picking up steam and velocity, but approximately one hundred miles from Barbados, they typically veer north due to the "Coriolis Force," sparing the island. Based on the expectation that Hugo would miss Barbados, we had positioned support teams and resources in the northern Caribbean, where we anticipated the impact would be widespread and therefore where a massive rehabilitation effort would be required. The day after it hit, we sent a team of staff members, led by John Wooten, the program officer to Antigua. John did an outstanding job and stayed through the entire reconstruction period at great personal sacrifice, as his family remained in Barbados.

Paul Bell, a former Peace Corps director from the 1960s, was the legendary leader of USAID's Office of Foreign and Disaster Assistance's regional program. Based in Costa Rica, where he headed up disaster mitigation, relief, and reconstruction programs, Paul worked tirelessly to create and maintain rapid response efforts through technical assistance partnerships between the United States and the nations in the region. He embodied that unique and rare combination of superb strategist and operational leader. Paul was a visionary who foresaw the need for an office that provided both critical assistance and capacity development—one that's still in place. He was a special friend and mentor who I will always remember fondly.

During Hugo, Paul had pre-positioned himself with his team on the northern island of Antigua. We knew it would be a massive hurricane, and it certainly resulted in devastating consequences for the Windward and Leeward Islands, except for Barbados. So the very day after it passed through, I flew up to Antigua to meet with him. As I deplaned, I expected him to debrief me on his operational plan, but he was already in action mode.

"Let's get on my light airplane and fly to Montserrat," he said. He knew from people there that the beautiful place, otherwise known as Emerald Isle, had been wiped out. A guy with a walkie-talkie said the island looked like a forest fire had been through it. When we arrived, we could see that the once verdant-green paradise had been entirely devastated by Hugo. There was no remaining foliage; the island had been rendered a brown desert.

Since there was no longer a control tower at the damaged airport, we landed with the assistance of the walkie-talkies on the ground. We found a cool, calm, and collected Chris Patten, governor-general of Montserrat and the man in charge that day, sitting in a tent on a hill overlooking the harbor; it was all that was left.[3] Members of the donor countries were lined up to find out how they could help. After receiving Chris's assessment, we compared notes and flew back to continue our evaluation of the rest of the islands. With Paul's assistance, we refined our initial plan for immediate relief, and I flew back to Barbados. That's when the donor coordination kicked in.

After briefing Larry Armstrong and the mission staff, I met with the directors of the British and Canadian aid programs: Michael Bawden, head of Official Development Assistance for the British, and Art Saper, head of the Canadian International Development Agency, both of whom were very experienced and brilliant development experts. The three of us quickly became disappointed and frustrated by the slow pace of the UN-led donor coordination. The United States, the UK, and Canada controlled 90 percent of all the resources planned for hurricane relief and reconstruction. So we decided to hold a separate meeting in Bridgetown, and we chose the brand-new McDonald's restaurant as a fitting place for our lunch conversation. We called the results of our rump meeting the "McDonald's Protocol."

It was quite obvious what needed to be done, by whom, and how. The British had a destroyer in the region with a contingent of British marines very much like the United States Seabees—a naval construction force that could immediately provide reconstruction services. The Canadians had built most of the original airports in the islands and could handle their reconstruction. USAID had teams of electric utility companies currently working to rebuild Jamaica due to the previous year's hurricane, and I knew that we could move them to the eastern Caribbean to handle electrical wiring and to restore electricity. The United States was also the lead donor in the region for agriculture and road construction programs.

The three of us very quickly consulted with the prime ministers of the affected islands and agreed to assume responsibility for our sectors and the implementation of the reconstruction effort. And so the McDonald's Protocol was formalized. We requested our respective government's approval via cables to our capitals and received nearly instantaneous support for the effort, which became widely known and applauded throughout the bureaucracy of all three capitals. The implementation of the recovery work began, and we managed to provide funding commensurate with the stated needs of each affected island.

It was unfortunate that we had to dedicate a large portion of our efforts to hurricane reconstruction instead of targeting those resources toward the development strategy of the respective island nations; however, it was also fortunate that we could do so in such an efficient way.

It was a very satisfying period of my career, having the opportunity to work with extraordinary leaders like Paul Bell, Art Saper, and Michael Bawden. We remained lifelong friends after we weathered that monster storm together. Unfortunately, some islands never recovered, like Montserrat. Between the devastation of Hurricane Hugo and the volcanic activity that occurred there, the economy collapsed and most of the residents immigrated elsewhere.

Hugo, however, was not my last test as a new mission director. A different kind of "storm" had begun brewing on a distant shore during this time in my career. It would be unlike anything USAID had experienced in its history, and it resulted in a congressional delegation traveling to the eastern Caribbean to hold a hearing for the very first time.

The George H. W. Bush administration and the Democratic-led House of Representatives were engaged at the time in a major debate regarding the amount of US foreign assistance going to these Caribbean islands and the focus of it. Eventually, the House's Foreign Affairs Committee decided to hold a hearing—in the Caribbean—to ask the prime ministers to present their views, in person, to the committee, an unprecedented action at the time and one that has never happened since, to my knowledge.

I had excellent working relationships with all of the prime ministers and knew them to be proud leaders. As representatives of small independent countries, each worked to maintain their island's independence while balancing the weight of the giant countries there to support them—the United States, Canada, and Britain. Budget allocation always became a game of protecting each one's interests, and I had to personally engage with each leader about that issue regularly. We didn't always end in agreement, but I had excellent relationships with most of them. To prepare for the regional hearing, I needed an idea of what they might say to the visiting members of Congress.

The foreign assistance budget is a perennial political football; the shifting priorities of different stakeholders often leads to a standoff between the president's policy imperatives and congressional demands. The committee intended to request that the prime ministers testify as witnesses for their views, and most certainly, the entire USAID portfolio would be the focus of the discussion.

The committee scheduled two hearings—one in St. Lucia under my direction and one in Jamaica directed by Bill Joslin, the USAID/Jamaica mission director, and Marilyn Zak, the deputy director. The entire committee flew down under the chairmanship of Congressman George Crockett. The committee was a bipartisan mix of Democrats and Republicans, perhaps ten members altogether—a "who's who" of Congress. Since I had enjoyed an excellent relationship with Congressman Crockett and his staff during my time at headquarters, USAID leadership had confidence that I would be able to handle this "unprecedented historical event."

The event was so unusual that it required a unique action plan. My first move was to consult with all seven of the prime ministers. Those called to testify at the hearing also selected a delegation of cabinet members and prominent business executives to attend with them. The committee also planned to visit individual projects and speak to the target groups. The one-week affair in the two countries was a huge, complex planning exercise. Larry and I spent a considerable amount of time strategizing and prepping for my testimony, in full consultation with the Bureau for Latin America and the Caribbean leadership. Never was there a time when relationships mattered more! Bill Joslyn and I attended both committee hearings held at hotels in Jamaica and St. Lucia.

Three prime ministers dominated the discussion with the committee: John Compton of St. Lucia, James Fitz-Allen Mitchell of St. Vincent, and Eugenia Charles, otherwise known as Dame Mary Eugenia Charles, DBE of Dominica, and the only woman serving at the time. Eugenia Charles was first among equals. She was the second female prime minister in the Caribbean, and eventually she would hold her position for fifteen years, making her the world's second-longest-serving female prime minister behind Indira Gandhi of India and just ahead of Margaret Thatcher of the UK.

Prime Minister Charles endorsed the US invasion of Grenada in consultation with President Reagan to eliminate a communist threat in 1983. She received her title of grand dame from Queen Elizabeth, and in my judgment, she could have been the president of either the United States or Canada. The grand dame could easily dominate and control a meeting. She made sure the visiting congressmen got an earful about the Caribbean, and she made it her business to see that I got a fair hearing. No doubt, she scored well on both counts.

> No matter what the situation or circumstance appears to be, there will always be opportunities to create meaningful relationships, and you never know when they will be the difference between success and failure in future endeavors or events.

Issues concerning the best use of foreign aid dominated the discussion, as did trade issues, especially those regarding bananas. Given the importance of the crop to their island's economy, Prime Minister Compton and Prime Minister Mitchell led as experts on these issues. They were eloquent in their analysis of the trade situation. The debate was whether or not the US companies, Chiquita and Dole, the largest producers of bananas in the world at that time, would be allowed to export bananas duty free to the EU in exchange for allowing Caribbean bananas to be imported duty free into the United States.

In their testimony, Prime Ministers Compton and Charles praised the USAID Caribbean regional programs. I was extraordinarily grateful, pleased, and relieved all at the same time. Even the prime ministers who differed with me over some aspects of the program took a balanced, reasonable approach when they spoke to the committee—an outcome that left me quite surprised in a couple of cases. It became apparent that my consultations with the regional leaders had been a worthwhile investment.

It was during this visit that I initiated my working relationship with Congressman Don Payne. Highly regarded for his leadership in providing oversight for US government foreign policy regarding Latin America, the Caribbean, and Africa, Payne later served as both the head of the Congressional Black Caucus and as the chair of the Subcommittee on Africa and Global Health and Subcommittee on the Western Hemisphere.

The historic congressional hearing left the members with a very favorable impression of the work performed by USAID in the Caribbean and Jamaica. USAID headquarters in Washington breathed a great sigh of relief afterward, and so did I.

10 A New Opportunity at USAID Headquarters

Elections Have Consequences

The reward for work well done is the opportunity to do more.

—JONAS SALK

In 1991, Ambassador James Michel, the new assistant administrator for Latin America and the Caribbean, came to visit the region. Jim had a stellar reputation, having served as legal adviser to the secretary of state and ambassador to Guatemala. We traveled to Granada and St. Lucia to visit various project sites and meet with the prime ministers. During the trip, Jim asked me if I would be willing to curtail my assignment in Barbados and become his deputy in the bureau. I was, of course, very pleased with this offer and intended to discuss the idea with Rosa.

Rosa and I hosted a farewell dinner for Jim at our home. The invitees included the usual guests: the USAID senior staff, British and Canadian diplomats, Caribbean government members, and business leaders. As I recall, it was a typical lovely evening in Bridgetown accompanied by an animated dinner conversation. At the end of the evening, as we escorted Jim to his vehicle, he paused and surprised Rosa with a question.

"Are you looking forward to returning to Washington?"

"No, not really; I would prefer to stay here for another tour," my rarely undiplomatic wife responded in a polite but dead-serious manner. It would be the source of many chuckles over time. Still, I understood her feelings. We lived in a beautiful country, and our sons were very happy with their friends and school.

It was hard to leave, but leave, we did. I will always give credit for my career success to the woman that my best friend, Harry Simmons, calls a saint. No doubt, I could not have experienced or achieved the things I have in my career and managed a balanced family life without Rosa. The difficult decision to leave Barbados after two short years, however, turned out to be one of my best career decisions.

Jim Michel was an accomplished diplomat, a visionary leader, a superb mentor, and a man of high integrity. It was an honor and a privilege to serve as his deputy at headquarters. It was also the beginning of a thirty-year friendship and a terrific working relationship that included serving together as colleagues and in advisory roles at USAID and the Peace Corps. I have the utmost admiration for Jim's intellect, leadership philosophy, unique ability to develop effective teams, and willingness to take a moral stand on the major issues of our time.

We were very fortunate that Marlene Garcia and Georgene "Georgie" Hawe were our executive assistants; together, they had decades of experience managing the administrative tasks for senior officials. Marlene had worked for Jim for many years, at the State Department and USAID, and Georgie remained an essential colleague of mine until her retirement several years later.

Three decades after first meeting Jim, our friendship continues, and as founding members of the USAID Alumni Association, we still meet for our occasional lunch. Many of my business relationships evolved into lifetime friendships like the one with Jim. I consider the many excellent relationships I developed over the years to be a great blessing, as I do my opportunity to serve the US government in so many capacities.

The year 1992 turned out to be a particularly intense time to return to USAID headquarters in Washington, DC. The US presidential race between the incumbent Republican president George H. W. Bush and the Democratic contender Bill Clinton was in full swing. A lot of the political debate centered on the economy and the loss of US jobs to Mexico and other places. There was a heated debate about the anticipated impact of NAFTA signed between President Bush and the leaders of Canada and Mexico. Clinton and Gore attacked NAFTA during the campaign and framed it as a job-loss issue.

Despite the heated presidential campaign, there was a very pleasant interlude in October 1992. That month, Spain celebrated the five hundredth anniversary of Columbus's voyage and arrival in the Americas. As part of commemorating this historical milestone, several presidents of the Central America countries traveled to Seville to participate in Expo '92 and related festivities as guests of King Juan Carlos and Queen Sofia.[1]

This was also an historic moment in Central America because for the first time in history each of these countries had a democratically elected president as the head of government. "Many observers regarded President Vinicio Cerezo's assumption of the presidency in Guatemala in 1986 as a special moment in the history of Central America, because it meant that all five Central American republics were ruled simultaneously by elected governments for the first time in history. This remarkable 'outbreak' of elected regimes in the region was part of a larger process underway throughout the hemisphere, as many South American countries had also replaced military regimes with elected civilian government doing the 1980s."[2]

The Bush administration was eager to acknowledge and praise this democratic wave across Central America. So when we learned that the presidents would return to their home countries via Washington, DC, Jim Michel and I, in consultation with the State Department, suggested that we consider hosting a summit for the Central American presidents in a historic place in the capital region. The summit was sponsored by the Southern Governors Association, and it provided a forum in which the nineteen states of the association and the governments of Central America could establish a partnership.

Governor Doug Wilder of Virginia graciously agreed to host the summit at Monticello, the home of Thomas Jefferson, in Charlottesville, Virginia. The logistics for this event were quite elaborate, and our Latin America and Caribbean team worked closely with the State Department and its protocol staff to arrange it. The amazingly innovative lead organizers of the summit were Lindy Wood, head of the Latin America and Caribbean private sector office, and Debbie Meyers, special adviser to Enrique Iglesias, the president of the Inter-American Development Bank, with the able assistance of the savvy Karen Harbert, Jim's special assistant. Jim and I were accompanied by our wives, Connie and Rosa. The occasion beautifully combined both official business and social events. For example, as I recall, Connie and Rosa joined the first ladies for a tour of the governor's mansion in Richmond and Monticello, led by Governor Wilder's daughter.

The summit itself involved a general meeting, led by Jim Michel and Bernard Aronson, the assistant secretary for this region, that principally focused on issues of common interest, including trade and investment, democratic reforms and administration of justice, and social programs. Each topic's discussion was co-led by a governor and a president, an arrangement designed to create the basis for future partnerships.

The official dinner, hosted by President Iglesias, was held in a large tent on the candle-lit grounds of Monticello, hosted by Governor Wilder and his daughter. It was a beautiful fall day, and enjoyable for all concerned, and I will never forget Governor Wilder's toast to the group, in which he read a letter of welcome by the president of the Southern Governors Association. At the end of the letter Wilder noted with a broad smile that this was a message from "Governor Bill Clinton of Arkansas . . . the next President of the United States." This was a surprise of course, which was met with a small chuckle from the audience and annoyance from the Bush administration appointees in the room. One month later Bill Clinton defeated George H. W. Bush and won the election to become the forty-second president of the United States of America.

In this same period, USAID became a controversial media target in the debate over the shift of American jobs to Caribbean and Central American nations when the ABC network televised a damaging exposé on its show *20/20*. Investigative reporters went to a couple of the countries in question and filmed conversations between USAID officials and people posing as private company representatives interested in setting up assembly factories in the region. The nationally televised segment presented particularly unfortunate remarks made by a new and junior USAID staff member about the ease of working in these countries due to the lack of organized labor unions.

CBS's *60 Minutes* investigative news show also put a spotlight on USAID.[3] The show aired interviews with senior USAID leaders in Central America and Jim Michel, both as the head of the Bureau for Latin America and the Caribbean and senior Bush administration representative concerning the issue of US job loss. I sat in on Jim's interview with Ed Bradley—the late, legendary *60 Minutes* correspondent. It was a tough interview, but I thought Jim did a terrific job of presenting a balanced analysis of the issue and USAID's role in managing the US government's foreign aid in the region. But, as so often is the case in the world of investigative reporting, the producers of *60 Minutes* had their story—USAID was assisting companies that were sending US jobs to Central America and the Caribbean—and they stuck to it.

So there we were, caught in the throes of a very intense political campaign, grappling with this important national issue. We believed, based on economic analyses supplied by leading economists and corporate leaders, that we were contributing to the economic growth of the United States in the export sector. The opponents of that strategy believed that we were exporting US jobs overseas. That debate continues to this day, with no resolution in sight. Who or what people choose to believe depends on what side of the debate they're on.[4]

Without question, the nations in Central America and the Caribbean benefited greatly from the hundreds of thousands of jobs created by American companies and other companies in that region. Further, we also had data that pointed to the corresponding link between the job growth created overseas and the job growth produced in the United States.

President Bush ran out of time to get NAFTA ratified by Congress and signed into law while he was still president. Interestingly enough, once the election was over, President Clinton and Vice President Gore pivoted and became advocates for the passage of NAFTA by the Congress, thus illustrating, once again, how foreign aid and trade agreements are used as political footballs. It all depends on which side is tossing the ball around, at what time, and for what purpose.

As a result of the political debate, Congress added stipulations to NAFTA restricting the number of US jobs that could be exported. Funding for private-sector-led growth projects was drastically reduced in Latin America and other regions, and the role of USAID in executing such projects was cut back. Ever since this period, potential funding for trade and investment programs has been subjected to intense Congressional review. We shifted our strategic direction to other areas. Even though the official policy of the Clinton administration supported NAFTA, and trade and investment projects weren't prohibited, the scrutiny under which such projects had to operate became onerous.

With the presidential election, unexpected opportunities arose for me at USAID headquarters. During the transition in 1993, Jim Michel went on to serve as acting administrator of the agency, until Brian Atwood was appointed as the new administrator. With Jim's departure I assumed the acting assistant administrator role in the Bureau for Latin America and the Caribbean.

I had never met Brian before, but I knew about his vast experience in both the government and the nongovernmental organization world. After leading the Clinton-Gore transition team at the State Department, he was nominated to be undersecretary of state for management, but Senator Mitch McConnell placed a hold on all undersecretary nominations at the State Department as a means of forcing the Clinton administration to name a new USAID Administrator. During that period Brian was nominated to be administrator, the hold was lifted, and in the interim he served as undersecretary of state for management. Several months later, in May 1993, he was confirmed as the new USAID administrator. Prior to the Clinton campaign, Brian was the first president of the National Democratic Institute for International Affairs; during the Carter administration, he served as the assistant secretary of state for congressional relations. Also, interestingly, he began his career as an FSO at the State Department.

In my view, Brian's first brilliant decision was to handpick a group of experienced foreign policy experts for nomination to senior staff positions in USAID. All the nominees had long served as senior Senate staffers for leading Democratic senators.

Overall, I would say that the agency's staff was openly enthusiastic about the new administration and pleased to see a leader of Brian's stature at the head of USAID. However, I didn't expect an offer of any kind from Brian. Frankly, I had intended to return overseas as a mission director; having survived the "trade wars" in the political campaign, I thought a strategic move back to the front lines of development was the way to go. I had my eye on mission director positions in a couple of countries. However, in 1993, I was surprised and quite interested when Brian asked me to consider becoming the executive secretary for USAID. The idea was compelling, given Brian's impressive vision for USAID. Since we had not worked together, I assumed he'd made this offer based on recommendations from others, probably first and foremost Jim Michel. I would be the first career person to become part of Brian's leadership team, and from a historical perspective, the second African American to hold the executive secretary position for the agency.

After consulting with Rosa, Jim Michel, and several folks I respected, I agreed to take on this assignment, as long as Brian and I could reach an agreement on a couple of preliminary conditions. I wanted to remake the executive secretariat function in USAID. I envisioned an office that would be similar to and operate as efficiently as the executive secretariat offices at the State Department and the National Security Council. I thought this was an appropriate direction to take, and Brian readily agreed with me. He also approved the budget and the staff I would need to carry out my plans. Most importantly, I would need an accomplished deputy, and thankfully, Brian gave me the authority to select any officer in the agency. My first choice was Toni Christiansen-Wagner. Again, Brian agreed with me.

Toni was the deputy director of the Central American office at the time of my offer and a highly regarded FSO. Toni was one of the most outstanding of my colleagues from the Bureau of Latin America and the Caribbean, a terrific leader, a wise manager, a mentor to her staff, and very savvy in managing interagency relationships. She had garnered great respect in the field as the USAID lead in the demobilization and reintegration of insurgent soldiers, including Contra armed units and the FLMN (Farabundo Martí National Liberation Front), back into civilian life after the Central American wars.[5]

Because of her extraordinary efforts and experience in the field office, I knew it would be hard for the bureau to relinquish her. However, I was adamant that I have the best person I could find to be my deputy for what I considered to be a monumental task. This position would manage all affairs for the administrator—not just the paper flow, as it currently did. Fortunately, Brian's experience with this mode of operation at the State Department led him to agree that my choice was an excellent one. Fortunately, Toni accepted my offer. We made a great team and were successful in restructuring operations for the office.

Toni was a tremendous colleague and a great friend over the decades. She moved on after a couple of years in the position, and Paula Goddard replaced her. Both women were extraordinary colleagues; they took on a job that was not mainstream at the time and that therefore could have been a risky career move for each of them. However, in the State Department and the National Security Council, a leadership position in the executive secretary's office was a career builder, and I was determined to make it the same at USAID. I'm thrilled to say that the deputy executive secretary jobs turned out to be excellent career vehicles for both women.

Toni went on to serve as a mission director in Jordan and Egypt. Following her USAID career, she became a true pioneer as one of the few female chief operating officers in Middle Eastern–based global corporations. Paula eventually replaced me as executive secretary and then later became a mission director in Slovakia. Following her USAID career, she became a senior adviser to the United Nations Office of Drugs and Crime in Vienna and eventually a vice president at the Tetra Tech Corporation.

It's not always the best policy to play it safe with career decisions. Calculated risk-taking may create opportunities that eventually pay excellent dividends.

As I began the challenging process of developing a new approach for the executive secretary's office, my first step was to meet with and gain perspective from the executive secretaries at both the State Department and National Security Council. Fortunately, I benefited from the wisdom of two outstanding FSOs who went on to become among the most distinguished ambassadors and senior officials in the history of the State Department— William "Will" Itoh, the executive secretary at the National Security Council, and William "Bill" Burns, the executive secretary of the State Department. These highly respected professionals were very generous with their time, knowledge, and views on how I could approach my new job. We developed close collegial relationships that were instrumental in effectively managing USAID's involvement in the interagency process.

It was during this period that I met Helene Gayle, a senior public health officer at Centers for Disease Control who was selected to serve as the first director of USAID's new HIV/AIDS program. Our friendship has now spanned decades. Helene's distinguished career continued after her US government service when she became the CEO of CARE International, and after my USAID career I was honored when she asked me to serve on the board of directors of that legendary global organization.

As a small agency, the executive secretary office at USAID never had the staffing required to replicate that at the State Department or the National Security Council. But with Brian's support, I received the budget necessary to recruit excellent staff. When first Toni and then Paula, those two exceptional FSOs, agreed to join me in this crusade, it sent a strong signal across all of USAID. I asked Linda Whitlock, an outstanding FSO, and Pat Hamilton, a dynamic executive assistant, to join our front office team, giving us additional experience for managing our extensive responsibilities. We and our executive secretariat staff colleagues coordinated the internal activities of the various bureaus, managed the external interagency coordination with other US government agencies and the National Security Council, and supported the USAID/White House liaison and her staff.

One of the important opportunities my new position presented me with was the chance to build strong relationships with the administrator's political appointees and senior staff. Fortunately, I developed excellent and productive relationships with them, particularly with Brian's chief of staff, the highly regarded Dick McCall. I found him to be a man of extraordinary integrity and political skill with an in-depth knowledge of Congress, which he had acquired from his broad experience in senior staff positions in the Senate.

Dick had worked for a number of distinguished senators, including John Kerry and Hubert Humphrey on the Senate Foreign Relations Committee. He had played a key role in negotiating the end of the war in El Salvador, and he was the assistant secretary of state for International Organization Affairs for the Carter administration. Dick's world-class sense of humor was an added benefit and genuinely appreciated by all who worked with him. He was, first and foremost, a policy guy and one of Brian's confidants. Dick is an incredibly decent, honorable colleague and a good friend to this day.

Assuring that USAID had a seat at the National Security Council table was an essential part of my day-to-day duties, as it was an ever-present concern. At first, USAID did not have what we considered the appropriate access, even though Brian was well connected and widely respected at the White House. The council is the principal forum used by the president for national security and foreign policy decision making, with senior national security advisers and cabinet officials, and the president's principal arm for coordinating these policies across federal agencies. Typically, it conducts its business via two key decision-making meetings—first, one that the principals (i.e., the cabinet secretaries and agency heads) attend, and second, one the principals' deputies attend. Given that a significant amount of the council's business was covered in the deputies' meetings, we believed it essential that USAID senior officials be included in them.

I chose to be proactive in developing relationships at the NSC to ensure the inclusion of our agency into those vitally important meetings, but a few strong personalities in the White House didn't fully appreciate the importance of our participation in this forum. One example of the management challenges I faced was when a meeting was scheduled to consider policy shifts regarding the Horn of Africa, and I wanted Dick McCall—our lead person on the Horn of Africa—to be present at it. But a few individuals at the NSC thought that it would be adequate for USAID to be represented by the State Department, whose official would subsequently brief our leadership. We prevailed in that particular debate, and overall we won such bureaucratic battles for USAID about 75 percent of the time. I found the agency's success rate was related to the particular region, the importance of the topic or issue, and the quality of the personal relationships that our lead political appointees had with their counterparts at the NSC and the State Department.

The executive secretariat's office also consulted with various USAID bureaus and offices about their strategy and policy papers. Both Toni and I could play a useful role in this arena because of our field mission experience, which was especially helpful in building relationships with USAID's senior leadership. Brian always welcomed our input on most issues, and this approach set the tone for our excellent working relationships across the agency.

Most of the career staff I knew at USAID were dedicated civil servants and enthusiastic about working with the Clinton administration. However, some of the new appointees were skeptical at first about the commitment of a career staff that had spent so many years working for Republican administrations under Reagan and Bush. So, once again, I took on the role of bridging a gap—this time, one of trust. As I sought to provide context for the new team, I relied on my often-repeated pitch that "we're looking forward to working with the new team, and you may be surprised to discover that once you get to know us, we will be your best allies." I believe, at the end of the day, that that approach worked well and resulted in productive relationships.

During my time as executive secretary, I was drawn back to Haiti once again under a surprising set of circumstances. In September 1991, President Jean-Bertrand Aristide was removed from office when the Haitian army staged a coup against him. His life was saved only by the intervention of US, French, and Venezuelan diplomats. During the 1992 election campaign, Bill Clinton had promised to restore Haitian democracy and Aristide's presidency. In August 1994, the Clinton administration, under a UN resolution, launched "Operation Uphold Democracy," which effectively forced the capitulation of the Haitian military regime. In October, Aristide returned to Haiti to complete his term in office, accompanied by Secretary of State Warren Christopher and Administrator Atwood. A few months later, Brian was selected by President Clinton to lead the White House delegation for Aristide's formal assumption of his rightful office in May 1995.

In June 1995, Brian Atwood led the presidential delegation to observe the parliamentary and local elections in Haiti. I assisted in the coordination and planning for the three-day delegation and was pleased that Brian asked me to accompany him as part of the delegation. It was a homecoming of sorts for me. It had been nearly ten years since I had served in Haiti, but many of my Haitian colleagues were still at the mission or were officials in the Aristide administration. I had several USAID friends and colleagues at the mission, and it was very gratifying to be part of the restoration of Haitian democracy. The US ambassador was the legendary William "Bill" Swing, truly a diplomat out of central casting. I will never forget our arrival on an official US aircraft at the Port-au-Prince international airport. As we deplaned, at the bottom of the airstairs was the regal, ramrod stiff Ambassador Swing in an immaculately tailored white suit, without a drop of sweat on his brow despite the ninety-plus-degree temperature. At that time and throughout his thirty-year career he had taken on some of the most complex and demanding posts in the history of US foreign policy, and he was the ideal person to lead the US Embassy during this critical period in that tormented nation.

It was a unique time for US-Haitian relations, where the US government restored the democratically elected president, supported both national and local elections, and for a short period occupied Haiti in a peacekeeping mission. I traveled to a couple of regional capitals and observed this period of hope for Haiti and how optimistic ordinary people appeared to be at that moment. Thus, it has been very sad for me to see how that nation has continued to suffer since the 1990s from a continual barrage of manmade and natural disasters, unfortunately consistent with Haiti's centuries of tragic history.

In the early days of the Clinton administration, the announcement that the number of USAID missions worldwide faced reduction due to a tight operating budget loomed over our operations. As the incoming administrator, Brian made the hard decision to close down twenty-plus missions.

Realignment sufficed for some missions, while others had to consolidate offices for budgetary savings. For example, the eastern Caribbean operation where I had served as mission director closed and the portfolio moved to Jamaica. Missions in middle-income countries including Costa Rica, Ecuador, and Panama were also closed. A couple of them reopened or downsized before ultimately shutting down. It was a period of enormous stress in the field with many contentious issues to deal with.

The budget cuts also led to targeted layoffs. The situation was extremely problematic for USAID because it dramatically affected some of our best and brightest officers. Far too many talented, experienced people got caught up in a budget-cutting exercise that evolved into an organizational crisis. Most of the senior career officers vigorously opposed this action. It became the subject of a heated debate in which the pros and cons brought about lengthy discussions on more than one occasion. It often appeared that the individuals advocating for budget cuts didn't fully understand the magnitude of that decision. It took USAID about ten years to recover from the loss of most of our middle management, and the situation represented a severe setback for USAID. Given the wide variety of actors involved in government decision making—Congress, the executive branch, and various constituencies—such exercises can quickly become shortsighted; USAID, unfortunately, suffered from such a perfect storm.

Much of our effort in the executive secretary office focused on interagency work, through which we strived to build a presence for USAID every day. We engaged in various fronts with the Department of Commerce and other agencies with significant foreign affairs portfolios. We remained vigilant because many of those agencies zealously protected their turf, and we had to be equally devoted to retaining our voice and a seat at the policy-making table. When Vice President Gore formed his binational commissions for Russia, Egypt, Ukraine, Mexico, and South Africa, he hosted breakfast meetings on the environment and other shared issues. We wanted to be sure that USAID was included in policy discussions with the vice president and other senior officials in the Clinton administration. Overall, we maintained a pretty good batting average.

I believe Toni, Paula, and I did an excellent job in achieving our most important goal of assuring that USAID consistently participated in relevant policy conversations at the White House and the National Security Council. To this day, I consider the three of us as pioneers in fostering an operating bureaucratic principle that USAID must have a seat at the table.

Those first few years were very intense and dramatic for the Clinton administration. Bureaucratic battles were commonplace, and reengineering and cost-cutting measures were introduced that often focused on USAID. Particular senior staff members recommended elimination of or drastic cuts to funding levels of long-term training and secondments to the Senior Seminar, the Foreign Service Institute, and the United States Army War College. In response, I organized a small group of senior staff to present the case to Brian that it would be a mistake for USAID to relinquish these coveted positions that every government agency sought out.

Further, we believed that such a drastic elimination of training opportunities demonstrated shortsighted thinking and would send the wrong message to our most talented officers. Clearly, the loss of executive training slots and relationship-building opportunities would damage USAID's stature within the foreign affairs arena. Fortunately, the administrator agreed, and we saved the teaching positions and the student slots at the National Defense College and the Senior Seminar. What we lost in that battle were other important long-term-training positions and program scholarships at prestigious universities such as Stanford, Princeton, Harvard, and Syracuse. Those were valuable and important programs to USAID, but our key training programs survived, and so overall we were satisfied with the results of our efforts.

The battles were never ending with certain members of Congress, notably Jesse Helms, then chairman of the Senate Foreign Relations Committee. Senator Helms fought to abolish three foreign affairs agencies, one of which was USAID. Unfortunately, he successfully eliminated the United States Information Agency (USIA) and the Arms Disarmament Control Agency (ADCA). Among those in the DC foreign affairs community, the closure of those two independent agencies signaled a significant loss of policy expertise for the presidency, and I shared that view.

However, Senator Helms was unsuccessful in abolishing USAID because Brian Atwood led a well-fought battle to preserve an independent development voice in the US government.[6] The context for this battle was the US government's 1993 Government Performance Reporting Act (GPRA), which required strategic planning and management systems well beyond what USAID had in place. The administration, through Vice President Gore's National Performance Review (NPR), had embraced this legislation as a basis to "reinvent government," streamlining its processes and more clearly articulating the value of government to the general public. In response to the vice president's initiative, in 1993 Brian declared USAID to be a "reinvention lab" to pioneer the approach set forth by the NPR. Over a period of two years the agency's mission and development approaches were defined, building the basis for the agency's strategic plan as required by GPRA. In transforming the way it planned, implemented, and monitored its development efforts, the agency built on its own best practices.[7] These significant USAID reforms led to a review by the vice president's staff that demonstrated the value of this organizational reengineering and also resulted in the agency receiving an NPR award.

Overall, the reforms, plus Brian's dogged determination, were the key factors in assuring USAID's survival as an independent agency. The president, the first lady, and the vice president supported Brian's efforts, but later on his ultimate triumph cost him professionally.[8] Brian's appointment as ambassador to Brazil was withdrawn when Helms refused to consider his nomination.[9] Fortunately, this abuse of power did not hinder Brian's distinguished career. During the Obama administration, he was nominated and selected as the chair of the Development Assistance Committee of the Organization of Economic Cooperation and Development based in Paris with the rank of ambassador.

11 Mandela Magic
The Capstone of My USAID Career

As I walked out the door toward my freedom, I knew that if I did not
leave all the anger, hatred, and bitterness behind, I would still be in
prison.

—NELSON MANDELA

I made my first visit to the beautiful country of South Africa in 1995, when
I was the executive secretary of USAID. I traveled there at the request of the
Bureau for Africa as a member of a four-person team to conduct a management assessment of the USAID mission. During this trip, I got a brief
introduction to the historic democratic transition under the incomparable
Nelson Mandela and was given the opportunity to experience, firsthand, a
sense of the change to come. During his twenty-seven years as a prisoner
during the apartheid era, Nelson Mandela remained determined and refused freedom three times until it was offered under his terms. I would
later learn well during my years in South Africa that President Mandela was
a man and leader for the ages.

South Africa is a fascinating nation and a powerhouse in Africa. The fos-
sil record indicates humans have inhabited South Africa since prehistoric
times; during the modern era, the region was settled by Khoisan and Bantu
peoples. Dutch traders landed at the southern tip of present-day South
Africa in 1652 and established a stopover point, what became Cape Town,
on the spice route between the Netherlands and the Far East. After the British seized the Cape of Good Hope area in 1806, many of the Dutch settlers,
known as Afrikaners, who were also called Boers (farmers) at the time,
trekked north to found their republics, Transvaal and the Orange Free State.
The discovery of diamonds (1867) and gold (1886) created wealth, which
increased immigration from the metropole and intensified the subjugation
of the native inhabitants. The Afrikaners resisted British encroachments

but were defeated in the Second South African War (1899–1902); however, the British and the Afrikaners ruled together beginning in 1910 under the Union of South Africa, which became a republic in 1961 after a whites-only referendum. In 1948, the Afrikaner-dominated National Party was voted into power and instituted a policy of apartheid—billed as "separate development" of the races—which favored the white minority at the expense of the black majority. The African National Congress (ANC) led the opposition to apartheid, and many top ANC leaders, such as Nelson Mandela, spent decades in South Africa's prisons. Internal protests, insurgency, and boycotts by some Western nations and institutions led to the regime's eventual willingness to negotiate a peaceful transition to majority rule. The first multiracial elections in 1994 following the end of apartheid ushered in majority rule under an ANC-led government. South Africa has since "struggled to address apartheid-era imbalances in housing, education, and health care."[1]

In 1999, Thabo Mbeki, the deputy president and distinguished leader of the ANC, was elected as Mandela's successor. During his tenure in office, the South African economy grew at an average rate of 4.5 percent per year, creating employment in the middle sectors of the economy. The black middle class significantly expanded with the implementation of Black Economic Empowerment. This growth increased the demand for trained professionals but failed to address unemployment among the unskilled bulk of the population.[2]

Jacob Zuma became president in 2009 and was reelected in 2014, but he was forced to resign in February 2018 after numerous corruption scandals and gains by opposition parties in municipal elections in 2016. President Cyril Ramaphosa took office in 2018, and his administration has made economic growth a priority while pursuing efforts to reduce unemployment, poverty, and socioeconomic inequality; improve public service delivery; and unite a socioeconomically, geographically, and racially divided society.[3]

While there had been only informal discussions about my becoming the mission director in South Africa before my trip there in 1995, afterward, the seed took hold in the back of my mind. I saw the phenomenal potential of the South Africa mission. The management assessment revealed that Leslie "Cap" Dean and his extremely knowledgeable staff were instrumental in supporting the government and civil society in that nation. The South Africa mission had begun the process of transitioning its programs to align with the new government under the transformative, democratic leadership of Nelson Mandela, elected president in May of 1994. Before his election, all USAID work had been with antiapartheid and civil society groups and led by a wide range of nongovernmental organizations supporting the anti-apartheid movement.

After spending my entire USAID career in Latin America, South Africa was not on my radar as a possibility before the assessment. I had observed that postings in our embassies in Africa was often the road to leadership positions for African Americans in the foreign affairs agencies. However, given my years of experience in Latin American and the Caribbean, I continued to pursue assignments in that region and had turned down a few offers of senior positions in missions in Africa. Some USAID senior officers over the years had predicted this would set my career back. Looking back, I feel satisfied that I made the right decisions for me and my family.

Now, because of the management assessment experience, I had a deeper understanding of the importance of South Africa to US foreign policy. The excitement generated by the Mandela presidency in the Clinton administration in concert with its ambitious US foreign policy goals was contagious, and I decided to seek the mission director's position when it opened up. South Africa's democratic transformation was a global phenomenon. The surprising end of the country's apartheid system of governance created a palpable spirit of hope around the world in terms of advancing the ideals of racial and cultural equality.

Following the assessment, Cap and I participated in several review meetings in Washington on USAID's new strategy to assist the Mandela government. During this period, Brian decided that I was his candidate to be the new mission director in South Africa, and I was very pleased to be given this opportunity.

Rosa and I had spent most of my career in Latin America. Our sons were born and raised there; we all spoke Spanish and felt very comfortable in the region. Moving to South Africa would involve a trek across the globe, living worlds away from family and aging parents. Now that our sons were older, they also had opinions about moving that required consideration. Michael was preparing to head off to college at the University of Virginia, and Steven was about to enter high school. The idea of moving away at this time was an unpopular one. I had to convince everyone dear to me of the career wisdom in a move that impacted their lives more than usual.

South Africa presented me with an opportunity to lead the second-largest USAID mission in the world with oversight of a billion-dollar portfolio. This was years before the massive Iraq and Afghanistan reconstruction programs, a time when a billion dollars was still considered a substantive program amount. And there was the magic of Nelson Mandela to think about in connection with this historical moment in South Africa. No question, it was a fantastic opportunity. Finally, we reached a family consensus, and I accepted the mission director position. The idea of moving to South Africa had not been an easy sell, but we now view this as one of the best life decisions we made as a family.

I had my first personal encounter with President Mandela shortly after we had arrived in South Africa. While we were packing up for our move to the country, I got a call from Brian Atwood. He had been asked to join an honorary committee to support the eradication of polio campaign in Africa. The campaign, which was titled with the new soccer-themed slogan "Kick Polio Out of Africa," evolved from a partnership between the World Health Organization, Rotary International, and USAID. Nelson Mandela was the committee chairman, and Brian had been invited to attend the launch event in Johannesburg. However, since I would be arriving in South Africa during the same week, he asked me to represent him at the one-day event. It never occurred to me that Mandela would attend, as most celebrities and dignitaries who lend their name and fame to a good cause rarely attend ceremonial events. At that time, I wasn't aware of President Mandela's personal philosophy regarding his role in such matters.

Mandela inspired a new generation of leaders and set a high bar for humanity. He achieved the impossible while enduring great trials of personal adversity, setting aside anger and hate, disappointment and suffering, a feat which most human beings would find themselves incapable of. His strength and determination to overcome debilitating human emotions and instead look to a more positive future was beyond remarkable, and he managed to reconcile a diverse nation that had lived through the injustice, pain, and tragedy of the apartheid era and to establish democratic governance as a platform for historical transformation, the likes of which the world had never seen.

So we began our trip to South Africa—Rosa, Michael, Steven, and me. After a long twenty-hour flight from New York, we landed in Johannesburg during the early evening. The next day, still feeling quite jetlagged, I woke up to get ready for the kick-off event. Tired, I soldiered on and got into a suit, and then my family and I headed over to the convention center.

With President Obama in the Oval Office in 2009. (Pete Souza, the Obama White House)

As a Peace Corps volunteer in 1968 in Monte Plata, Dominican Republic, with my neighborhood buddies, "my informal language teachers."

With President Obama and Peace Corps volunteers serving in El Salvador in 2011 during a presidential trip to that nation. (Pete Souza, the Obama White House)

With Senator Harris Wofford at my Senate confirmation hearing in 2009. Harris was a friend and wise mentor, and he graciously introduced me that day. (courtesy of the Peace Corps)

With Caroline Kennedy in 2011 at the John F. Kennedy Presidential Library and Museum for an event held in commemoration of the Peace Corps' fiftieth anniversary and for the presentation of the John F. Kennedy Service Awards to Peace Corps volunteers and staff members in recognition of their outstanding public service, both at home and abroad. (courtesy of the Peace Corps)

With Senator Patrick Leahy in 2012 at the Patrick and Marcelle Leahy Center for Lake Champlain for an event at the University of Vermont to promote the importance of global service and to highlight the contributions of Vermont's current and returned Peace Corps volunteers. (courtesy of Senator Leahy)

With Senator Chris Dodd, our guest speaker at the Peace Corps headquarters in 2010. Chris was a famed returned PCV who served in the Dominican Republic, a distinguished senator from Connecticut, and a good friend. (courtesy of the Peace Corps)

With Susan Rice, US ambassador to the United Nations, as a guest speaker at the Peace Corps speaker series in 2012. (courtesy of the Peace Corps)

Meeting with the Peace Corps volunteers serving as counselors in Camp GLOW (Girls Leading Our World) in Macedonia. These camps, in all PC countries, encourage girls to become active citizens by building their self-esteem and confidence, increasing their self-awareness, and developing their skills in goal setting, assertiveness, and career and life planning.

With Vice President Joe Biden and Rosa at a White House event for agency heads in 2009. (courtesy of the Peace Corps)

With members of the Peace Corps senior staff at a White House picnic in 2010.

Michael and Angela and their sons, Ronin and Gabriel, in 2017.

Steven and Nga and their sons, Joseph, Eliot, and Lucas, in 2018.

On the University of Wisconsin–Madison campus in 2019.

Although I had checked with the administrator's staff to find out whether I would be expected to make any remarks and received firm assurance that I would not, based on past experiences with government communication, I was not wholly convinced by this assurance. So just to be sure I wasn't caught off guard, I did a bit of homework on polio and learned that because the disease had been eradicated, except in pockets of Africa and Pakistan, USAID no longer funded polio-eradication projects. I decided that if I were unexpectedly called on to speak, I would talk about USAID's global-health portfolio and our health projects in South Africa.

My family and I arrived at the Sandton Conference Centre, a place I would often visit in the future, given its role as a primary venue for national conferences and events.[4] We met the other "Kick Polio Out of Africa" committee members—the first lady of Ghana, the first lady of Congo-Brazzaville, the World Health Organization's director for Africa, and the president of Rotary International. I represented USAID.

A huge crowd had formed, and dozens of reporters, both international and local, were standing ready. Shortly after that, we heard loud sounds of sirens blaring outside and learned that President Mandela would be arriving within minutes. Further, the minister of health informed us that the president would like to have a private meeting with his committee before the event! At that point, the fog quickly lifted from my jetlagged mind, and reality sank in. I remember thinking, "Oh my God, my first day in South Africa, and I'm going to meet Nelson Mandela! Wonderful!"

After being led to an elegant, private meeting room with the other committee members, President Mandela entered. The minister introduced the committee and then issued a surprising directive.

"I'd like for each of you to brief President Mandela on what your organizations are doing to combat polio in Africa."

There I stood, overcome with emotion in meeting Nelson Mandela, after having been assured I would not have to speak or brief on polio. Luckily, I wasn't the first to speak, and I had my backup plan as to what to talk about given that USAID was no longer funding polio eradication

When my time came to speak, I used the tried-and-true device of all public speakers—a personal story or anecdote—which is usually effective with an audience for two reasons: it happens to be true, and it's also memorable. I told President Mandela that on the drive to the convention center, I'd asked my two sons, aged eighteen and fourteen, what they knew about polio. I related how my oldest son, Michael, a premed college student, had some idea of the disease because he was interested in public health issues. My youngest son, Steven, like all children of his generation had fortunately never even heard of polio. I described my personal story of growing up in Chicago, a big urban area, where we lived in abject fear of the disease. I relayed how wealthy people sent their children to the mountains or a distant rural area during the summer. Everyone was concerned about garbage collection and the need to keep the streets clean. My mother wouldn't let me swim in a public pool during the summers. Newspaper stories with pictures of crippled children and children in iron lungs stoked our fears of polio. I told President Mandela that I happened to be a member of the fortunate generation that became the first or second cohort of children who received the Salk vaccine. And after that, polio just disappeared from our lives entirely—and summers were very different for us thereafter. I wrapped the story up by extending my desire to see a world in Africa where children have a polio-free future, just like in the United States and the rest of the industrialized world.

Following my story, President Mandela patted me on my back and thanked me for sharing my personal story. It was a moment I will never forget. What an honor it was for my family to share the incredible opportunity to meet President Mandela as part of our first experience in South Africa. I would have the privilege to sit down with him in various settings in the future with small groups of people in relaxed venues, including a management retreat, where I would hear his views on multiple topics. On a few occasions, he would attend quarterly board meetings of an organization supported by USAID, in which his new wife, Graca Machel, served as the board chair. Thus, my tour of duty began as I met one of the world's most admired leaders. Without a doubt, that experience ranks at the top of my South African memories, and I dare say, my family's memories, as well.

We had learned as a family that every new overseas assignment presented unanticipated experiences, and although we were looking forward to living in South Africa, our transition once we got there was tough. The first six months in the country proved especially hard for us. The US Embassy is in Pretoria, the administrative capital, located sixty miles north of Johannesburg with a population at five hundred thousand. It's also known for being a university town because it is home to three major universities and as the Jacaranda City because it has thousands of Jacaranda trees (the purple beauty of spring was very striking) planted in its streets, parks, and gardens. Thanks to these lovely trees, its often said that the city goes from urban gray to an amazing purple as the Jacaranda trees flower.

South Africa was not always the most comfortable living environment we experienced. We sometimes faced difficult cultural challenges in a post-apartheid society as black and brown Americans. We had to maneuver a somewhat treacherous social landscape, but we have always considered ourselves lucky to have had the magnificent experience to witness such a historic transformation. We were the only black family in an all-white neighborhood. Of course, 90 percent of the white population in Pretoria was Afrikaans, who had lived with a cultural ideology of "apartness" since the adoption of apartheid in 1948. They spoke Afrikaans, a language derived from Dutch and spoken by the protestant settlers in the Cape region in the seventeenth century. When we went to the nearby Brooklyn Mall for brunch, we were usually the only black people who were not sweeping floors or serving food. We waved to our white neighbors from a distance the entire first year. Only once were we invited to dinner in their home. Frankly, we would have preferred not to go, but there was an unspoken obligation that came with being a diplomat in a new country and we would typically welcome such an invitation.

The dinner itself was lovely, but there were uncomfortable moments, nonetheless. Servants brought our food to us in the formal dining room, reminiscent of a southern plantation scene from a *Gone with the Wind* world in America. None of these people, the servants or neighbors, had ever entertained American black people, so I imagine the experience was as foreign to them as it was uncomfortable for us. After dinner, dessert and drinks were served outside on the patio in the delightful December summer weather. The evening had gone fairly well until our host challenged me on a point concerning race in America.

"I want to know why blacks in America feel discriminated against."

I doubt my response was particularly well received. I used a comparative analogy to describe the similarities between apartheid and the Jim Crow Laws in the United States. The brief discussion ended the evening, and in any case, it was our last invitation to that home, for which we were thankful.

I admired Rosa and Steven's ability to successfully navigate in that complex society. Steven met the challenge head on and succeeded academically and athletically at a new high school, the American International School of Johannesburg, and also forged lifelong friendships with his classmates. Our older son, Michael, while attending the University of Virginia during our tour, came to South Africa three times a year. Although we deeply missed being near to him during his first two years of college, we were proud to see how he excelled in a prestigious scholar program and with his premed coursework. Our family also experienced a terrible loss during this time. Rosa's mother, Encarnacion Mustafa, died on Christmas Eve in 1997. We left our sons with friends and headed back to the Dominican Republic. That twenty-hour flight was nearly unbearable due to our grief and sadness in anticipation of what we would experience upon arriving in Santo Domingo. Being so far away from our families proved to be the difficult downside that we anticipated early on; this sad loss brought that realization home to us in a very personal way.

We had some extraordinary experiences in South Africa, with our sons taking advantage of the exceptional outdoor experiences made possible by the country's geographical diversity—scuba diving, jungle safaris, and the like—with other students and friends. We found the South African countryside beautiful, with mountains, rolling plains, lush green valleys covered with vineyards, and jungle areas. It was the only USAID mission in the world where we were engaged in activities in four major cities: Cape Town, the beautiful legislative capital; Pretoria, the administrative capital, comparable to Washington, DC; Johannesburg, the business center of the country, similar to New York City; and Durban, a lovely port city on the Indian Ocean. Durban was also well known because Mohandas "Mahatma" Gandhi started his law practice there in 1893. There, he launched his nonviolent civil disobedience campaign in support of the resident Indian community's struggle for civil rights until he was expelled by the British colonial authorities in 1914.[5]

Rosa and I, as well as my senior staff, had significant representational duties that saw us hosting and attending numerous government, business, or civil society events in these four cities. We had many official events in Pretoria to organize, and VIPs from around the world wanted to visit South Africa during this historic time, widely reported on in the media, and so we often entertained visitors in our homes. Those high-level visits were time consuming and required a lot of planning and preparation by my staff and me to manage them effectively. I have a methodology that I have used throughout my career to organize official VIP visits. I've always believed that it's essential to identify a project or point of interest that's readily accessible to the visitor at sites that are within a reasonable travel range. If the site requires a four-hour drive, you're not going to convince the visitor's staff to visit it. Fortunately, Gugulethu Township is close to Cape Town, and that's where we arranged for the site visit of First Lady Hillary Clinton and her daughter, Chelsea.[6]

For this special event I specifically chose a project that highlighted a grassroots program demonstrating women's empowerment led by a very unprivileged group of people. It was a renowned housing project, called Victoria Mexenge, managed by the Homeless Peoples' Federation, where homeless women had formed a co-op to build their own homes. The success of this project, the dedication of the women, and the high quality of the sound brick homes they were constructing was astonishing. Carleen Dei, our terrific director of the Housing and Urban Development Office, and I worked with the advance team to walk through every step of the visit beforehand. I wanted to offer the first lady a hands-on activity, one that would allow her to help with the construction, which her staff assured me she was willing to do. Pam White, our brilliant executive officer, was our principal liaison to Mrs. Clinton's team and handled numerous calls, emails, and cables back and forth as the planning crescendo built up to the actual visit. She led our team in creating the script for the trip, based on the events recommended by our colleagues, the technical office directors. All of this hard work led to the organization of four events that USAID would participate in.

The overall visit was very successful, and we were praised by the first lady's staff for our impeccable planning and follow-up. Most importantly, the first lady and Chelsea clearly enjoyed the events and interactions with the South Africans they met. It created such a memorable visit for Mrs. Clinton that she mentioned the project to the presidential advance team, which included the site in President Clinton's historic visit to South Africa in March 1998. I was happy to learn that Mrs. Clinton returned to the same project site in 2009 as secretary of state.

I feel fortunate to have been in South Africa when Hillary Clinton made her two visits. I'd never met her before, and it was an honor to accompany such an impressive leader who was well informed and knowledgeable about all the issues we had to deal with in South Africa. In every meeting— whether the subject was education, health, or governance—she conducted in-depth conversations on the topic at hand, and she gracefully interacted with both senior officials and ordinary people on the street during her visits to various project sites of nongovernmental organization.

The first lady delivered an inspiring speech at the University of Cape Town in honor of the thirtieth anniversary of Robert Kennedy's speech against apartheid. A standing-room-only audience gathered to hear her thought-provoking words, which were well received by the students, faculty, and both the national and international press. It made us all incredibly proud to be represented by this intellectual giant and dynamic leader.

In 1996, President Clinton appointed the brilliant and dynamic leader James Joseph as ambassador. Joseph was a legendary business and philanthropic executive who had worked with Martin L. King Jr. as a founding co-chair of the civil rights movement in Tuscaloosa, Alabama, during the brutal years of the civil rights movement. A graduate of the Yale Divinity School, Joseph also taught at Yale University and the Claremont College, where he once served as a university chaplain. As a senior executive at Cummins Engine Company in the 1970s, he was a pioneer in shaping the corporate social responsibility movement in America.

Joseph had served four US presidents, including as the undersecretary of the interior during the Carter administration, and had survived a plane crash in Micronesia; a minister and man of God, he believed he had been saved for a purpose, and he lived his life accordingly.[7] Ambassador Joseph was married to the dynamic Mary Braxton Joseph, an Emmy Award–winning television journalist and media consultant. Together, they made a superb team that skillfully represented the United States, successfully pursued the Clinton administration's foreign policy goals, and developed excellent relationships with both the government of South Africa and the greater South African community.

Ambassador Joseph played a vital role in the Binational Commission, co-chaired by Vice President Al Gore and Thabo Mbeki, the deputy president of South Africa. The commission was a major strategic initiative put forth by Gore in 1993 to advance US government foreign policy objectives and support the Mandela government's strategic goals. The US–South Africa Commission was also referred to as the Gore-Mbeki Commission. It included practically every US cabinet secretary and their South African government counterpart minister; the members participated in the commission twice a year, which was held alternatively between Washington, DC, and Pretoria or Cape Town.

The principal players on the US side of the commission were the secretaries of commerce, education, housing and urban development, agriculture, the interior, health and human services, transportation, and energy, and of course, the USAID administrator.[8] By definition, the members were a high-powered group of prominent leaders and close allies of the president and the first lady. However, only a few of the departments had international affairs' budgets. So any initiative or program they wanted to carry out in South Africa would eventually have to be funded by the USAID budget. That made life interesting for me as the mission director.

Ambassador Joseph and I, in concert with the head of USAID, Brian Atwood, had to figure out the most strategic and equitable manner in which to work with the other members of the commission. We wanted to support the commission through an effective and coordinated process. We assumed that USAID's development strategy, which supported the Mandela administration's national priorities, would be a logical program umbrella for the cabinet departments. We sought to avoid new initiatives that did not reflect this strategic vision. Still, it was a challenge to coordinate with a dozen cabinet department officials in both the US and South African governments.

To aid in the coordination, I proposed that USAID serve as the executive secretariat for the commission. Ambassador Joseph and Administrator Atwood concurred with my proposal and agreed to present the idea to Leon Fuerth, the vice president's national security adviser. Fuerth also supported the plan and secured the approval of the vice president. This change led to a more organized process for identifying and using US government funds for commission-designated projects. In practical terms, when any given cabinet secretary proposed a new initiative for funding out of the USAID budget, the mission would determine the strategic fit and level of funding. It didn't change the level of intensity in the interest of the cabinet departments to participate in the South African development program, but it did make the process more coherent. Our headquarters coordination was skillfully managed by our secret weapon in DC, Will Elliot, our energetic and very knowledgeable South Africa desk officer.

The bottom line was that everyone wanted funding for their priority projects. Sometimes we managed to provide them with resources—as long as the request reflected an interagency-reviewed approach for South Africa and the priorities of its government. But, as always, what sounds logical on paper can be difficult to implement, especially when dealing with powerful people of influence, such as ministers and cabinet secretaries. Most of the time, the mission's position was viewed as reasonable, rational, and strategic, but occasionally a decision was reversed for the greater good and our foreign policy.

Deval Patrick, then the assistant attorney general for the Civil Rights Division of the Department of Justice, was the force behind one of the most significant accomplishments of the commission. Deval had his roots in the same South Side Chicago neighborhood that I did and used his experience, education, and passion for justice to engage in issues of racial injustice. He and Paul Weisenfeld, the USAID regional lawyer, assisted the South African government in the writing of South Africa's first affirmative action plan, another product of the special relationship between South Africa and the United States under the Clinton administration. Deval Patrick later became the first black governor of Massachusetts in 2006 and was reelected to a second term in 2010.

I consider myself fortunate to have had the honor and privilege to work for James Joseph, a true visionary and leader with immense integrity who backed me up every step of the way. He became an important mentor, and both he and his wife, Mary, became lifelong friends. Always very thoughtful, he faced every major issue head on. He and his deputy chief of mission, Robert Pringle, a highly regarded former ambassador, assembled an extraordinary country team, and we worked together as a cohesive and innovative unit. As an exceptional servant leader, Joseph gained the respect of President Mandela and the entire South African cabinet. He also carried significant influence in the White House and formed an active and productive alliance with Vice President Gore and the First Lady.

There was another aspect of working in South Africa that I found, and still consider in retrospect, to be quite remarkable. In most of our bilateral relationships with developing countries, especially where we had an extensive USAID program in place, the mission typically took the lead in designing the strategic framework for the use of US government funding, based on the host government's priorities. In South Africa, however, that was not the case. The South African government declined to be a part of any foreign donor-led effort, including the customary consultative group headed up by the World Bank and the International Monetary Fund. It did not borrow money from such entities. I think many members of the South African government had the mindset that this was an oppressive, imperialistic approach to development. Consistent with this perspective, the government insisted that any donor assistance be specifically in support of its national strategic plan.

There were times when the South African government questioned why we were still providing substantial funding to the nongovernmental organizations instead of to the new government. We stood our ground and argued that it was in the country's best interest to continue to support the same institutions that had been the ANC's allies in the antiapartheid movement and the democratic transformation. The South African government's representatives concluded that this was a reasonable approach given our interest in continuing our efforts to strengthen civil society and understood that we were seeking ways to support the policies of the South African government in every way. Our ability to develop and maintain productive working relationships across the South African government was tied to the experience and caliber of our South African staff. Our wise and knowledgeable staff included outstanding leaders such as Nomea Masihleho, Farooq Mangera, Mathata Madibane, Anita Sampson, and many others who were instrumental in our efforts to work effectively in our multiple program sectors. Throughout my career, I, like many other FSOs, often observed that our local staff (Foreign Service nationals) were clearly the unsung heroes of USAID's work in the missions around the world. They provide the knowledge, experience, relationships, and continuity that is essential to the success of the American FSOs in any given country.

Of course, many of those discussions with the South African government officials ended up debated in the press by print and broadcast journalists. The South African government had its own strategy from day one, however, and it was determined to be fully involved in all the decisions.

The new government under Mandela proceeded to manage the bilateral relationship in a way I'd never seen any other nation attempt to do. Crucial to its success was that it had brilliant people in critical posts responsible for leading the government. Unfortunately, that's not often the case in other developing countries.

Because of the compelling story of the South African transformation and the dynamic leadership of Nelson Mandela, many celebrities and global leaders visited the country. When I heard that George Soros, the billionaire and philanthropist and founder of the Open Society Foundations, was planning to visit South Africa, I requested a meeting. The Open Society Foundations is the world's largest private funder of independent groups working for justice, democratic governance, and human rights. His local representative was initially skeptical that he would be interested in meeting with us, but I insisted that Mr. Soros would undoubtedly want to know what the US government's aid program was doing to support South Africa. I advised his team that I would like to brief him on how our broad democracy and governance program supported local civil society organizations in that country. The team agreed, and I flew down to Cape Town with Dick McCall, who was on an official visit.

I had prepared a concise briefing to make the most effective use of the thirty minutes we were scheduled to have with Mr. Soros. I was very pleased when, during the meeting, Mr. Soros very graciously asked to extend our conversation. We ended up speaking for about an hour. Following our meeting, he told his local representative that he wanted to explore ways that Open Society could collaborate with the USAID program to strengthen local civil society organizations.

Two other American "giants" visited South Africa during my years there, and I was honored to have the opportunity to work directly with them on a couple of programs. First, the legendary Reverend Leon Sullivan, a leader in fighting apartheid in his pioneering role as the first black board member of General Motors, traveled to South Africa in 1997. In 1977, Mr. Sullivan had drafted guidelines to help persuade American companies with investments in South Africa to treat their workers there in the same way that they treated their workers in the United States. He later worked with the United Nations on drawing up a code of ethical conduct for multinational corporations. As journalist Paul Lewis notes, "as originally stated, the Sullivan Principles called for racial desegregation on the factory floor and in company eating and washing facilities; fair employment practices; equal pay for equal work; training for blacks and other nonwhites so that they could advance to better jobs; promotion of more blacks and other nonwhites to supervisory positions, and improved housing, schooling, recreation, and health facilities for workers."[9]

His organization, OIC International, worked on vocational training programs in South Africa, and I wanted to learn more about their activities there. Reverend Sullivan—the "Lion of Zion"—used his pulpit and his position as longtime pastor of North Philly's Zion Baptist Church to organize for local African American causes, particularly in employment. From 1959 to 1963, he led area black preachers in organizing "selective patronage" boycotts of local companies deemed to discriminate against African Americans in their hiring, urging black consumers with the slogan "Don't buy where you don't work."[10]

The other visitor was William "Bill" Gray, a former congressman from Pennsylvania who in 1989 was the highest-ranking African American elected official. Rising to the number three job in the House leadership, he later headed the United Negro College Fund.[11] His trip to South Africa in 1998 focused on providing fund assistance to South Africa's historically black universities. I had previously worked with Mr. Gray in 1994, after he had been appointed by President Clinton as special envoy to oversee the elections in Haiti and the restoration of President Aristide to the presidency following a coup in that country.

Reverend Sullivan and Mr. Gray were acutely aware of the high stakes in South Africa and didn't allow any obstacle to deter them in their efforts to assist President Mandela and his administration. What I greatly admired about them was that they used their positions of influence and power, in corporate boardrooms and congressional committees, to fight for policy reforms that would benefit disadvantaged African Americans, and in this case, the new South Africa. I think it would be accurate to say that during the Mandela administration, the South African government had more influence in managing its relationship with the US than any country in the world at that time, including China and Russia. This new approach signaled country ownership, and the South Africans were in charge.

The South African government's approach was to call for a review meeting in Pretoria of all donor assistance organizations to learn about the details of our programs. Each donor nation (US, UK, Canada, the European Community, Nordic countries, World Bank) was asked to present its strategy and related programs to the South African Department of Planning. Each presentation was reviewed and critiqued, in real time, by the South African officials. Many of the ideas we presented were eventually endorsed and supported by the South African government. I believe officials were surprised to see our collegial and collaborative engagement and participation with the organizations that we funded. With this new dialogue and our demonstrated mutual respect, I think we changed their minds and earned their trust.

This level of involvement on the part of the South African government signaled a breakthrough moment and an incredible accomplishment for a recipient nation, and it was unprecedented. The process the government put in place demanded that we treat it as an equal partner, which was not how it typically worked in the case of donor-recipient relationships.

The government's insistence on this approach was impressive, as was its astute management of the process. In the end, despite the dismay of many of the donor agencies, I applauded this important, significant move forward for a nation that was undergoing a historic transformation. What we were witnessing was just another dimension of the impact of "Mandela magic."

In March 1998, we were honored and privileged to participate in the historic visit of President Clinton, Mrs. Clinton, and the president's delegation to South Africa. My team arranged one of the president's site visits to Victoria Mexenge, the Homeless Peoples' Federation housing project, thanks to the first lady's recommendation. I escorted the president and Mrs. Clinton and the ambassador and Mrs. Joseph on a tour of the project, where they received an enthusiastic and emotional welcome by the ladies of the cooperative.

Observing an overseas presidential visit is awe inspiring in its breadth and depth, and I have witnessed a few during my career. Dramatically, in this case, the president was on a six-nation African trip and was accompanied by some eight hundred persons on Air Force One and an accompanying plane. The delegation included a press corps of sixty reporters and photographers, sixteen members of Congress (fourteen Democrats and two Republicans), several cabinet members, senior administration officials, business executives, labor leaders, mayors, church leaders, and White House staff.[12] I will always remember the joint press conference held by President Mandela and President Clinton at Tuynhuys, Mandela's Cape Town residence. President Mandela was clear in his remarks that South Africa pursued an independent foreign policy, and expected the US government to respect its global perspective concerning all issues.[13] This event took place in the estate's lovely gardens, and I was seated next to several congressmen and journalists, all of us awestruck by this historic event and the obvious mutual respect demonstrated by both leaders. President Clinton commented that he was "the first American president to visit South Africa on a mission to Africa to establish a new partnership between the United States and the nations of Africa and to show the people of America the new Africa that is emerging."[14] It was gratifying for Rosa and me to interact with the members of the president's diverse delegation over the three-day visit, to witness their emotional engagement with all segments of South African society, and to see the extraordinary interaction between these two world leaders.

12 South Africa's Miracle

Without forgiveness, there's no future.

—ARCHBISHOP DESMOND TUTU

A crucial part of the South African "miracle" was the creation of the Truth and Reconciliation Commission, which was the brainchild of Dullah Omar, an influential South African lawyer of Indian descent and a lifelong human rights activist who became the spokesman for Nelson Mandela at the end of his imprisonment. Declared an enemy of the state for his efforts to help Mandela, Omar escaped assassination by the apartheid government many times. He was charged with high treason but became the minister of justice in President Mandela's cabinet and later the minister of transport under President Mbeki. Omar played a crucial role in transforming the South African justice system. One of his most important actions was to establish the Truth and Reconciliation Commission in July 1995 with Archbishop Desmond Tutu as its appointed chairman. The purpose of the commission was to investigate the crimes committed during apartheid and offer a platform for victims and their families to confront the perpetrators of crimes against them with an offer of amnesty to encourage them to come forward. The model served as an inspiration for other post-conflict societies in places such as Sierra Leone and Rwanda.

The process established by the commission became the gold standard for how a divided society with a violent past might work through that past and move forward. Even as the country learned that working through a complicated past takes time, the commission provided a way to openly address the individual and systemic wrongs committed under forty-three years of apartheid—a government-imposed system of discrimination and separation based on skin color.[1]

It's understandable that Mandela would have realized the importance of such a commission, considering he spent twenty-seven years jailed as a political prisoner. The white warden and guards tried to turn other prisoners against him, but Mandela converted them into followers, which only strengthened the ANC's position. His captors thought they could break his leadership role with other prisoners by isolating him from them, but it only created a rebellion among his followers.

He came out of captivity with no anger toward those who persecuted him. He even invited some of his jailers to his inauguration. The kind of peace and purpose that Mandela was able to create out of his terrible situation probably resulted from a higher sense of forgiveness, which he mastered. The Truth and Reconciliation Commission equipped the people of South Africa with an invaluable method with which to find peace by facing and forgiving those who had committed a wide range of crimes against them during the long years of the antiapartheid struggle.

Along with a few other donor-countries that were instrumental in funding a portion of its budget, including the British and Canadian aid agencies, USAID worked closely with Desmond Tutu, the brilliant leader and Nobel Prize–winning archbishop. We witnessed the compassionate and caring way he managed the commission process as the chairman who presided over hearings. Tutu and Mandela felt that everyone should be held accountable to the same standard for their actions—no matter which side of apartheid the wrongdoers were on and regardless of whether they were Afrikaners or ANC members.

Tutu would often travel to hearings in various regions of the nation to chair a specific case of national importance. The hearings were complex and well-planned sessions. I vividly remember one, in particular, that was led by Archbishop Tutu in Paarl, the heart of wine country in the Cape Town region. This scenic, idyllic part of South Africa had been the location for terrible, heinous crimes during the apartheid era. I accompanied a US government delegation to observe the hearing, which was being held during President Clinton's visit. John Shattuck, the US State Department assistant secretary for human rights, and Susan Rice, then-assistant secretary of state for Africa, led our group.

The hearing took place in the auditorium of a local school, flowers surrounding the stage. The families of the victims and the perpetrators were seated in separate sections of the hall. The process allowed the accused to present themselves to families they had harmed to apologize and express their remorse for what they had done and to ask for reconciliation and amnesty.

Translators were present to manage the five major languages of South Africa, and the hearing used simultaneous translations. Psychologists were available to deal with the anticipated emotional breakdown of the accused and the victims' families during and after the testimony.

It was a surreal setting with heavy security in place. Archbishop Tutu led the hearing about a case involving a young black man who had disappeared in the Paarl region in the 1980s. He had gone out drinking with friends at a bar and never came home. Missing for ten years, his family wanted to know what happened to him.

The local Afrikaner police commander, who had led a squadron that killed the young man, came forward to testify and admit to his guilt. The murdered man, who was simply at the wrong place at the wrong time, had been mistaken as an antiapartheid activist. The policeman enabled closure for the family by telling the family where they had buried the man, so his remains could be recovered. The man's widow was there with his children. This tragedy was just one of the hundreds of thousands that occurred during the bloody apartheid era.

In the second case, the accused were a cadre of the ANC who kidnapped an Afrikaner policeman, then tortured and killed him. They tossed his body in a pit, where it remained unrecovered. These men came forward and testified before the victim's family about the events of that night. They asked for amnesty. After two hours of highly tense and emotional testimony, we went to a break room to join Archbishop Tutu and the rest of his commission for coffee. The archbishop, crying from the emotional toll of the testimonies, explained that his tears were not just of sorrow but also of joy, because people were confronting their demons in a way that could improve the greater society.

It was, indeed, one of the most heart-wrenching days I had ever experienced, and I believe the same can be said for most everyone present in the school that day. Although no other country has been able to replicate the Truth and Reconciliation Commission's process with the effectiveness of the South African authorities, it has set a global standard and proven a useful model in the aftermath of horrific events in various nations.

Another inspiring example of truth and reconciliation was my experience with the extraordinary Biehl family. This was a family I ended up forming a rewarding relationship with, and I observed the lesson that they taught

the world about how to respond to a tragic loss. Theirs is a story of incredible compassion and forgiveness that lives on to this day. Amy Biehl
was a staffer for the National Democratic Institute who was tragically killed
in Gugulethu Township near Cape Town in 1993 during the run-up to
Mandela's historic election. I had not yet arrived in South Africa and learned
of her death from Brian Atwood because Amy had worked for him at the
institute.

As reported by the *New York Times*, Amy Biehl was driving three co-
workers who needed a ride to their homes in the township when a mob of
young men who were members of a black nationalist militia group started
throwing stones at Amy's orange Mazda. Amy was beaten and stabbed to
death as she tried to run away, as her friends screamed in vain that she
was a comrade and begged for the men to stop. The men ignored the loud
protests of her distraught black friends. At the trial, Amy's roommate said
her friend died because she was white. The *New York Times* reported, "After
memorializing Miss Biehl with freedom hymns and African laments, friends
and colleagues paraded through Gugulethu with placards declaring, 'Comrades Come in All Colors.'"[2]

In the face of this tragedy, the Biehl family demonstrated one of humanity's most astonishing displays of compassion and forgiveness that I have
ever seen. In 1997, during a hearing of the Truth and Reconciliation Commission, the young men who murdered Amy confessed and expressed their
sorrow and regret.[3] Amy's parents, Linda and Peter Biehl, forgave them.
In Linda's own words, "In 1997, when the four men convicted of her murder applied for amnesty, we did not oppose it. At the amnesty hearing, we
shook hands with the families of the perpetrators."

After I arrived in South Africa, I got a call from Brian Atwood, who told
me about the Biehls and related their personal story. He explained that
the Biehls, as part of their reconciliation process, wanted to establish a
trust, the Amy Biehl Foundation Trust, with donations that had arrived,
unsolicited, from strangers moved by the news of their daughter's death.
Peter and Linda planned to live in South Africa for most of the year to
manage the foundation. Brian asked that I meet with them to learn more
about their goals. I was honored to get to know such amazing people.
At that time, I only knew about Amy's work in South Africa, but I soon
learned the life story of this incredibly accomplished young woman. She
had been a star swimmer at Stanford University and a Fulbright scholar.
She was committed to participating in the transformation of South Africa.

Her memory will live on as others come to know of her as the young activist who made it her mission to support the end of apartheid rule. She looked outward and stepped up like mission-driven leaders do to make a difference for people who may not look the same as them and who may not even live on the same side of the world. She sought to empower South Africans to improve their lives.

Though Amy lost her own life in the process, her legacy lived on through her parents. As I became friends with her parents, I came to see why she had been so remarkable. During my conversations with the Biehls, they told me about the goals of the Amy Biehl Foundation Trust and their determination to empower poor South Africans in the townships of Cape Town. They planned to create small businesses, such as bakeries and small factories. They wanted to develop community outreach activities for young people in the townships that would support programs for education, sports, arts, and music. The Biehls submitted a proposal for USAID funding that included a matching-grant formula. Their project was endorsed by the South African government and Archbishop Tutu, as the chairman of the Truth and Reconciliation Commission.

We considered this a worthwhile initiative and decided that the mission should provide some funding for this empowerment and reconciliation program. My colleagues Henry Reynolds and Jim Harmon worked closely with the Biehls on this strategic initiative, and I am proud that USAID contributed to the foundation and that we had the opportunity to work with the Biehls. For decades, they continued their work in South Africa through the foundation. Despite the distance between California and South Africa, Peter and Linda traveled to South Africa all those years and resided there almost ten months out of the year. Today, the foundation runs programs that provide life skills, practical skills, and vocational skills to thousands of children and youth from the townships around Cape Town, desolate places that took root during the apartheid era on the Cape Flats.

The Biehls poured their hearts and souls into this project in the memory of their daughter and the work she wanted to accomplish in South Africa. Unfortunately, Peter fell ill on a flight back to California in 2002, and soon after, he died of colon cancer. The world lost a hero, but before he died, Peter urged his wife to continue what they had started. She promised she would, and she has. Linda has continued to do this work to this day, and in recent years has spent much of her time in South Africa, where a large number of young people fondly call her "makhulu," which means "grandmother" in Zulu. The Biehls were revered in South Africa by Nelson Mandela, Archbishop Desmond Tutu, and everyone who ever met them. I feel genuine pride that USAID contributed to this organization, which truly represents the very best of humanity.

In the crucial years before the historic election of President Mandela, an important organization was established by the brilliant leader Vasu Gounden. Vasu was on the ANC team that led conflict resolution efforts during crucial moments of the run up to the 1994 elections, and later he was on the team of the Independent Electoral Commission that assisted in the successful negotiation of an agreement that convinced the leader of the Inkatha Freedom Party, a powerful Zulu tribal party, to put its name on the ballot for the election. This was a critical factor in ensuring a peaceful election and ushering in a democratic South Africa under the leadership of Nelson Mandela. In 1992, Vasu founded the African Centre for the Constructive Resolution of Disputes (ACCORD), the goal of which was "to bring creative African solutions to the challenges posed by conflict on the continent."[4]

I met Vasu around the time when we were holding the first couple of meetings with the Binational Commission, which is when he shared his dream of establishing a conflict resolution institute that would address and mediate conflicts across the African continent.

Vasu explained, "My vision is to create an eminent group that would include distinguished leaders like President Mandela, Olusegun Obasanjo of Nigeria, Julius Nyerere of Tanzania, and other people of similar stature. These prominent and highly respected leaders of great integrity would mediate in conflicts like Rwanda, Burundi, or the Sudan and negotiate peace before they become armed wars." I told him that I thought he had a terrific idea, and I believed it was an important initiative that should be supported. However, I explained to him that USAID/South Africa funding was solely for development programs in South Africa and that such a continent-wide program was outside of our purview. Still, because I was intrigued by his idea, I offered to arrange a meeting for him with Brian Atwood. Vasu had a grand vision and had already carried out a feasibility study, created architectural drawings of what the center would look like, and researched a location.

So on Brian's next trip to South Africa to attend the Binational Commission sessions, I arranged a meeting. Vasu's brilliant presentation captured Brian's attention. As I recall, one of Vice President Gore's senior advisers attended the meeting as well and was also impressed with his conceptual framework. They asked me to determine how this initiative could be supported. I suggested that we consider developing a feasibility study for an Africa-wide program funded by the mission.

We funded the feasibility study, Brian was impressed with the results, and he asked us to obtain funding to support the Africa-wide program, for which his chief of staff, Dick McCall, strongly advocated. ACCORD arranged a small dinner meeting where they invited President Mandela and where Dick McCall and I would be present. At this meeting, the president personally asked for the US government to support the work of ACCORD. The principles that guided the organization were, according to Mandela, "the very ideals for which humanity has striven for centuries—peaceful resolution of conflict, human rights, and good governance."[5] Thanks to Vasu's stellar leadership, it rapidly gained recognition as one of the leading conflict management organizations in the world and the largest in Africa. Graca Machel, Nelson Mandela's wife, later became the chair of its board.

In 2020 the African Centre for the Constructive Resolution of Disputes was named by Pennsylvania University as the twenty-third-most influential think tank in the world, and number one in Africa. It has achieved monumental success, and Vasu and his colleagues have gone on to establish conflict resolution programs across Africa. It is currently creating an Africa Wide Conflict Prevention Network, which will be the largest of its kind in the world. The UN has recognized the organization's intervention approach as a viable model for supporting peace. In September 2005, Vasu, in his capacity as president of the organization, became the first African nongovernmental organization in history to address the UN Security Council. Vasu's story illustrates the power of a great idea. In 2022 ACCORD will be thirty years old, and USAID will have supported this organization for a record twenty years. ACCORD is a notable success story of USAID's efforts to support peace and security in Africa. I'm grateful I could assist Vasu in realizing his vision for Africa by presenting this initiative to USAID leadership.

Leadership requires an open-minded attitude when special people appear with extraordinary ideas. Become entrepreneurial when determining an approach to support new ideas.

During the era of Mandela, South Africa was a nation where one encountered some of the most remarkable emerging leaders and organizations in the world. These leaders were also considered the vanguard in shaping this new society. One stellar example of such a partner was human rights activist Kumi Naidoo, widely admired, both in South Africa and around the world, as the secretary-general of Civicus, an international alliance for citizen participation, and highly regarded for his leadership in the anti-apartheid movement.

Kumi was arrested several times for violating provisions against mass mobilization, civil disobedience, and violating the state of emergency. Due to his activities against the apartheid regime, he was forced underground before finally deciding to live in exile in England. I had great respect for Kumi's wisdom, judgment, and determination to strengthen civil society as a fundamental pillar of this new democracy. His astute insights and wise counsel were instrumental in shaping our programs in support of civil society. In 2009 Kumi became the executive director of Greenpeace, and in 2018 was appointed secretary-general of Amnesty International. He is a widely respected global leader, and his courage and determination is unsurpassed.

Another important area USAID was involved in at this time was children's education. In 1997, we entered into a partnership with the Children's Television Workshop to create a local version of *Sesame Street* as a co-production with South African Broadcast Company. This initiative, envisioned as part of our pre-K education program, had the brilliant Michelle Ward Brent, an experienced and innovative early-grade reading and communications technology expert, as the project manager.

However, the plan ran into high-profile opposition from Jesse Helms, then chairman of the Senate Foreign Relations Committee. It would take a novel to retell this story in full, but suffice it to say that Helms attacked *Sesame Street* because it was a Public Broadcasting Service program, an organization he repeatedly tried to defund. And at the same time, in some circles in South Africa, *Sesame Street* amounted to "cultural imperialism," which triggered several harsh media stories about my colleagues and me.

This potential partnership became a political football, and I often asked incredulously during this contentious period, "Who could be against Big Bird?" The fierce backlash concerned the South African Broadcasting Corporation, but despite these worries, Michelle courageously proceeded to finalize the project with both the broadcasting company and other local partners, and Ambassador Joseph and Administrator Atwood remained steadfast in supporting this education initiative for young South Africans.

In the end, the mission and Big Bird prevailed, and as a result, South Africa's *Takalani Sesame* enjoyed a fifteen-year run as one of the most popular children's shows in the nation. It received wide praise for its significant contribution to preschool education and its positive impact on millions of children. The show even created an HIV-positive character to teach children early on about the AIDS virus.

"Can USAID help us with this ethics project?" That was the question posed to me in 1997 by Pat Keefer, the regional director for the National Democratic Institute. The South African government, to its great credit, had decided that it wanted to create a code of ethics for the South African cabinet for the first time in the history of the nation. As Pat further explained, the South Africans wanted to review the ethics codes and practices of Ireland, the UK, Canada, Australia, and the United States. However, they needed funding to cover the senior team's travel budget assigned to carry out this study. We recognized this was an extraordinary opportunity to assist the Mandela administration in an important policy area, and we seized the moment in an innovative manner.

An experienced and dynamic leader, Pat Keefer was highly regarded and very well connected with the ANC leadership. Our extensive working relationship and her successful projects had led me to trust her judgment. I explained to her that funding the travel to several countries presented us with a complicated policy issue, but that this endeavor was clearly a worthwhile one.

Pat told me she wanted me to come to Cape Town the next morning so that I could meet with Mandela's general counsel to talk about this idea. This invitation implied that we would have the chance to be engaged in a very high-level initiative and in the planning to figure out how to make it happen. So the next morning, I flew down to Cape Town. Pat and I met with Nicholas "Fink" Haysom, President Mandela's general counsel. Haysom, a white South African, was a human rights lawyer who joined the ANC and eventually became a member of the ANC's negotiating team for a new constitution. He told me about this marvelous idea and explained that the ANC hoped the US government might be able to assist. I determined that the US government had to be at the forefront of this historic policy initiative, one that, in my view, was too important to miss; we had to step up and find an innovative way to support this initiative.

I immediately briefed Ambassador Joseph, and he agreed with me. I advised Administrator Atwood and Carol Peasley, the head of the Bureau for

Africa, about our plans. Everyone that I spoke to in USAID enthusiastically agreed that we needed to be involved. USAID/Washington and our team came up with an innovative funding plan and we covered the travel expenses for the South African government delegation's study tour to the UK, Ireland, Canada, and the United States.

The project became a joint initiative between USAID and the National Democratic Institute. Pat Keefer and I accompanied a delegation consisting of Valli Moosa, minister for provincial and constitutional affairs, and Haysom to Washington, DC. Moosa, a highly regarded leader who had played a significant role in the antiapartheid movement, was probably the youngest cabinet minister in the South African government.

We met with several senior White House staffers and congressional leaders and engaged in extensive conversations with Chairman Henry Hyde (IL-R) and Bobby Scott (VA-D), the ranking member of the House Judiciary Committee (the committee responsible for initiating the historic Watergate hearings). The delegation met with a few senators who were on the Senate Judiciary Committee and with the USAID and State Department officials responsible for the administration of justice and the rule of law programs. One of the highlights of the delegation's trip was its meeting with two Supreme Court justices.

Just as we prepared to leave for a scheduled meeting in the office of John Lewis, the legendary congressman from Georgia, we got an unexpected call from his chief of staff. Unfortunately, the congressman would not be able to meet with us due to a crucial vote about to occur. Interestingly enough, it was the final vote on NAFTA, and every Democratic vote was vital for President Clinton at that point. Disappointed, I responded that I understood.

We continued to our next appointment in the Rayburn (House Office) Building, where incidentally, Congressman Lewis also had his office. As we walked by the front of the building, we saw the congressman walking toward us on his way to the Capitol to vote. Surprised upon seeing him, I quickly decided to use the opportunity to introduce him to the members of the delegation. They were, of course, well versed in the history of the American civil rights movement and felt honored to be able to meet him and shake his hand.

As I approached him, I said, "We understand that you cannot meet with us, sir, but I want to introduce you to the South African delegation."

"Oh, no, no, no, we are going to meet! I'm just going to vote. I'll be right back. Please go wait in my office."

We then went to the congressman's office and waited for about an hour until he returned, and, as always, he was so very gracious. We met with him for nearly an hour and a half, and it was an excellent meeting. How fortunate for members of the delegation to have the honor to converse with an icon of the American civil rights movement, one who marched and worked with Martin Luther King Jr. Congressman Lewis was generous with his time, a testimonial to the person he was known to be. The South Africans were delighted with their experience, and I am very proud that we played an essential role in organizing the study tour, another memorable and unifying moment for US–South African relations.

I consider my role as mission director in South Africa to be my most rewarding experience in USAID. It was a unique opportunity that offered me a front-line level of engagement in US foreign policy and, more importantly, also enabled me to witness firsthand the unparalleled leadership of Nelson Mandela—one of the most important figures of the twentieth century.

Heading the South African mission proved to be an exhilarating and gratifying experience. It was the most significant assignment of my USAID career, as I managed a broad and complex portfolio that encompassed many sectors—democracy and governance, education, economic policy reform, housing, and urban development, and small to medium business development.

Successful management of such a complex program required careful coordination with the ambassador and the embassy country team and regular communication and team building between the South African government and the mission to ensure that USAID was effectively represented in the four major cities of Pretoria, Johannesburg, Durbin, and Cape Town.

As in all large, high-profile missions, it was necessary to develop productive relationships with the South African government, civil society as represented by the major nongovernmental organizations, the private sector, the university community, other interested parties, and the media. Constant communication with USAID headquarters, the administrator, the Africa regional bureau, and the technical offices of one of our major allies in this region was required to support this complex portfolio. I made it a point to travel to Washington, DC, at least quarterly to communicate our accomplishments and challenges to the executive branch, Congress, and key interest groups such as the university community and think tanks. Securing the level of support I thought the mission needed required a lengthy fourteen-hour flight every three months, which I cannot say I enjoyed.

Fortunately, thanks largely to Brian Atwood, I was given the necessary latitude from the beginning to both recruit and retain exceptional staff, which included a particularly distinguished senior mission staff. All of my office directors attained the highest level of leadership and career rank in both USAID, the State Department, and in the corporate world. We led and managed this broad project portfolio and developed excellent working relationships with all sectors in South Africa. I have highlighted the tremendous career success of my South Africa senior team in the acknowledgments section of this book. It was an honor to serve with these outstanding officers, and I am grateful that our strong friendships have continued since that historic moment in our careers.

When I reflect on the time I spent in South Africa, I realize just how magical a time it was. What a joy and an honor to share the presence of such incomparable, determined, intelligent, and brave individuals as I witnessed life-defining history in the making. I thought it impossible to imagine any future career engagement that could come close to my experience in South Africa.

But then, I'd thought that before.

13

Recruited by the International Youth Foundation

The Nonprofit World

The purpose of life, after all, is to live it, to taste experience to the utmost, to reach out eagerly and without fear for a newer and richer experience.

—ELEANOR ROOSEVELT

In 1998, at the end of my two years as the mission director in South Africa, I wasn't sure what might be next for me in USAID or if there even was a "next" there. Would I consider a second tour in South Africa if offered one? Leaving the country would be difficult for me. It had been a challenging experience, but a very successful and engaging assignment. I had formed superb relationships with the ambassador and the country team, as well as with my counterparts in the South African government, business community, and civil society. The country had become an enormously satisfying place to live and work.

Rosa and I had raised our children in the Foreign Service world, and I truly loved working at USAID. While overseas, we enjoyed being part of the USAID family, sharing experiences with my colleagues and their families. Many of them became lifelong friends—which may sound like a catchphrase at this point—but I can assure you, those friends remain very special to me.

I'd worked with talented and dedicated counterparts all over the world. I couldn't fathom a more fascinating, creative, and mission-driven life and career. I wasn't at all sure I was ready to leave it. I had a few helpful conversations with Brian Atwood about my future, and we discussed a couple of different offers for my next mission director assignment. Further, the State Department offered me an ambassador post in Mali, which after much agonized consideration, I turned down. I had always planned to have a second career once my Foreign Service career ended. But, when the actual time came to consider retiring from USAID, I found myself struggling with the thought of leaving the life and work I had loved for twenty-two years. Could I be successful if I returned to the private sector? It was a challenging and emotional decision for me to make.

However, after long family discussions, I finally came to the conclusion that after serving in USAID as an FSO for more than two decades, it was time for my family and me to return home. Rosa and our sons—Michael in his second year of college at the University of Virginia and Steven in his second year of high school in Johannesburg—along with my mother and my siblings all agreed that it was time for me to retire from the Foreign Service. I was especially concerned about my mother's health. She had been ill and for the first time in my career could not visit us in a new country. In hindsight, I'm glad I made the transition when I did because it gave me a long runway in terms of a second career. I immediately began contemplating alternatives for what that work would be.

After my decision was final, I turned to thoughts about who the best USAID leader would be to succeed me as the mission director and continue the success that my team and I had enjoyed in South Africa. You don't give your heart and soul to an enterprise and not care about what happens to it after you leave it. I recommended to Brian that he consider one of the agency's most outstanding senior officers as the next mission director for Pretoria. We hit the jackpot when Stacy Rhodes agreed to shift from his intended post of Peru to South Africa instead.

Stacy had tremendous experience, was highly regarded throughout the agency, and was respected by his State Department colleagues. He was a terrific leader and ideal for the mission director position, in my view. I knew he would embrace this unique opportunity to engage in the transformation of South Africa in an innovative and determined fashion. I was truly grateful because we had the perfect candidate ready to step in and take the reins in South Africa, and I was pleased that the administrator agreed.

I had found purpose and great satisfaction working for mission-driven organizations like the Peace Corps and USAID, and I wanted to continue to do so in the second part of my career. I now had the opportunity to consider working in the nonprofit world, consistent with my goal of working in all three sectors—corporate, government, and nonprofit.

So I was pleasantly surprised when an executive recruiter reached out to me while conducting a search for the International Youth Foundation (IYF) to ask if I would consider the newly created executive vice president of global partnerships. The IYF mission of improving the lives of young people "wherever they lived, learned, worked, or played" resonated with me.

Further, Rick Little, the founder and CEO, was a visionary leader and brilliant social entrepreneur who had assembled a terrific, highly motivated staff. I met with him and my long-time friend Bill Reese, who had recently assumed the position of the chief operating officer of IYF. Bill and I had been friends since his days as president at Partners of the Americas, and he recommended me for the position. Rick liked the fact that I had both business and government experience; however, he initially expressed a degree of skepticism about my fit for IYF. He wondered whether a senior government executive would be comfortable or flexible enough to perform successfully at a small, fast-moving organization like IYF. My response to him was that during my entire USAID career, I had always operated with an entrepreneurial mindset, which proved integral to my success.

I was intrigued by Rick Little's unique life journey and how he created IYF.[1] After being severely injured in a horrific car accident, he dropped out of college to create a life-skills coaching program for high school youth. For two years, Rick lived out of his car, doggedly determined to follow his dream, and endured over 150 grant proposal rejections from youth-centered foundations. He finally received acceptance for a proposal from the board of trustees at the prestigious Kellogg Foundation.

He then went on to raise over $150 million to fund his dream. After resounding success with his first youth program, he became the 1989 recipient of the single largest commitment ever made by the Kellogg Foundation and the second-largest grant in the history of American philanthropy at that time. The reported $70 million he received from Kellogg enabled Little to expand his dream and fund the IYF. Rick's view was that "every child deserves at least one adult who is irrationally committed to them." Pursuing the global development of youth life skills, he created a successful partnership with Lions (Clubs) International.

My confidence in Bill Reese as an outstanding executive played a significant role in my consideration. After meeting with board members and other senior staff, I was even more impressed by IYF's global mission and corporate culture. I also liked the idea of building alliances with world-renowned corporations to support youth development. I had spent most of my career at USAID building partnerships, and I believed my experience would be useful to IYF. So I signed on with the organization in 1999.

Rick had the great foresight to assemble an influential board of directors, and he was skilled in picking the members. Each one was a brilliant global leader who introduced us to their network and literally gave us access to anyone in the world.[2] Sir David Bell, the chairman of the IYF board and an inspirational, brilliant leader, illustrates the point. At that time, Bell was the chairman of the *Financial Times*, and subsequently, director of people at the Pearson Group, which included under its corporate umbrella the *Financial Times* and the *Economist*.

Due to the influence and credibility of David and other board members, we received personal introductions to the CEOs and senior executives of global corporations. Thus, we were able to secure buy-in from the corporate leadership, which greatly facilitated an open-minded and often enthusiastic reception from middle management. Visionaries need a team around them to organize, implement, and manage their vision; IYF could only be successful as a team effort, and that it was. The entrepreneurial executives and senior staff were agile, hardworking, and creative. Though we were a small foundation, located in Baltimore, we were determined to position IYF as a global player in the international arena of youth development.

Because we were a small organization, Rick delegated full responsibility of the separate portfolios to each of his vice presidents, under Bill's management lead. Our senior team included Esther Benjamin, Don Mohanlal, Carol McLaughlin, Cathryn Thorup, and me. We derived tremendous creative energy from the support of many talented colleagues.

I was fortunate to work with two superb executive assistants—first, the creative Emma Lozano, and then a recent immigrant to America, the talented Nilufar Kurbanova. We traversed the world while creating a strategy, designing programs, troubleshooting problems, establishing strong partnerships with our global clients, and supporting our partner organizations. There was never a dull moment working with our network of global partners.

When Bill and I arrived at IYF, the foundation had some eight international partners. Before my arrival, Rick and the IYF board had decided to grow the IYF footprint by linking the foundation with established non-governmental organizations rather than creating brand new ones as IYF had done in Germany, Poland, and Oaxaca, Mexico. Within a year or so, we successfully brought into our network organizations in Argentina, Brazil,

Paraguay, and Tanzania. New innovative partnerships with Nike, the Inter-American Development Bank, and Nokia gave us the bandwidth to expand into new countries. We partnered with Intel and introduced Intel "clubhouse" programs in Jordan, the West Bank, and Russia. With Rick's inspiration, our team embarked on a crusade to convince global corporations that IYF should be the preferred global partner to support their goal of broader engagement with the world's youth. Given that IYF was a small organization, it could not set up offices around the world, so IYF created a local partner operating model, years ahead of the time when such an approach became popular. The model centered around identifying the leading youth development organization in any given country and partnering with it. Typically, such organizations also had stellar leadership and an influential board of directors in place.

Based on this success, we created a strategy for outreach to the private sector. I drew up a target list of Fortune 500 companies and we proposed to the leaders of these corporations that IYF was an excellent investment if they wanted to engage in youth development. I soon recognized the secret of IYF's success. Rick's particular genius, in his role as visionary and speaker, was his unique ability to convince potential donors of his value proposition. Of course, another key asset was that IYF had influential national partners in every country in its ten-nation network.

We worked broadly in both the industrialized world and the developing world. We had youth organization partners in Ireland and Germany, Argentina, Brazil, the Philippines, South Africa, and Thailand. The magic of IYF, in my view, was its unique selling position. Rather than trying to reinvent the proverbial wheel at great expense, we showed global corporations how they could invest in the excellent programs our country partners already had in place. Then I introduced and marketed IYF as a turnkey-project system they could use to accomplish their goals. I employed basic logic to demonstrate how they could benefit quickly by using successfully positioned global programs run by prominent child development experts and business leaders—the ideal network.

My typical sales proposition would be, "Your managing director in country X is engaged in building your business there. As good corporate citizens, they are called upon and expected to support worthy projects in local communities and local society. But that's not their primary job. IYF can align them with influential leaders in youth development organizations already operating in country X. We offer a turnkey program that will result in an impactful national youth development program you'd be proud to sponsor. Your managing director can show up at all of the preorganized events, without having to dedicate his or her valuable time managing the youth project. And not only that, it would seem wise to work with our national partner organization, comprised of influential youth development experts and respected business leaders."

I would give them examples of the people and organizations aligned with us. In Brazil, the former first lady was the head of one of the foundations; we worked closely with the Association of Toy Manufacturers and with the former vice president of the country. Further, one of the country's leading sociologists was an adviser who focused on youth. Those types of alliances would be invaluable resources for the corporations we wanted to work with, and they were benefits that came as part of our program. It was a win-win for everybody.

Since it was an argument that made sense, it worked. We created and implemented new global, multiple-country, multimillion dollar programs with some of the world's leading corporations. Companies like Nike, Nokia, and Lucent Technologies embraced our model and became advocates for IYF, referring us to other corporations. Building these corporate relationships created a gateway for our rapid growth with global partners like British Airways, Cisco Systems, Coca-Cola, the Gap, Intel, the Inter-American Bank, Johnson and Johnson, Kellogg, Mattel, Microsoft, the Prince's Trust (Prince Charles's foundation), Shell, the Tommy Hilfiger Foundation, the World Bank, and many other prominent organizations.

IYF's partnership with Nokia was an exciting initiative, and I was privileged to work on the design and execution of this program.[3] During that era, Nokia had a market footprint that could be compared to Apple of today; it was truly a successful global brand. For more than a decade, we teamed with Nokia to connect youth in sixty-eight countries to their communities so they could get a better education and improve their job prospects. In this effort I thoroughly enjoyed my superb partnership with the dynamic Nokia executives leading this program, Martin Sandelin and Kimmo Lipponen. With Nokia's investment of nearly $50 million, IYF reached more than 650,000 young people directly and another 5.4 million children, youth, and adults indirectly.

Lucent Technologies Corporation proved to be another innovative partnership.[4] As part of its efforts to provide the next generation of leaders with the educational opportunities necessary for future success, the Lucent

Technologies Foundation provided IYF with a $15 million grant to support increased access to training and development opportunities for educators and young people in twenty-four countries over four years. For example, in Poland, schoolteachers in rural areas received innovative training to improve the quality of education. In Venezuela, girls from low-income backgrounds received life-skills education, vocational training, and job placement support. In this effort, I supported my colleague Carol O'Laughlin, a wizard of creativity, working with the visionary David Ford, president of the Lucent Technologies Foundation.

Our creative leadership team crafted projects that fit the vision and goals of our corporate partners, which I saw as a crucial strength of IYF. Simultaneously, and consistent with our mission of improving the lives of young people, we carefully designed projects that included a few key components (e.g., youth engagement, local partnerships, potential for scaling up, and monitoring and evaluation) that reflected our organizational mission. IYF has always believed that educated, employed, and engaged young people possess the power to solve the world's most challenging problems.

Our partnership with Nokia exemplifies this approach. The "Make a Connection" program was designed to help young people connect with their communities, families, and peers. From the beginning, local ownership was key to the Nokia-supported programs. IYF and its in-country organization partners worked closely with Nokia staff in designing locally relevant and locally branded programs. Employee engagement and communication strategies were codesigned, with an emphasis on helping to develop essential life skills, such as confidence, goal setting, conflict resolution, and teamwork. By developing such skills, young people were able to improve their school performance, increase their literacy, enhance their job readiness, and contribute to their communities. Nokia was a forward-looking corporation, its senior executives were hardworking and creative, and we enjoyed our relationship with them. On our various trips to their headquarters in Helsinki, we also enjoyed some memorable moments experiencing Finnish culture, such as the Savonlinna Opera Festival, and Finland's natural beauty.[5]

While programs initially focused on helping young people become active citizens, their focus eventually expanded to address youth employment needs. In 2001, Nokia and IYF began exploring ways of recognizing and supporting the work of exceptional young leaders around the globe. Soon after that, YouthActionNet was born. Originally conceived as an awards program, YouthActionNet evolved into a multifaceted global youth leadership initiative.[6] Led by Ashok Regmi each year since 2001, YouthActionNet's Laureate Global Fellowship program has selected twenty young social entrepreneurs, ages eighteen to twenty-nine, to participate in a year-long fellowship, which provides access to training, networking, and advocacy opportunities.

It was an exciting time at IYF as we began to grow our portfolio. We were delivering practical projects that were viewed as innovative and led to new ideas to present to our country partners. Once our local partners understood that our suggestions made sense for their national strategy, we would market it to the corporations. During my time at IYF, not one corporation ever refused out of hand to talk with me about a potential partnership. They might've said, "Not now" or "You're asking for more than we are willing to invest" or "I want you to change an aspect of this proposal." But I never heard, "No, this is a bad idea."

An unusual opportunity led to an unexpected joint project between IYF and Nokia, because of the tragic events on September 11, 2001. This was the single most shocking and traumatic terrorist attack on the United States in its history. Like virtually every American, I remember the day well, but in a very personal way.

The crisp, cloudless sky seemed a deeper shade of blue than usual. A slight chill hung in the air on that sunny Tuesday—a perfect day for flying. I remember it that way because I was headed to Washington Dulles Airport near my home that morning to catch a flight to Dallas, Texas. I planned to attend a regularly scheduled quarterly meeting with senior Nokia executives who had flown in from Finland to Nokia's US headquarters in Dallas to review our collective, ongoing work.

Nothing seemed unusual as I sat waiting for the call to board American Airline's flight to Dallas—the idea that I was sharing space with five terrorist hijackers was inconceivable. At that time, American Airlines only operated a few flights from Dulles, and that morning three flights were scheduled for takeoff in the 8:00 to 8:30 a.m. time slot; all passengers sat waiting in a relatively small common area.

Four planes involved in the attack flew out of various American airports that day, all on planes filled with plenty of fuel for the long flights and enough to trigger the destruction planned. Fifty-three passengers and six crew members unknowingly boarded the third plane at Dulles with five al-Qaida terrorists. They would overtake the crew and head the aircraft into its intended target—the Pentagon—which housed the headquarters of the US Department of Defense in nearby Arlington County.

My plane to Dallas was the last plane to leave Dulles that day, and it had already left the ground before President Bush shut down all air travel. With telephone communication lines jammed up by people trying to check on loved ones, Rosa woke up that morning to the horrifying news of the day, frantic in not knowing which flight I flew on out of Dulles. It was a terrifying and surreal time for the whole country and especially for frustrated people trying to connect with those they cared about through normal lines of communication. On that day, and for a long time after that, nothing was *normal* in America.

The only good news from that horrible day was how Americans rallied together, united from within and from caring support worldwide to heal emotionally, physically, psychologically, and financially. Help was almost immediate in many cases. After landing in Dallas, I met up with the Nokia executives from Helsinki, Finland. As we all sat in the Nokia offices in shock, we started to wonder aloud if there was anything we could do to help.

From my experience with incredible people in the Foreign Service and USAID missions all over the world, the question "How can we help?" is a typical response to a crisis. Those who have led lives geared toward serving others often look outward first rather than inward.

Shortly after the tragedy, the Nokia-IYF Fund was born. The decision resulted from six hours of brainstorming with our always thoughtful and innovative partners Veronica Scheubel, Martin Sandelin, and Kimmo Lipponen. We created an education fund designed to help pay the college tuition of young people who had lost a parent in the terrorist attack. We also recommended that this should cover all affected students, no matter their nationality or citizenship.

We consulted in the middle of the night (Helsinki time) with our respective senior leadership, and Nokia immediately donated one million dollars to get the fund up and running. Additional early funding came from the generosity of Nokia employees—after receiving that initial corporate donation—and we began to solicit support from other corporations and individuals. We were not alone. Our fund was eventually joined together with many other similar ones under the umbrella of the Families of Freedom Scholarship Fund.[7]

Getting home after the Dallas meeting was a challenge in the aftermath of 9/11. No one could predict when air traffic would resume, so for the time being we were stranded in Dallas. My Foreign Service experience kicked in, and I decided that if plan A (a return flight back to DC) did not materialize soon, I would execute plans B or C: a rental car or a train trip. With this in mind, I immediately called Hertz Car Rental, and fortunately, I was able to secure one of the last cars available for a one-way rental.

I then called my sons, Michael at Harvard Medical School and Steven at James Madison University. I asked them to contact Amtrak and secure reservations for a cross-country rail trip, no matter the routing (via Montana to Michigan or Louisiana to Florida) for me and two IYF colleagues. Alan Williams from South Africa and Michael Strubin from Germany were willing to join me in the journey back to Washington, DC. The train option turned out to be a logistical nightmare, so I opted for Plan B—the rental car—and we began a several days drive across the American South during which we also stopped to tour prominent places of interest.

We stopped to visit the Clinton Library site (then under construction) in Little Rock, Arkansas, as well as Memphis and Nashville, Tennessee. It was a trip the three of us will never forget; we had some heartfelt encounters with our fellow Americans along the way. To this day, we occasionally exchange messages with each other on September 11 to celebrate life and our friendship and in remembrance of those who lost their lives on that terrible, historic day.

Overall, the biggest difference between working for USAID versus IYF was that I had broad managerial latitude in a private organization. Our leadership decided what strategic focus to adopt, who to hire, how to use our resources, and what level of risk the organization could withstand. A combination of proven management practices, sound auditing methods, and wise guidance from the board guided our oversight. One has far more latitude in the private sector than in the US government, given the at times contentious push and pull between Congress and the executive branch.

During the incomparable period of professional growth I experienced at IYF and the fulfilling work I did there, I also treasured the time spent with the many exceptional people I worked alongside—the corporate partners, youth leaders, terrific friends, and committed colleagues. I particularly loved the purpose of the organization; being able to associate with smart people, doing excellent work, while striving to make a difference in the lives of young people all over the world was very rewarding. We had dynamic leaders in Germany, Thailand, Brazil, Philippines, Ireland, the UK, Kenya, and Jordan. Many of the programs continue today, all these years later.

I had a fifty-mile commute from my home in northern Virginia to the IYF headquarters in Baltimore, but the exciting work adventure provided such satisfaction that the commute never bothered me. However, the job also put extensive global travel demands on our small executive team, which became a significant challenge for me over the ensuing years, and more pertinently, a hardship that Rosa and my sons had to endure. I was in Baltimore maybe only once or twice a week due to my extensive travel schedule. Four years on the road had taken a toll on both my family and me, so I promised my family that I would make a change, and I decided to leave IYF.

My IYF family of friends and associates created a special going-away gift for me. They called it "Williams's Rules," which they had printed on small cards. The rules were: Be kind to everyone. Hire the smartest people you can find. Give them far more responsibility than they can handle. Don't get mad if they make a mistake. Always acknowledge good work. Don't meddle. If the situation requires, create a new rule.

The sentiment continued to be a touching reminder that I left a positive impression of my business and personal values on those I worked with at IYF. The little things do mean a lot in life and relationships—that's an understatement worth embracing. It has certainly paid off for me.

My longtime friend Bill Reese served as the chief executive officer of IYF from 2005 to 2019. And in 2019, upon his retirement, my former USAID colleague and distinguished senior USAID official Susan Reichle was appointed president and chief executive officer. It's good to know that IYF continues to be led by brilliant, determined people who lead mission-driven lives.

Meeting like-minded people of such high caliber and working with them to help change the lives of youth all over the world was a privilege and a highlight of my time spent at IYF.

14 Reconstructing Iraq

Research Triangle International

I feel that luck is preparation meeting opportunity.

—OPRAH WINFREY

Some have said that a recurring theme in my life is that opportunities suddenly appear before me at the perfect time. I would agree that I have been fortunate, blessed even. But I would prefer to think that opportunities have come to me primarily as a natural result of my focus on forming and nurturing meaningful relationships.

This time, it was through a conversation with Luis Crouch, a good friend and former colleague in South Africa, who had been the senior adviser to the South African Ministry of Education. He was one of the most prominent thought leaders at the Research Triangle Institute, or RTI International—a global research institute and international development consulting organization.

Luis, a well-known and preeminent education economist, had also served as a senior technical adviser for the World Bank's highly regarded Education for All program. I had long admired Luis's research leadership and contributions to literacy programs around the world. He asked me if I would be willing to consider working for the institute. It was a pivotal moment in RTI's history. Ronald Johnson, RTI's vice president for international development and former professor of public administration, had launched an aggressive revenue growth strategy aimed at expanding the institute's global development project portfolio. At the time Luis was talking to me about joining the organization, RTI was an important USAID partner but not one of USAID's top five international development contracting firms in terms of revenue. RTI's USAID-funded projects included policy and technical assistance projects in education, local governance, and public health. Ron and his team were recognized for RTI's stellar work in assisting the governments of

Indonesia and El Salvador in broad-scale local government projects and in supporting local finance and governance projects for USAID, the World Bank, and the Asian Development Bank.

RTI was one of the few major international development contractor firms working with USAID that did not have a principal office in Washington, DC. Most of its competitors were either based in DC or had their largest office there. RTI wanted to grow its USAID business, and an expanded base in DC was an important component in the international development plan. Luis introduced me to Ron, and we had a few intriguing and productive conversations before he asked me to consider a position as RTI's representative in DC. I would quickly learn that Ron was an extraordinary leader, a visionary, and a person of exceptional integrity.

RTI represented an opportunity for me to once again work with a highly regarded, mission-driven organization whose mission is "to improve the human condition by turning knowledge into practice." I anticipated that I could also significantly reduce both my commute time and international travel in such a position, and cutting back on travel was a priority for my family and me. So in December 2002, I resigned from IYF and immediately joined RTI. This outstanding research institute was founded in 1958 with support from the North Carolina government and business leaders, and in collaboration with North Carolina State University, Duke University, North Carolina Central University, and the University of North Carolina at Chapel Hill. I could not have anticipated that it would result in a career move that would span a decade in two phases, an amazing period of professional growth and unique experiences.

I was also pleased that I would be reunited with my friend and former USAID colleague Derick Brinkerhoff. Derick was a distinguished expert in international public management and comparative public administration and was hired by Ron as an RTI fellow. I had had the good fortune to work with Derick for the first time in Haiti. In 2005, Derick collaborated with his wife, Jennifer Brinkerhoff, a professor of Public Administration and International Affairs at the George Washington University, on a groundbreaking book titled *Working for Change*, in which they explore career paths in international public service through the profiles of six public service professionals that illustrate how individuals manage the choices they are presented with over the course of their careers. I was one of the profiles. Little did I know at the time that this was the beginning of a periodic collaboration that would lead to a future book project with Jennifer in the foreign affairs arena.

In my previous twenty-two years at USAID and my four years with IYF, I had worked in numerous countries and every region of the world. But my first phase of work at RTI would lead me on a surprising challenge in the most unexpected nation in the world—Iraq! Following 9/11, President Bush and his top advisers determined that Iraq was an ongoing terrorist threat under its dictator Saddam Hussein.[1] Citing the existence of weapons of mass destruction, the United States and its allies under Bush invaded the country in 2003. This action would result in a decade long, $60 billion commitment to the reconstruction of Iraq.[2]

The invasion, called Operation Iraqi Freedom, was the first stage of the Iraq War. It began on March 19, 2003, and was launched by a combined force of troops from the United States, the United Kingdom, Australia, and Poland. This early stage of the war formally ended on May 1, 2003, when Bush declared a cease of combat operations and announced the toppling of Saddam Hussein's government. After a nine-month manhunt, forces captured Saddam Hussein on December 13, 2003. When the short war ended, the US and the UK formed a coalition of nations to reconstruct Iraq. The Coalition Provisional Authority, headed by L. Paul Bremer III, a senior American diplomat, became responsible for the governance of Iraq. Bremer in turn appointed an Iraqi governing council that had limited powers. The primary goal of the Coalition Provisional Authority was to maintain security and rebuild Iraq's badly damaged infrastructure.

The reconstruction program would become the most massive undertaking of this type since the Marshall Plan in 1947. Along with the economic reform of Iraq, reconstruction projects included the repair and upgrade of Iraqi water and sewage treatment plants, electricity production, hospitals, schools, housing, and transportation systems. The Iraq Relief and Reconstruction Fund, under the management of the Coalition Provisional Authority, funded much of the work.

In early 2003, USAID awarded five major reconstruction contracts in the following sectors: infrastructure, primary and secondary education, public health, agriculture, and local government. The local governance contract (covering provincial, district, and neighborhood level governance) went to RTI. As described in the final report of the special inspector general for the reconstruction of the country, USAID's award to RTI was to fund a local governance program that would include "activities to help the Iraqis create a more favorable environment for local governance" and that would "build the capacity of representative councils and subnational offices of central government ministries to manage more effective, efficient, and responsive customer services."[3]

Our responsibility included providing technical and advisory services to the newly formed local government committees at all three levels (neighborhood, district, and provincial). At the time, it was the largest contract ever awarded to RTI and a major step forward in our new international development strategy.

Ron was the home office project team leader for the Iraq local governance program. He was an expert in local government, municipal service delivery, decentralization, public infrastructure financing, and post-conflict governance. Also heavily involved initially at the corporate level was Sally Johnson, RTI's vice president for corporate affairs and a key executive in supporting this new and unprecedented contract in Iraq. Her office effectively managed the interest that this high-profile contract elicited from Congress and the media.

Peter Benedict, our chief of party and in-country leader, was a very experienced former USAID mission director who was well versed in the Middle East. He had a broad understanding of the history, culture, and politics of that area of the world, having studied the region while completing his graduate work at the University of Chicago, where he received his PhD. He was also an expert on Iran, Iraq, and the United Arab Emirates, where he once managed humanitarian programs for the Ford Foundation before he took the job working for USAID.

Other outstanding leaders in our Iraq project included a longtime friend and former USAID colleague Peter Bittner, then a vice president at Chemonics International, a private international development contractor firm. He played an essential role in recruiting a senior team in record time and was instrumental in convincing Peter Benedict to serve as our chief of party. The wise foreign policy expert Dick McCall, then a senior vice president at Creative Associates, a leading international development contractor firm, also joined our senior project management team, giving me another opportunity to work with him.

Another former USAID colleague, Chuck Costello, agreed to come on board as the deputy chief of party. I had also previously worked with Chuck, a highly regarded former Latin America mission director. We were also fortunate that another member of the RTI corporate leadership, Bert Maggart, joined our project management team as the chief of staff to our CEO, Victoria Haynes. Bert was a retired US Army major general and one of the tank commanders in US Operation Desert Storm. I was the final member of our veteran six-person leadership team for the local governance project, and I took on the job of DC liaison with USAID.

We were responsible for the design and management of the largest project in RTI's history in which we were supported by the tremendous creative and courageous work on the front lines by thousands of Iraqi and expatriate staff. Due to the size of this project, scores of individuals in RTI's headquarters played important roles in the successful implementation of the local governance project. Our leadership team greatly benefited from the expertise and dogged determination of our colleagues in the areas of project management, accounting and finance, contracting, logistics, IT, HR, staff recruitment, communications and public relations, security and risk management, and procurement. In many ways, RTI was uniquely qualified to lead this project on behalf of USAID, given its extensive experience over two decades in sizeable local governance projects in countries such as El Salvador and Indonesia. This highly regarded technical expertise was clearly a key factor in winning the Iraq contract. This contract continued for five years, with total awards of $900 million, and would be a cornerstone of USAID's assistance program in Iraq.

We bonded together as we carried out this intense, demanding work. Every day presented us with new, unanticipated issues and logistical problems. We interacted with both the US and British military forces as they carried out the occupation of Iraq. At the same time, we helped rebuild Iraqi governance at the local government level and worked closely with the Iraqi people. Our team relied on each other in surprising ways, and never once did any team member fail in their individual or collective efforts. What we saw and experienced would indeed be worthy of a book or a movie.

The situation in Iraq created a need for what many observers considered nation building. To effectively respond to the multiple challenges of operating a national program in a country that had become nearly dysfunctional called for maximum flexibility on the part of our staff, innovative thinking, and physical stamina. After three decades of Saddam Hussein's repressive rule and culture of corruption, "Postwar looting and the exodus of government bureaucrats from public service—both voluntary and involuntary—caused a complete collapse in governance capacities. The country's broken systems required a virtually complete reconstruction, literally and figuratively."[4] The demise of Saddam Hussein was initially a welcome development as far as Iraqis were concerned, especially among members of the Shia population, who had suffered for decades under the dictatorship. We saw a wave of optimism throughout the country as we deployed our teams. Unfortunately, this groundswell of optimism, both in Iraq and America, quickly began to disintegrate once the violent insurgency began in 2004.

The March 2007 report of the special inspector general for the reconstruction of Iraq, "Lessons in Program and Project Management," noted several factors that characterized the management of US relief and reconstruction efforts in Iraq, including continual change in the overall management and increased complexity from 2003 to 2007 in program management, resulting in hundreds of contractors and thousands of projects. US policy makers repeatedly shifted strategy in response to the constantly changing circumstances in Iraq. In the face of this monumental challenge, "thousands of talented and dedicated men and women worked long hours under challenging and often dangerous circumstances to manage and execute the Iraq reconstruction program; they developed, in a very short period of time, a relief and reconstruction endeavor of unprecedented complexity and magnitude."[5]

Seasoned professional development experts were highly sought out for this project, and they responded to the US government's call, given the magnitude of the multibillion-dollar endeavor. One such expert was my friend and former colleague Hank Bassford, who was the "mayor" of Baghdad during the period of governance by the Coalition Provisional Authority. Hank was an ideal choice for this position, given his extensive USAID experience, his ability to develop viable relationships with a complex array of stakeholders and constituents (American military and civilian, coalition reps, and Iraqis), and his tested leadership skills in some of the most challenging missions in the world, such as Egypt and El Salvador. RTI's local governance team worked closely with Hank, who took on some of the most demanding situations one can encounter in this fluid and treacherous operating environment during his tour in Baghdad. It was a very productive partnership.

While working on the Iraq project, I also reconnected with my good friend and former USAID colleague Philip Gary. Phil and I had first met in the mid-1980s when we both worked at USAID headquarters; he was in the Bureau for the Middle East during the time I was in the Bureau for Latin America and the Caribbean. Phil and his wife, Viviann, were a dynamic power couple in USAID. Viviann was a superb officer and thought leader, serving both in field missions and in headquarters in senior USAID positions, including as head of the Office of Democracy and Governance in the Bureau for Europe and Eurasia and head of the Office of Environment in the Global Bureau. Phil had an amazing career, moving easily and expertly between government, academia, and the consulting world. Phil is a true foreign affairs intellectual, and I have always valued his knowledge, experience, and sage wisdom. He took on some of the toughest assignments during his USAID career and his career as a consultant, including stints in both Iraq and Afghanistan. He served as team leader of our local governance project in Iraq and subsequently as the director of the post-conflict group in RTI headquarters, and it was a pleasure to reconnect and work with him on this unprecedented project.

People have often asked me if we felt safe working on the local governance project in Iraq. During the first year, we had no significant security concerns. But no one anticipated the future deterioration of the so-called semi-secure "permissive zones." Therefore, when faced with this situation and later the insurgency, RTI, like all foreign organizations operating there, hired a special security firm to protect our staff and provide onsite protection. Without a doubt our teams in both the provinces and in Baghdad faced danger. In the latter years of the reconstruction program, some of our staff worked on the provincial reconstruction teams, combined units that brought together US government political, military, and economic experts that assisted the Iraqi provincial officials. Our governance teams worked with each team, and occasionally these teams faced rocket attacks on their and our compounds or other threats due to the persistent and evolving insurgency as they carried out their normal day-to-day operations.

RTI established offices in seventeen of Iraq's eighteen provinces by early 2004, including two offices in Baghdad (in the Green Zone in one of Saddam's sons' residences and one in the central city). The office and housing conditions were unlike any encountered in a typical developing country setting owing to the collapse of the infrastructure across the country, but we were innovative and adapted. At first, both in the provincial capitals and towns throughout Iraq our living conditions were rudimentary at best. We lived in tents or bombed out Iraqi government buildings or we staked out space in the US or British military compounds. Eventually, the contractor firms brought in trailers and converted truck containers that served as both living quarters and offices, and living conditions improved substantially.

We hired scores of former city managers and civil engineers from the United States and other countries as advisers. We then created teams, matching these experienced expatriate professionals with our newly hired Iraqi staff in each province. We employed thousands of Iraqis with different technical backgrounds; most of them were very talented and well-trained professionals. At that time, Americans knew very little about Iraq, due to our decades-long isolation and complex, hostile bilateral relationships. Under the brutal dictatorship of Saddam Hussein, Iraqis had confined themselves to their respective ethnic and religious groups to survive, and they were not yet prepared to work together. Confronted by this reality, we had to build our project support systems so that they could operate in a radically new environment.

In my role as USAID/DC liaison, I traveled to Iraq at least once a quarter for the first couple of years, usually spending at least a month there as part of the team. My principal responsibility was to serve as the coordinator between USAID/Washington and our local governance project team, and so I was involved in addressing all the major implementation issues that we faced. I was also part of the start-up team to help set up our offices in the provinces. Ron, Peter, and I spent considerable time briefing congressional staff and occasionally senators and representatives about our implementation challenges on the ground. There were extensive coordination meetings with the frontline US government agencies and continual conversations with interested journalists. There was widespread interest in the Iraq reconstruction program and a strong desire to see immediate, positive results, given the massive funding provided across several sectors.

RTI was perceived to be operating on behalf of the Iraqi people, given our work at the local level to empower Iraqis to govern themselves for the first time in their history. In the past, Saddam appointed the governors and other local officials in the provinces, so this was a new phenomenon. We helped set up a process for some of the first democratic elections at the local level. Our provincial teams created systems and ran programs that trained and provided local officials with the tools to interact with the citizens of their area. We spent a lot of time talking about why citizen participation was necessary if a democracy were to work. Across the nation, we joined forces with the US and British military and Iraqi government officials to organize the first citizen-led committees. These committees operated at the neighborhood level, the municipal level, and the provincial level. It was gratifying to see how the Iraqis embraced the opportunity of democratic, citizen-elected governance. We saw this trend all across the country, despite the ethnic and religious schisms that local committees dealt with in real time. Key to establishing decentralized leadership in Iraq was the local governance project's work with provincial leadership to form an organization of all eighteen provinces (governorates). A singular result of this collaboration was the association's drafting of the Law of Governorates Not Incorporated. The association then lobbied Parliament for passage of Law 21 of 2008, colloquially known as the Provincial Powers Act.

But, of course, none of this happened in a vacuum. The geopolitical issues of the day were reflected in US government policy in Iraq, in the violence of the insurgency, and in the internal politics of Iraq, and today, these issues remain major challenges for both the United States and Iraq. In my view, USAID did an excellent job of trying to provide resources to help Iraqis become a self-governing nation and of moving them along the road to democracy. However, complicated external and internal forces, both political and religious, operated against the US government effort. The environment for change was challenging and complicated, and the situation continues to be complex and difficult to this day.

Iraq is a country with a talented workforce due to its historically high quality, broad, and secular education system. Of course, it also has enormous oil and gas resources and wealth. If the Iraquis could create a governable nation that would allow peaceful coexistence between its multireligious, multiethnic society, Iraq could become the leader of the Middle East. It is also an agricultural powerhouse. After all, we're talking about the historical Fertile Crescent region between the Tigris and the Euphrates Rivers! I can still see in my mind's eye the moment we first arrived in the city of Hillah on the banks of the Tigris near the legendary site of Babylon—the very cradle of civilization. What incredible potential exists there. During our time in Iraq, Ron and I had a chance to tour the ruins of Babylon. We had a quick visit in April 2003, under the protection of a US Marine detachment one afternoon. Under Saddam Hussein, the Iraqi government excavated Babylonian ruins and attempted to reconstruct certain features of the ancient city, including one of Nebuchadnezzar's palaces.[6]

Overall, the local governance plan in Iraq was the most intense project I have ever worked on in my career. Clearly, many of my colleagues who worked out there or in Afghanistan had similar experiences. I spent 80 percent of my time on the local governance project. Due to the project, RTI's international development business greatly expanded, as we began to bid on larger projects across all sectors funded by USAID. Working closely with Ron Johnson and his team at RTI for six years was a productive and exciting period of my career. I enjoyed being back in the private sector and continuing my work in international development.

However, something quite amazing had begun to emerge on the horizon of American politics at that time. Barack Obama, a uniquely charismatic senator from Illinois, appeared on the Washington scene, seizing national attention and opening up a new chapter in American politics. His story is now mythical in American history, as he went on to become the first African American elected to the office of president of the United States. Early on, I found myself inspired to step up and contribute to his campaign.

I first met Barack Obama years earlier when I supported his bid for the US Senate. I attended a few fundraisers in DC, thanks to the encouragement of my sister, Hilda, and her enthusiasm for Obama. He was then a state senator, and she was very impressed with his record in the Illinois General Assembly. I didn't know him personally because he arrived in Chicago many years after I had left for the Peace Corps. However, I later learned that Michelle Robinson Obama's family lived on the same street on the South Side of Chicago as my grandmother, ten blocks from where I spent much of my time growing up. Also, my cousin Heather graduated in the same class as Michelle Robinson at Whitney Young High School.

By the next time I met him, he was an exciting potential candidate for president of the United States. Like millions of Americans, I was captivated by his message of hope and change, and I became very interested in his campaign. My entire family, including our extended family in Chicago, became enthralled with the Obama candidacy. Rosa and I watched every news program we could, following every minute of his campaign.

Eventually, I volunteered for his campaign, first in Virginia. After his victory in the Iowa caucus in early 2008, Senator Obama lost to Senator Clinton in the New Hampshire primary, and the Obama campaign faced an uphill battle in the next critical primary state, South Carolina. My son Steven and I drove to Columbia, South Carolina, to work as campaign volunteers, and it was an exhilarating experience for both of us. I will never forget the excitement and joy we found working as a team on the Obama campaign. We manned a phone bank and canvassed voters in the neighborhoods of the capital city. We have memories of many rich experiences with other volunteers and ordinary citizens that we met in their homes, on the streets, and in the historically black colleges.

I recall how, in the twilight hours of the final day of campaigning, Steven and I stopped to distribute campaign literature to two elderly black gentlemen who were rocking in chairs on their porch. The house looked like a scene from the old TV show *Sanford and Son*. At the side of the house was a virtual automobile junkyard. When we asked the men if they planned to vote, the response we got reminded us of just how much this election meant to so many and brought tears to our eyes.

"We already voted early for Obama," one of the men exclaimed with great enthusiasm. "Give us more of those brochures because he's gonna win, and we want the souvenirs."

Steven and I had the good fortune to cross paths in Columbia with several terrific leaders who would be appointed as members of the Obama cabinet. We reconnected with Susan Rice, who would become US ambassador to the United Nations and later national security adviser, and met Samantha Powers, who would serve as special assistant to the president on the National Security Council and then as US ambassador to the United Nations. I am incredibly proud of Steven for his willingness to immerse himself in the campaign. We will always have the beautiful memory of our time stumping together on the Obama campaign.

Senator Obama won a decisive victory in the South Carolina primary, and he went on to capture the Democratic nomination and then the presidency. Steven and I were there at the University of South Carolina's Koger Center for the Arts when Barack and Michelle Obama arrived for his victory speech—an electric, joyous moment for the surging crowd. I continued to campaign for him and rejoiced in his victory—something I never thought I'd see in my lifetime. I only wish that my parents had been alive to experience the miracle of Barack Obama, his glorious victory, and the magical moment several months later when the first African American took the oath of office as president of the United States.

Our family in Pretoria, South Africa, in 1998.

As USAID mission director in Cape Town, South Africa, greeting first lady Hillary Clinton on her 1997 visit to a housing project led and built by homeless women in the black township of Gugulethu.

With Rosa in Cape Town in 1998 at an awards dinner in honor of Archbishop Desmond Tutu, the South African cleric and theologian known for his work as an antiapartheid and human rights activist as well as the chairman of the Truth and Reconciliation Commission.

I was RTI's liaison for the USAID-funded Iraq local governance program. I was on the start-up team that launched the project in Iraq as part of the US government's massive Iraq reconstruction program. Here I am upon our arrival in the city of Basra in 2003 with our start-up team, including Bill Fuller (regional rep), Peter Benedict (RTI's chief of party), an unidentified consultant, Chuck Costello (deputy chief of party), and Sam Tadesse (monitoring and evaluation specialist). Behind us is the bombed local headquarters of Saddam Hussein's Baath Party

A visit to Basra's municipal water treatment plant in 2003 with the head of the city's public works department, the manager of the municipal water treatment plant, and Bill Fuller. Under the project, this plant system became a top infrastructure priority for major investment and rehabilitation.

Visiting a school in Baluchistan, Pakistan, in 2004 as vice president of RTI International with Suzanne Olds, our chief of party. This school was supported under the USAID-funded Pakistan Education Sector Reform Assistance Project.

Visiting a maternal-child health clinic in 2007. The Jakarta clinic was supported under a USAID-funded project, where RTI was one of the implementing partners.

With students in a Peace Corps-supported computer training course in Ghana in 2011.

A 2009 visit to a girls high school in Thailand where Peace Corps volunteers are on the teaching staff. (courtesy of the Peace Corps)

With family and friends before my Senate confirmation hearing in 2009. My brother Phillip, niece Ellen Thompson, my friend Carrie Simmons, my sister Hilda, my friend Harry Simmons, Rosa, and Steven. (courtesy of the Peace Corps)

With Rosa and Peace Corps staff on a 2010 trip to Morocco. During this trip we made a site visit to meet PCV Rachel Maher and her students at their rural school. This was a special day for all concerned because of the visit of her mother and the hospitality of her host mother. (courtesy of the Peace Corps)

With Dr. Eric Goosby, the head of the President's Emergency Plan for AIDS Relief in 2010. We formed an outstanding partnership between our two agencies, supporting Peace Corps volunteers who worked in Africa on HIV/AIDS programs and the launch of the Global Health Service Corps program, an innovative public-private partnership to place doctors and nurses as adjunct faculty in medical or nursing schools in Africa. (courtesy of the Peace Corps)

With Congressman Sam Farr, our guest speaker at the PC headquarters in 2011. A passionate and tireless advocate for the expansion of the Peace Corps, Sam was also a returned PCV who served in Colombia and a great friend. (courtesy of the Peace Corps)

As graduation speaker at the Monterey Institute of International Studies in 2011. (courtesy of the Peace Corps)

A special fiftieth anniversary panel with the "Shriver Team—The Legends of 1961," who came together in 2011 to pay tribute to the Peace Corps (left to right): C. Payne Lucas, who ran the first programs in Africa and later founded AFRICARE; Maryann Orlando, office administrator in the earliest days; Senator Harris Wofford; and Charles Peters, the journalist, author, and founder of *Washington Monthly* magazine. (courtesy of the Peace Corps)

The annual meeting of the Peace Corps Country Directors in 2012. Flanking me are my esteemed front office team: Elisa Montoya, Stacy Rhodes, Carrie Hessler-Radelet, and Esther Benjamin. (courtesy of the Peace Corps)

With Stacy Rhodes on my last day at Peace Corps in 2012. (courtesy of the Peace Corps)

15 The Honor of a Lifetime

Director of the Peace Corps

Two roads diverged in a yellow wood, and I—
I took the one less traveled by,
And that has made all the difference.

—ROBERT FROST

I was deeply honored when Gayle Smith invited me to be part of the Obama-Biden transition team for the foreign affairs agencies. Gayle, a good friend and former colleague from our USAID days, asked me to join her as the co-lead in this endeavor. I requested a leave of absence from RTI to take on this exciting and historic assignment.

So I joined the Obama and Biden transition team leadership. It consisted of three co-chairs: John Podesta, former Clinton White House chief of staff and the CEO of the Center for American Progress; Valerie Jarrett, one of Obama's longest-serving advisers; and Pete Rouse, Obama's Senate chief of staff. Gayle was uniquely qualified to lead the foreign affairs transition team, given her vast experience in development and democracy issues and her significant senior US government policy expertise. She had served as the special assistant to President Clinton and held senior positions in the National Security Council.[1]

As a first step, we selected team members who had substantial experience within the primary agencies. We were fortunate in recruiting several outstanding development experts, such as Rick Barton and Wendy Chamberlain, a former ambassador and veteran diplomat. Rick launched and led the Office of Transition Initiatives at USAID, which is often referred to as the "crown jewel of USAID." Rick went on to have a series of senior positions in the Obama administration.[2]

The experts we assembled for the team—Valerie Dickson-Horton, Esther Benjamin, Sheila Herrling, Natasha Bilimoria, Larry Knowles, Jayne

Thomisee, and Semhar Araia—had substantial USAID and foreign affairs experience. We also had the great fortune to have some talented young professionals from the Obama campaign, including the dynamic Dar Vanderbeck (our executive assistant), Adam Poswolsky (our IT-plus wizard), Kitty DiMartino, Kate Brandt, and Alex McPhillips.

One of the overarching goals of the Obama-Biden transition team was to assure that we engaged in the broadest possible open and transparent dialogue with the development community, across all sectors. With that goal in mind, we held hundreds of meetings with stakeholder groups in the foreign affairs arena. Our goal was to hear new ideas and engage in healthy debates about existing programs. We wanted to provide an opportunity for these experts to speak openly about policy positions and specific programs that the new administration should pursue.

Our transition team received tremendous support and cooperation from each of the target agencies. We had an especially productive working relationship with USAID, thanks to the outstanding leadership of Alonzo Fulgham, the acting USAID administrator, and Barbara Feinstein, the lead USAID coordinator. I had first met Alonzo when he was a PCV in Haiti, in one of the historic first volunteer groups. He went on to have a distinguished USAID career, including as mission director in Afghanistan, the largest US government assistance program. Further, he made history in becoming the first African American to serve as the head of USAID. Alonzo had created a superb internal transition team that provided excellent support, working tirelessly to provide access to critical agency leaders and major USAID partners as well the critical documentation that our team required for this exercise.

We fully briefed Secretary Clinton's team and Alonzo Fulgham's team regarding our findings and our recommendations, which were well received by the transition team leadership. Being on a transition team proved to be a rewarding period in my career; the unique experience allowed me to engage in a historical process that, in many ways, defines American democracy—the peaceful transition to a new administration.

The opportunity to observe the steady stream of prominent visitors to the transition team's headquarters provided daily inspiration. At any given time, the leaders of our society were coming and going into the headquarters building. I recall seeing a wide range of notable people, including Ralph Nader, Zbigniew Brzezinski, T. Boone Pickens, Warren Buffet, and

Bill Gates. We also often saw former Carter and Clinton administration cabinet members. It's difficult to put the substantive impression of that experience into simple words. Being in the presence of so many prominent and respected figures in our government gave me a feeling of great optimism and hope.

With the transition work completed, I considered offers of a few senior positions, but none of them were immediately appealing to me. Besides, I had made a solid promise to Rosa that I would remain at RTI. So I returned to my work at RTI, as planned. And then it happened—the call of a lifetime from the White House Presidential Personnel Office. "You're going to be nominated by the president as the next director of the Peace Corps." And there it was, the one government opportunity I could not turn down. Rosa, Michael, and Steven were very positive about it. I was delighted to accept this incredible, once-in-a-lifetime offer, and I was nominated in July 2009.[3]

The offer to serve the Obama administration as director of the Peace Corps was monumental for me, considering my years of service with this unique agency and the impact it had had on my life. My Peace Corps experience, as a volunteer and staffer, had transformed my life and set the stage for my personal growth and professional career going forward. Accepting this offer would give me a chance to connect with a new generation of Peace Corps volunteers, and the timing could not have been more meaningful. If confirmed, I would be serving in this position during the 2011 fiftieth anniversary of the Peace Corps—the perfect opportunity to demonstrate the mission of this amazing organization!

It was gratifying to see the tremendous reception that my nomination received from the returned PCV community. I learned that Judy Harrington, a former PCV who lived in Lawrence, Kansas, started a national petition movement when she became aware that I was under consideration.[4] As a returned volunteer, that level of support is always valuable; it's a rallying cry for the returned PCV community, and I was grateful for Judy's gracious initiative. In that way, the Peace Corps is similar to the military; we never forget our "global service comrades."

During my Senate confirmation hearing on July 29, 2009, I had the distinct honor to be introduced by former senator Harris Wofford, and the hearing was chaired by Senator Chris Dodd, who had also served as a PCV in the Dominican Republic.[5] The legendary Wofford had been President Kennedy's civil rights adviser and one of Sargent Shriver's principal advisers in creating the Peace Corps. He had a storied career of distinguished public and national service as a government official, university president, US senator, and adviser to several presidents.

After my nomination had been announced, David Weiss, a long-time friend and part of the Peace Corps family, graciously offered to introduce me to Senator Wofford. As president of Global Communities, a prominent international development organization, David had served as the special assistant to former Peace Corps director Dick Celeste, during the Carter administration. It meant a great deal to me when Senator Wofford agreed to introduce me at my confirmation hearing. I had no idea that it would be the beginning of one of the most heartwarming friendships of my life. In our frequent lunch or breakfast meetings, Harris always emphasized the importance of increasing the size of the Peace Corps, and he was a tireless advocate with both congressional leaders and the Obama administration's foreign policy team. I greatly valued his wisdom and advice.

This great man dedicated his entire life to improving the human condition, and since his death in 2019 the world has been a lesser place. He died, quite poignantly, on the holiday he had advocated for in honor of Martin Luther King Jr., a truly great American for whom he had once served as an adviser during the civil rights movement. His obituary in the *New York Times* aptly read, "Harris Wofford, a former United States senator from Pennsylvania whose passion for getting people involved helped create John F. Kennedy's Peace Corps, Bill Clinton's AmeriCorps, and other service organizations and made him America's volunteer-in-chief, died on Monday night in Washington. He was 92."[6]

I vividly recall my first lunch meeting with Harris, when I had brought along his book *Of Kennedys and Kings: Making Sense of the Sixties.* We spent most of our two-hour conversation talking about the decade and his experiences with the Kennedys and Dr. King and his family during the civil rights movement. Friends of his knew well that while in his presence, they were in the shadow of a giant. The thousands who attended his memorial service at Howard University became the final testimonial to the incredible life he had led and his powerful influence on all of us.

I was confirmed by the Senate on August 7, 2009. That was a glorious day for me as I stood in the Sargent Shriver conference room at Peace Corps headquarters and took the oath of office as the eighteenth director of the United States Peace Corps and as the first African American man in this position. I asked my son Steven, who, within the year, would begin his service as a Peace Corps volunteer in Nicaragua, to hold the Bible as I took the oath of office, a formality I had been through several times before in my career. My appointment by President Obama had been voted on and confirmed by the Senate the day before. As is customary for senior positions in the US government, this informal portion of the swearing-in process was carried out quickly to allow me to assume my new position immediately.

Carl Sosebee, my former USAID colleague and now general counsel for the Peace Corps, administered the oath. Carl would become one of my most trusted advisers, and a source of great wisdom and expertise throughout my tenure as director. As I took the oath of office, I thought back to my early years of growing up in Chicago and the dreams I had had. None of them included what I was about to embark on; *this* dream I owed to President Obama and his foreign affairs team for presenting me with this tremendous opportunity. I also felt a deep appreciation and gratitude to the Peace Corps for leading me toward a transformed life, starting back in 1967.

Soon after that I met with Jody Olsen, who had been the acting director of the Peace Corps during the transition period, and she graciously briefed me on the current state of the agency and key issues that I would inherit. Jody and I knew each other through our development community connections. She was a highly regarded development professional who began her career as a PCV, and we were contemporaries, as she served in Tunisia in the late 1960s. It was widely known that she had more Peace Corps executive experience than any other person in the organization's community owing to the multiple leadership positions she held overseas and in headquarters. During the Trump administration, the community was delighted to see that she was appointed as the twentieth Peace Corps director.

Later that month, a formal swearing-in ceremony with the Peace Corps staff would be held at the agency's headquarters. Rosa, my sons, my daughter-in-law, my sister and brother, their families, my friends, and my former colleagues would witness the momentous occasion with me. Such ceremonies are customary for senior positions in the US government. I've always felt that they appropriately honored the government agency and our democratic institutions and illustrated the importance of the leadership position. The ceremony also gave me a platform to present my initial vision for my tenure in the Peace Corps and set the stage for what our team planned to accomplish under the Obama administration.

As news of my appointment to director spread across the media, I received a message from my long-lost Peace Corps training roommate, Dennis Kroeger. He read about my new role in *USA Today* while on vacation in San Diego and immediately called the office. We quickly reconnected. We had stayed in contact after our time in the Peace Corps ended and on into the late 1980s but then lost touch. I couldn't find Dennis after that, and I had always wondered where my friend landed. I now learned the reason I hadn't been able to contact him was because he and his wife, Cheryl, had spent much of their careers overseas. They had lived for a decade in South Korea, Iceland, and the United Kingdom—thus without a US address—while teaching in various overseas Department of Defense schools for dependents. They had returned to California and continued their careers as high school counselors and administrators. We had a joyful reunion in Los Angeles and have remained in close contact ever since.

At the time of my appointment, more than two hundred thousand Americans had served as PCVs. Over nearly five decades they had promoted world peace and friendship between Americans and the people of 140 host countries in Africa, Asia, Eastern Europe, Latin America, the Caribbean, and the Middle East. During my tenure, an average of eight thousand or more PCVs would work in local communities in almost eighty host countries.

As the director, I had assumed the leadership of an American agency with an esteemed global brand and a mission to promote world peace and friendship. As described on the official Peace Corps website, "Returned Peace Corps Volunteers have gone on to achieve extraordinary success in all kinds of fields. Some, inspired by their service, stay in education or health-related professions or choose to join the Foreign Service. Others pursue careers in business, from entrepreneurial startups to management at major companies; Returned Peace Corps Volunteers are working as journalists, writers, members of Congress, and even astronauts."

It was an agency known as one of President Kennedy's signature achievements, and it has always enjoyed bipartisan congressional support. I recall a conversation I had with Caroline Kennedy at a fiftieth-anniversary event at the John F. Kennedy Library in Boston. She told me that, throughout her life, she had heard stories from thousands of Americans who explained how their lives were transformed by their Peace Corps service and who told her how grateful they were to her father for creating this agency. Another remarkable characteristic of the Peace Corps had always impressed me. For nearly fifty years, it has remained true to the great legacy of Sargent Shriver Jr. and the three goals he established for that new agency: to help the people of interested countries meet their need for trained men and women; to help promote a better understanding of Americans on the part of the people served; and to help promote a better understanding of other people on the part of Americans.

PCVs work on a wide variety of jobs in Africa, Asia, and Latin America, assigned to rural communities and towns where living conditions and transportation limitations can be physically demanding. Volunteers typically work side by side with communities on pressing global challenges. The principal program areas are agriculture, community and business development, education, health and HIV/AIDS, environment, and youth development. All PCVs have a primary job in one of these areas, but most quickly acquire a second job as they come to recognize the needs in their communities. In nearly all cases, PCVs find themselves surrounded by the youth of the country they are in and become engaged in youth development. PCVs often focus on the ignored segments of the population, and they therefore end up becoming models of "global citizens" who return home with rich overseas experiences and insights that contribute to America's understanding of the world. Most PCVs work in the "last mile"—areas where no other US foreign affairs agencies or nongovernmental organizations have a presence.

It was a great pleasure during my first year as director to visit three countries that illustrate this broad engagement by PCVs—the Dominican Republic, Tanzania, and Thailand—and observe the magnificent work of these dynamic and passionate Americans. It was particularly fascinating for me to be back in the rural countryside of the Dominican Republic and to see PCVs working on youth development projects. Volunteers in this fieldwork collaborate with local counterparts to reach out to youths aged ten to twenty-four to teach them life skills, employability skills, and sexual and reproductive health education through regular engagement with them in clubs and mentoring activities.

Education is a primary focus of the Peace Corps in most countries, and many volunteers work with schools. In Tanzania, I observed PCVs working as high school math teachers in rural villages, where they taught algebra and even calculus to students aged twelve to twenty. Volunteers prepared lesson plans using a variety of teaching methods and syllabi developed by the Ministry of Education. To connect classroom concepts to real-world applications, volunteers organized experiential learning activities like field trips and guest speakers. In Thailand, I visited PCVs teaching English as a second language, with a particular emphasis on STEM subjects for rural students.

Further, in every country that I visited over the next few years, I was repeatedly impressed by one of the most time-relevant Peace Corps projects— GLOW (Girls Leading Our World). GLOW grew to become the agency's most widespread gender-empowerment initiative. PCVs have empowered tens of thousands of children and young adults worldwide through Camp GLOW programs that encourage and build self-confidence and leadership skills. GLOW challenges campers to think beyond traditional gender roles and address the unique societal and health issues girls and women face in their cultures.

One of Sargent Shriver's most important legacies and success stories that I believe to be unique within the federal government but that often goes unmentioned or unappreciated in the history of the Peace Corps is the commitment to women and minorities. From the very beginning, Shriver insisted that they be given equal opportunity to serve as both volunteers and as staff in this American enterprise created to promote peace and friendship worldwide. This policy was especially significant because he implemented this practice in 1961, before the passage of both the Civil Rights Act in 1964 and the Voting Rights Act of 1965. To my understanding, this represents one of the first times in American history that a federal agency mandated equal rights as one of its founding principles. Shriver's historic initiative fostered a gender-equal culture within the Peace Corps; today, more than 60 percent of the volunteers are women, as are a majority of staff members.

During my tenure, consistent with the Obama administration's policy and our collective beliefs, my team and I actively pursued diversity and inclusion in our hiring practices. We maintained above-average hiring percentages for both minorities and women in our senior staff and country director positions.

A wise foreign policy expert, my former colleague Philip Gary, once told me that "one of the reasons Peace Corps is so successful is that it is premised on putting individuals in dynamic situations for relatively short durations *where their individuality is the institutional action lane*. . . . It is absolutely unique among governmental institutions, and these individuals often bring creativity, dynamism, and positive development outcomes." I was eager to do everything I could to foster this type of resilience and sense of service among volunteers and to provide them with the support they needed to succeed.

As the director of the US Peace Corps, I engaged in a wide range of policy matters, global initiatives, and management and program issues, and in 2009, we launched a comprehensive exercise to create a vision for a modern twenty-first-century agency. However, my immediate task was to focus on a plan of action for my first one hundred days in office.

16 My First One Hundred Days

Leading an Iconic American Institution

Boldness be my friend!

—WILLIAM SHAKESPEARE, *Cymbeline*

The first one hundred days have been the focus of all US presidents since the days of Franklin D. Roosevelt, when he coined the phrase during a radio address in July 1933. It has taken on such symbolic significance that the period is considered a benchmark for measuring early success, and so since that era the members of a president's cabinet and subcabinet have followed suit in leading their departments and agencies.

With this in mind, I wanted to move quickly to capitalize on the strong White House and congressional support for the new Peace Corps expansion plan I envisioned. A plan to build a reliable and experienced team at the Peace Corps was my top priority. I had the good fortune to have a group of outstanding leaders in mind as candidates for my senior staff. During my career, I have observed many great leaders, both close up and at a distance, from which I learned a fundamental lesson about leadership—always hire or appoint the best people available for your team and have that team poised to join you on day one.

Whether one is selected to be a cabinet secretary or head of the Peace Corps, it's imperative to put a strong team in place; I wanted to make sure I had a core group of executives that I had a shared experience with who would be eager and honored to work at the Peace Corps and who would help me plan and implement significant initiatives.

Don Gips and Nate Tibbits, the experienced and wise executives who were the director and deputy director of the presidential personnel office, gave me a great deal of latitude selecting the Peace Corps senior appointees. Due to my long career in the foreign affairs arena, many excellent candidates came to mind. I had the great fortune that the Obama-Biden transition team had selected Elisa Montoya as the White House liaison to the Peace Corps, which made her the first senior appointee at the agency after the election. We met for the first time over lunch, which was the beginning of a tremendous working relationship and friendship. A skilled lawyer, Elisa played a key role in the Obama-Biden campaign, and I quickly observed that I could rely on her judgment and integrity in all matters. In speaking with Don and Nate, Elisa and I found them to be open minded about my slate of candidates. Happily, 80 percent of my candidates came on board.

Diversity and inclusion were crucial elements on my mind regarding our staff, consistent with my personal and professional views and those of the Obama administration. I am proud of those stellar professionals that we brought on board, which resulted in a diverse senior staff in terms of race and gender.

Never assume a key leadership role with a group of strangers. Effective leadership requires that you hire or appoint the best people available for your team and have that team poised to join you on day one.

Once offered the director position, my first call went out to Stacy Rhodes, my long-time USAID colleague, since our Haiti days together dating to 1979. Stacy, an experienced and highly respected development expert, was then working as a senior executive at the Millennium Challenge Corporation. Immediately enthusiastic about working together at our beloved Peace Corps, he agreed to join me as my chief of staff. To this day, I feel immensely fortunate that we traveled this journey together.

The White House Presidential Personnel Office had an outstanding candidate for the Peace Corps deputy director position in Carrie Hessler-Radelet, a widely respected international development executive and a returned PCV who had served in Samoa. Carrie would bring a high level of energy, global public health expertise, and a strong commitment to gender equity to our front office team. Further, Carrie and her family represented a wonderful Peace Corps legacy, in that her husband Steve, her aunt Virginia, and her grandparents had served as Peace Corps volunteers and staff. We both shared great respect for our beloved Peace Corps and the PCVs, and together we were a strong and innovative leadership team.

I created a new position, associate director for global operations position, because I wanted a unified overseas command structure to manage the regional offices that directly oversaw the work of our country directors. My candidate, the dynamic executive Esther Benjamin, had worked with me at IYF and on the Obama-Biden transition team. I knew that she would bring the intellect, vision, passion, and superb leadership skills needed for this crucial position and provide overarching strategic support and management of the agency's direct volunteer operations. My idea was that the person who assumed this role would encourage efficiencies by streamlining agency operations, disseminating best practices among the regions, providing an organized, cohesive voice to agency leadership, and coordinating the activities of all overseas operations. The global operations office would manage the development and coordination of global and regional initiatives and track both progress and impact of the Peace Corps overseas posts.

Next, I looked to hiring the associate directors for Africa, Europe/Middle East/Asia, and the Americas and Pacific regions. Working with Esther, they would provide direction and oversight over the Peace Corps' global program and operations. Again, we struck gold in recruiting one of the foremost African experts in America, Dick Day. As a former USAID colleague, he had spent decades leading programs in Africa with three different government agencies. Like Stacy Rhodes, Dick also moved to the Peace Corps from the Millennium Challenge Corporation. I credit the CEO of the Millennium Challenge Corporation, Daniel Yohannes, my Obama administration colleague, for his generosity in allowing two of his senior executives to join me at the Peace Corps. Collegial and transparent interactions characterized the working relationships among senior officials I encountered across the entire Obama administration.

I was pleased when the White House Presidential Personnel Office recommended Helen Lowman, a returned PCV who had worked in Thailand and was the former country director in China and Mongolia. Helen's terrific experience was precisely what was needed to serve as the director of our most diverse and complex region—Europe, the Middle East, and Asia. Further, during this period, as we completed the selection of my new team, I was pleased to see the continued outstanding leadership that was provided by the acting heads of each region, Roger Conrad (Americas and Pacific region), David Burgess (Europe, the Middle East, and Asia), and Lynn Foden (Africa).

Thanks to Elisa Montoya's careful and skilled management of this process, we were able to work quickly with the White House to fill more than thirty vital senior staff positions. Also, I was pleased that my former executive assistant at RTI, Claudia Calderon, joined our front office team. I knew I could rely on her to smoothly plan and manage both my complex schedule and the vagaries of my new position.

Given the importance of Peace Corps country directors, I instituted a new approach for selecting those critical leaders who represent the face of the Peace Corps on the front lines around the world in their host countries and who serve as the guiding lights for the PCVs and our local staff.

Peace Corps country directors supervise a staff made up largely of locals (i.e., the core staff at each post) but also a few Americans. They coordinate with the national government, local governments, community organizations, and local nongovernment organizations to design and implement programs through which PCVs address specific challenges and opportunities in each host nation. They also work diligently every day to find creative and innovative ways to inspire and support our volunteers. Each of the country directors brings years of management and leadership experience to their work, playing a vital role in the Peace Corps family.

Those of us who were returned PCVs have vivid memories of our country directors in our formative years and their strength, compassion, and moral leadership. I strongly believe that the leadership skills of the country directors and their engagement with the PCVs are the keys to the success of our country programs. I insisted that our front office leadership team collectively interview and agree on the final hiring decision for every new country director. Of course, our goal was to find the most qualified executives with substantial international experience, a passion for the Peace Corps' mission, and a special ability to inspire and lead PCVs. We were determined to pursue these objectives while also looking to create a diverse and inclusive leadership corps that reflected America's diversity. Further, I was pleased in those rare instances when former senior State Department and USAID officers applied for country director positions. This included my former colleague in South Africa, retired ambassador Greg Engle, who we were delighted to assign to Ethiopia, a historic and major program.

I was pleased with the initial results of my staffing plans. I then turned my attention to my next principal task. As I have typically done throughout my career when I assume a new position, I began assessing the organization's current strategy, significant issues, and overall operations. Because the Peace Corps was a fifty-year-old institution, I thought a comprehensive review of the organization to prepare a blueprint for the twenty-first century was especially appropriate.

At the time, the Peace Corps' budget had plateaued, and to launch any new initiative or meaningful reform would require additional funding. During my confirmation hearing, I indicated that one of my primary goals would be to expand the Peace Corps. I noted that additional funding for such an expansion would be necessary, explaining that I would carry out an assessment of the agency that would become the plan for the Peace Corps in the twenty-first century. Once installed, I asked for a significant budget increase from the administration, and subsequently worked diligently on Capitol Hill to garner support for incremental funding over time from Congress. My proposal received a very favorable bipartisan response, and to my great pleasure Congress approved the largest budget increase in Peace Corps history in December 2009, increasing our budget for the fiscal year 2010 to $400 million. The addition made it possible to plan to increase our overseas presence to ten thousand volunteers by the end of fiscal year 2011. This number of volunteers would finally bring the agency into compliance with the provision of the Peace Corps Act, which states that the policy of the United States is to maintain at least ten thousand volunteers overseas, subject to the availability of funds. Our leadership team was fully committed to this expansion, which would have to be carefully coordinated with the regional directors and the affected country directors.

Included in this legislation was a provision I had suggested to the relevant committee staff that would require the director of the Peace Corps to submit a report to the appropriations committee on the findings of a comprehensive assessment in six areas:

- recruitment and selection process for volunteers,
- training in medical care for volunteers and staff,
- long-term placement that would reflect US priorities and host country needs,
- coordination with international and host country organizations,
- reduction of early termination rates, and
- strengthening of management, evaluation, and oversight.

I knew I would need to form a special team led by an outstanding de-velopment professional to carry out this large and complicated process. I decided to reach out to Carlos Torres, my former colleague and a highly regarded executive. As convinced as I was that he was the right person to lead this large-scale endeavor, I knew he would have to be persuaded to step out of his leisure-filled and rewarding early retirement. Initially, Carlos had expressed interest in the possibility of joining the Peace Corps as a country director, a job for which he was extraordinarily well qualified. However, I quickly realized that he could make a permanent contribution as the leader of the agency's comprehensive assessment. Happily, he agreed to come aboard in this position; he created a formidable team of superb profession-als with substantial international development and agency experience, and they produced a product of immense value for the future of the agency.[1]

As I envisioned, this was one of the most important decisions of my ten-ure at the Peace Corps. I was sure that the assessment would provide criti-cal information and guidance to position the agency for strategic growth. I anticipated that it would serve as a guide for agency programming and infrastructure investment for the present and future years. This strategic plan would give us the path for managing the Peace Corps over the first term of the Obama administration and provide a flexible framework for responding to the inevitable challenges of leading any federal agency, espe-cially one with global reach and responsibilities.

The assessment team asked a critical question; namely, what would the Peace Corps look like if it were created today? The answer to which was that it should "be a leader, in partnership with others, in the global effort to further human progress and foster understanding and respect among people." The assessment was conducted from January to June 2010 and became the basis for the report titled "A Vision for the Peace Corps at Fifty" that we presented to the White House and our principal committees in Congress.[2] In essence, it presented a blueprint for growing and strengthen-ing the Peace Corps over the next four years, which could be summarized as making the Peace Corps "bigger, bolder, and better." Carlos and his team, an outstanding group of talented Peace Corps staff, did a superb job of securing input from the critical stakeholders for the organization, both in the United States and overseas.

The assessment proved to be an essential road map and action plan for leading the agency. It allowed us to effectively address every significant issue and challenge we faced over the next four years. It was precisely what

Carlos and I had envisioned, and it gave me a great sense of satisfaction that the process and analysis resulted in such a valuable product. I will always be grateful to him for his outstanding leadership in this crucial endeavor. I was delighted that after completing the assessment, Carlos then agreed to an appointment as the regional director for the inter-America and Pacific region. From there, he continued with the Peace Corps until the end of the Obama administration, serving in his final position as deputy director.

At the time I assumed the position of Peace Corps director, I had only seen Senator Obama briefly during the presidential campaign and in group meetings during the transition. My first official one-on-one meeting with him as the Peace Corps director occurred in December 2009. Although I had participated in several White House meetings throughout my career, this would be my first visit to the Oval Office. Interestingly, that day as I waited for my meeting, I had a brief conversation with Charles Bolden, the new NASA administrator, who also had an appointment to meet with President Obama. It made for a unique shared experience for us because, like the Peace Corps, NASA also ranked among President Kennedy's most significant achievements as president. I was very proud to be able to experience that moment outside the Oval Office with Administrator Bolden. I later found out that this distinguished Marine Corps general, fighter pilot, and NASA astronaut had served as the captain of the most flights in space shuttle history. Later that month, I extended to him an invitation to be a special guest speaker at the Peace Corps as part of the Loret Ruppe speaker series.

The most auspicious moment in my life was entering the Oval Office and being greeted by the president of the United States. So many memories rushed through my mind as President Obama warmly welcomed me into his office as we shook hands. My thoughts immediately returned to the wish that my mother and father could have lived to see the day when Barack Obama was elected, and that they could now share with me the honor in knowing that their son would be a part of his administration. I would have liked for them to be able to realize how far my Peace Corps journey had taken me.

I thanked President Obama for my appointment and indicated how honored I was to serve in his administration. I also mentioned, jokingly, that I was probably the first graduate of Chicago State College to receive a presidential appointment and that my service as a PCV and USAID FSO had led me to this day.

He asked me about my plans for the agency, and I shared with him that the global requests for PCVs far outstripped the available resources and that

I intended to expand the number of volunteers in all regions of the world. We also discussed the importance of promoting diversity in the ranks of the PCVs. I acknowledged that the Peace Corps lacked the diversity it needed, and I explained that this was an area that would receive my special attention. I indicated to him my intention to recruit volunteers who would embody the rich diversity of America. I was pleased to have the opportunity early in my tenure to meet with the president and express confidence in my plans to expand the Peace Corps.

It had been more than a decade since I had observed PCVs in the field, and I wanted to see firsthand what the Peace Corps of the twenty-first century looked like. Also, I thought it was important to make my first official trip to our overseas posts during my first one hundred days. As someone with substantial Washington experience, I was well aware that, as director, I would have to balance my time between the field and headquarters. Both your team in DC and your leaders at more than seventy overseas posts must feel your equitable interest in their work as you address their issues. While it was absolutely critical to demonstrate my strong interest in the country directors and the work of the PCVs in the field, I also knew from my USAID experience that my most important task would be to develop strong bipartisan support for the agency in the Congress. That would require an extensive investment of my time, and I looked forward to this opportunity.

Naturally, my initial trip would be to the Dominican Republic, my first Peace Corps home. The Dominican Republic had the benefit of proximity to the US and a long-term, strong partnership with the Peace Corps and connection to my own PCV service. I added to my trip a visit to Nicaragua, another long-time partner country in the Americas region. When I traveled, the official director's delegation usually included three to four people. Each overseas trip was designed and staffed by the country directors in the host countries in concert with our regional directors at headquarters.

My core travel team included Elisa Montoya and Jeff West, a returned PCV from Ukraine, who was my special assistant for trips and events. Jeff did an outstanding job for me for two years as the point man on all planning details, including preparing the essential briefing book for all of my trips. I will always be grateful for his superb work. When Jeff moved to a new position in headquarters, Conor Sanchez took over the position and did an outstanding job for the remainder of my tenure. Elisa provided the strategic view and objectives for all my trips, working with the regional team on themes, speech messages, and planned activities. Trip strategy and management was only one of her responsibilities at the Peace Corps. I was very fortunate to have her stellar insights, wisdom, and brilliant managerial abilities as a senior adviser.

A typical official visit by a senior US government official's delegation follows a well-rehearsed format. It's usually divided into the following segments: a formal country background and issues briefing by the ambassador and the country team, which includes opportunity for the senior official to present his or her vision for the agency he or she represents and to introduce his or her accompanying staff; a series of courtesy meetings with the president or prime minister and their senior cabinet officials; special meetings with the agency's principal counterpart government, nonprofit, or business executives; and an all-hands staff meeting with the agency's staff. In my case, I also met with volunteer leaders and made a field trip to visit selected PCVs at their sites.

Upon my arrival in the Dominican Republic, I received a warm welcome from country director Romeo Massey and his team. It was quite amazing to return as the Peace Corps director, and I still had extensive connections across Dominican society in the government, civil society, and the business and university communities. I also received an enthusiastic welcome from the American Embassy's deputy chief of mission Chris Lambert—the number two person in the embassy. As luck would have it, I had first met Chris, a returned PCV from Costa Rica, during my USAID/Costa Rica assignment. He reminded me that I had assisted him in resolving a problem he had while working on a USAID-funded project; this is one of the scores of examples that illustrate the small "international development community" that we work and live in!

On our first day in the country, we visited volunteers in the morning and received a briefing about the plan for the day from Romeo Massey. Our trip director that morning was Adele Williams, who had been working in the country for several years and was very experienced and highly regarded by the volunteers. For my part, I looked forward to seeing volunteers in action, to witnessing the same type of experience that had transformed me during my years of service in the Dominican Republic. Education was one of the principal program sectors for the Peace Corps, and so we were en route on this bright, sunny Dominican day to a rural school where we would see volunteers teaching science and working on improving the computer systems in the school.

Upon our arrival at the site, the school director, district superintendent, head of the PTA, and volunteers who served in that school greeted us. The expressions on their faces conveyed both pride and amazement that a former PCV who had lived in a similar rural area had become director of the Peace Corps and chose to visit their school. In anticipation of our group's arrival we heard the buzz of excitement from a distance. Young students the world over love visitors, and these students were no exception. Many memories rushed to my mind of my own teaching experiences in schools across the Dominican Republic many years ago. The PCVs' rapport with students and the bonds between the volunteers and their teacher colleagues transcended time.

We engaged in a delightful conversation with both the volunteers and their counterpart teachers, who were also very proud to be hosting the director of the Peace Corps. We observed a demonstration lesson with their students, and we all told the children that they were special because only a school as special as theirs would be chosen to meet with visitors who had traveled all the way from the United States.

It's always inspiring to see the dedicated volunteers, excited to serve in this endeavor, the love they have for the children, and the children's excitement about being engaged in this new relationship with people from afar. The dedication and skillful support that the Peace Corps staff provided to the PCVs was impressive, just as it was when I was a PCV. The volunteers also served as counselors in youth clubs and GLOW camps that were a Peace Corps staple worldwide.

Driving back to Santo Domingo, I felt very proud of the contribution our country was making in this school and others like it. In line with national education priorities, volunteers were working hard to assist their Dominican partners in enhancing the education of a new generation of students. I was overcome with emotion, feeling privileged to be on the ground once again, seeing these volunteers in action as they promoted peace and friendship around the world. What a privilege it was to have the opportunity to lead this extraordinary organization. It was a glorious three-day return trip for me, given my Dominican Republic history. I could hardly imagine a more delightful visit.

For the second part of the trip we flew to Managua, the capital of Nicaragua. Country director George Baldino met us at the airport. Blessed with a dynamic and lovely personality, the former Catholic priest had an in-depth knowledge of Latin America from his extensive service as a parish priest in Peru. Within a year, I would ask George to reopen a historic country program in Colombia, a special job that called for a special man.

Things had changed since my first visit to Latin America as a PCV in 1967. Now, unlike in the past, one could fly nonstop from Santo Domingo to Nicaragua. This visit was somewhat subdued due to the historically luke-warm relationship between the Sandinista government of Daniel Ortega and the US government. The overthrow of Nicaraguan president Anastasio Somoza in 1979 is a well-known story. The triumph of the Sandinistas, led primarily by the revolutionary Ortega, ended the Somoza family's forty-three-year, American-backed dictatorship.

It seems a bit astonishing in retrospect, but President Ortega had a very favorable impression of the PCVs who had served over decades in his coun-try. As a result, I received a cordial welcome by the president and Rosario Murillo, the first lady. As an indication of his respect for the Peace Corps, he insisted that I attend a cabinet meeting, and he directed each of his prin-cipal ministers to present their most significant programs and describe the Peace Corps' roles in projects under the relevant ministries.

I saw firsthand the positive reputation of the Peace Corps among the Nicaraguan people during the rest of my visit, as I met with PCVs who were working with organizations to assist small and microenterprises. This visit provided another example of how the Peace Corps can transcend strained bilateral relationships and continue to create friendships by working at the grassroots level to promote the national priorities of the people in a given country.

On August 25, 2009, Ted Kennedy died after a long battle with cancer.[3] He had served as a US senator from Massachusetts for almost forty-seven years, from 1962 until his death. His long tenure and influence earned him the title of "the lion of the Senate." I knew that his state funeral in Boston would be of great historical significance because of his national leadership stature and contributions to America.[4] I had previously attended two prom-inent state funerals at the Washington National Cathedral: the first for the legendary William Colby, the former director of the CIA, and the second for Ron Brown, the famous political leader, chairman of the DNC, and secre-tary of commerce. Both men had died in tragic accidents.

Former presidents George W. Bush, Bill Clinton, and Jimmy Carter, Vice President Joe Biden, as well as many members of the Obama cabinet attended the funeral. I was part of the official delegation transported by a

Coast Guard C-130 plane to Boston from Andrews Air Force Base for the service at Our Lady of Perpetual Help Basilica on August 29, 2009. I was privileged to have the opportunity to pay my respects on behalf of the Peace Corps, one of his brother's greatest legacies and an agency that enjoyed Senator Kennedy's total support throughout his entire career. As befitting such a great leader, President Obama delivered the eulogy.

> "It's better to send in the Peace Corps than the Marine Corps."—Ted Kennedy

People have often asked me what a typical day is like for the director of the Peace Corps. The customary flow of an ordinary day of any given week when I was in the office went as follows. Because my top priority was the safety of our PCVs, I started each day with a global check-in with the director for global operations and her regional leadership team and, as appropriate, with the Office of Safety and Security. Once a week, I also held a senior staff meeting with some thirty office directors and their deputies, received a briefing and update by the assessment implementation team on each of the strategic areas and progress being made against stated objectives, and conducted a walk-around and office staff meeting with each of the technical, admin, and program offices in headquarters. Planning meetings were held to coordinate my next series of overseas or domestic trips and daily updates were provided on press opportunities as well as opportunities for events or conferences at which I might make a presentation or give a speech.

In recognition of the importance of the 535 members in Congress to the future of the Peace Corps, I also sought out a wide range of congressional meetings with leading members from both parties. I learned the lesson of seeking such support early on during my twenty-two-year career at USAID and made it the cornerstone of my leadership approach. I knew to avoid the undesirable situation where one has to meet with a senator or a representative for the first time because one requires their help to resolve an issue or problem quickly. The way to prevent that situation was by having regular conversations with them. Further, the existence of healthy and productive relationships with the primary committee chairpersons and ranking members, and their respective senior staffers, in both the House and Senate is crucial when encountering the inevitable issues that are bound to occur when leading and managing a global agency.

On a given day, I might go to the Hill with my congressional affairs team, Paul Weinberger and Suzie Carroll, a dynamic duo who covered the Hill thoroughly and strategically, to meet with a member or her or his staff. The subject of the meetings might be appropriation, oversight and policy, or particular issues of concern to the leadership in the House and Senate. My focus from the very beginning, starting with the courtesy calls to the senators on the Foreign Relations Committee as part of the confirmation process, was to operate in a transparent and broad consultative manner with the representatives, members, senators, and their key staff on all matters. Our regular consultation on every step of the assessment illustrated my management style in this arena. This approach certainly aided the appropriators' willingness to support the most substantial Peace Corps budget increase in decades.

Typically, at least quarterly, there would be an interagency meeting with USAID, the State Department, the Millennium Challenge Corporation, and occasionally at the National Security Council in the White House. I would also frequently meet with US ambassadors from Peace Corps countries on their visits to DC, and we would often receive visits from foreign heads of state or ministers from countries with PCVs or seeking Peace Corps programs. Periodically, I would meet with the leaders of international non-governmental organizations to discuss potential partnerships between our agencies in countries where we were both active.

One of my favorite events was to attend the "staging" for a new group of trainees about to embark for their host countries for training and their PCV assignment. I used these sessions to thank them for their decision to serve, to offer encouragement as they entered this new unknown phase of their lives, and to welcome them into the Peace Corps family and an experience that would no doubt transform their lives.

As my first one hundred days came to an end around Thanksgiving, I felt quite satisfied with the launch of our new team at the Peace Corps and what we had accomplished in a short time. I wrapped up that period with trips to Thailand and South Africa with two objectives in mind. First, I wanted to see how our marvelous PCVs in two historically significant countries for the organization were faring. Second, I wanted to fulfill my plan to visit each of the Peace Corps' three geographic regions during my first one hundred days. I was especially pleased to return to South Africa, a homecoming in many ways where I reunited with my former colleague Carleene Dei, now the USAID mission director, and many other local

USAID staff. The Peace Corps had a long and rich history in Thailand, and the country director there, John Williams, was one of our most respected leaders. He had extensive experience in Thailand, having started out there in his volunteer days, and he would later be instrumental in our efforts to open a program in Vietnam. Further, I was pleased to have the opportunity to meet with Princess Sirindhorn, the royal family's long-standing supporter of the Peace Corps, and share stories with her about the current cohort of PCVs.

17 Raising the Profile of the Peace Corps

Embracing the World

You are never strong enough that you don't need help.

—CÉSAR CHÁVEZ

In the summer of 2010, I received a request to meet with the new US ambassador to Nepal, Scott DeLisi. Ambassador DeLisi wanted to talk to me about the Peace Corps returning to Nepal. His counterpart, Shankar Sharma, the Nepalese ambassador to the United States, joined him. I was pleased to meet with both ambassadors because of the special place that Nepal has played in the Peace Corps' history. Sargent Shriver started the program in Nepal, and several of my friends served there. However, the Peace Corps had not had a presence there since 2004 due to the civil war, which ended in 2006.

I invited my senior staff to join me for this meeting. I was surprised that the Nepalese delegation, led by the ambassador, also included the finance minister, the deputy minister of planning, and the embassy's political officer. The State Department's Nepal desk officer accompanied Ambassador DiLisi. This meeting embodied the ethos of the Peace Corps in many ways, illustrating the significant role the agency has always played in the relationship between our two nations. This meeting resulted in a preliminary agreement to assess reopening the Peace Corps program and sending PCVs to serve there once again. It was an ideal opportunity, and we quickly determined that a new program was viable there with the full support of both ambassadors.

I was fortunate that my friend and former USAID colleague Nisha Biswal was the head of USAID's Bureau for Asia at the time; she was an enthusiastic supporter of this initiative. The relaunch of this historic program occurred in

2012, and Stacy Rhodes represented the Peace Corps in the relaunch ceremony in Kathmandu. Stacy had served as USAID's deputy mission director in Nepal in the late 1980s, making this event a full-circle "homecoming" for him. I was happy that he was our representative at this event.

The Peace Corps is a relatively small though highly revered agency. I felt it was important to further raise its profile with the other foreign affairs agencies, the White House, Congress, and the American public. So I decided to expand and diversify our speaker series, known as the Loret Miller Ruppe Speaker Series, in honor of Loret Ruppe, the longest-serving Peace Corps director and the driving force behind the agency's revitalization in the 1980s.

I saw this initiative as valuable for a couple of reasons, one of which was that it would provide an opportunity to introduce the new members of the Obama administration to the modern Peace Corps and expose our staff to these new leaders. I wanted to revitalize this speakers' platform by inviting cabinet and subcabinet leaders, foreign leaders, and all leaders across our society to speak. It presented the Peace Corps staff with an opportunity to engage with the founding generation of the agency—including some of the legends of the Shriver era, and to develop new partnerships with other US government agencies.

I decided that I would host an Oprah-style conversation, after which the guest speaker would open the floor to a question-and-answer session with the audience. I'm very proud that our team created a very robust speaker series. It included leaders such as Susan Rice; Charles Bolden, NASA administrator; Ellen Johnson Sirleaf, president of Liberia; Senator Chris Dodd; Tammy Duckworth, assistant secretary of Veterans Affairs (now senator); each of the returned PCVs serving in the House of Representatives; Tim Shriver, chairman of Special Olympics; Cheryl Dorsey, CEO of Echoing Green; and Sonal Shah, the director of the White House Office of Social Innovation and Civic Participation.

In each of our host countries, our country directors were on the ambassadors' country teams, and it was essential to have a positive relationship with the State Department. My team and I had a very productive and warm working relationship with Secretary Clinton and her staff. Whenever the secretary traveled to a Peace Corps–affiliated country, her staff scheduled a visit with PCVs whenever possible. For example, on a trip to Morocco, Secretary Clinton met PCV Muriel Johnston during a meet-and-greet session with US Embassy officials and other Americans in Marrakech. Ms. Johnston, an eighty-five-year-old nurse from Florida and the oldest PCV in the world at that time, worked as a health worker in rural Morocco. Secretary Clinton swore in several Peace Corps groups worldwide, always an honor for the organization and a meaningful experience for the PCVs.

If ever there was a significant initiative to consider or an issue to resolve concerning PCVs or programs in any given country, we always received superb cooperation from Cheryl Mills, Secretary Clinton's chief of staff, and the regional assistant secretaries. Many of them were my colleagues and friends from my days at USAID. This level of cooperation characterized the working relationships that my staff and I enjoyed with each of the foreign affairs' agencies in the Obama administration. This collegiality was also typical of the Obama administration's interagency team in the foreign assistance sector.[1]

I also relied extensively on the excellent judgment and skillful management of the interagency relationships by Stacy Rhodes, Esther Benjamin, and Cathryn Thorup, the director of strategic information, research, and planning. Cathryn, my former USAID and IYF colleague, was especially adept and creative in managing our involvement in the National Security Council strategic planning process and the architect of the annual performance plan and report for both the National Security Council and the Office of Management and Budget.

I can't fully capture in words the extraordinary level of cooperation, leadership, and bipartisan support we enjoyed with our six esteemed returned PCV members of Congress, the Peace Corps Caucus. The caucus included Chris Dodd (Dominican Republic), Democratic senator from Connecticut; Sam Farr (Colombia), John Garamendi (Ethiopia), and Mike Honda (El Salvador), all Democratic representatives from California; Steve Driehaus (Senegal), Democratic representative from Ohio; and Tom Petri (Somalia) Republican representative from Wisconsin. Further, I was pleased that upon leaving the House following the 2010 election, Representative Driehaus accepted our offer to serve as a country director in Swaziland.

Representative Farr graciously initiated and hosted a quarterly breakfast meeting for me and my leadership team with the Peace Corps Caucus. This session gave Carrie, Stacy, and me an opportunity to update them on progress of the Peace Corps, to discuss our budgetary concerns, to present issues and challenges to them, and to listen to their ideas and recommendations regarding policies and programs. I also enjoyed the special Peace Corps day hosted by the congressmen on Capitol Hill every summer that was in essence a special briefing for, and a recruitment appeal to, all congressional interns. It was an opportunity to demonstrate our camaraderie and enthusiasm for our beloved Peace Corps to some two hundred perspective PCVs, held in the new impressive venue, the Capitol Visitors Center.

We received strong and consistent support in Congress and in the administration led by Gayle Smith, special assistant to the president and senior director for development and democracy at the National Security Congress.

Operating in a transparent and consultative manner builds trust, which is essential in building relationships; without relationships, broad success is rare in any organization.

An important part of raising the profile of the Peace Corps is opening new country programs. In 2010 we expanded to three new countries with the reopening of programs in Colombia, Indonesia, and Sierra Leone. After a lengthy forty-five-year absence, the Peace Corps returned to Indonesia in 2010. Sierra Leone saw the return of PCVs after a sixteen-year hiatus due to the civil strife that had plagued that nation. The returned PCV Friends of Colombia group, bolstered by the strong advocacy from Congressman Farr and well-known author Maureen Orth, was instrumental in the Peace Corps returning to Colombia after an absence of twenty-nine years. This initiative benefited from a fortuitous alignment of factors, including the endorsement of Secretary Clinton, the efforts of the Friends of Colombia, and the skillful diplomacy of Colombian ambassador Carolina Barco and President Uribe. This led to our return in 2010, and we concluded our consultations with a memorable signing ceremony at the Embassy of Colombia, graciously hosted by Ambassador Barco and attended by our colleagues from USAID and the State Department.

That same year, I began to explore the possibility of opening up a Peace Corps program in Vietnam for the first time. I felt that this would both expand our footprint in southeast Asia and provide the organization with a historic opportunity. We consulted with the staff of the senators and representatives influential in US-Vietnam relations, including senators John McCain and John Kerry. I also conferred with the National Security Council and Secretary Clinton's staff on this matter, and we received encouragement to pursue negotiations with the government of Vietnam. Throughout these consultations we relied on the vast knowledge and expertise of the

Peace Corps' associate general counsel, the indefatigable Lien Galloway, who guided our deliberations in both the US and in Vietnam, in conjunction with Esther Benjamin, Helen Lowman, and Elisa Montoya.

As a first step, we presented our proposal to the Vietnamese ambassador to the US and our ambassador in Hanoi. In both cases, the conversations were positive, and both ambassadors instructed their staff to explore the concept of an English-language teaching program with the relevant government officials in Hanoi. As in all such exploratory cases, we proposed to begin with a small pilot effort of no more than ten to twenty volunteers, and the initial reaction to that was also positive. These preliminary conversations led to my official visit to Hanoi in March 2012.

During my visit, we received tremendous cooperation and support from our colleagues at the US Embassy in Hanoi. I was particularly grateful to David Shear, ambassador to Vietnam, for his advocacy with the Vietnamese government and our liaison officer, the deputy economic officer Nicole Johnson, who set up all our meetings and provided valuable insights every step of the way. It was during this visit that I first met Nicole's husband, Eric Johnson, a returned PCV who had served in Kazakhstan and who was a USAID/Vietnam officer. Eric was a talented education policy expert, and a few years later we would become colleagues at RTI International.

Despite some initial skepticism on the part of Vietnamese cabinet ministers about the Peace Corps, I had several productive meetings with them. Further, I had the great pleasure of giving a speech at the US Embassy's American Center in Hanoi to a standing-room-only audience, which I later learned was quite common when a senior US government official gave a speech.

However, despite our best efforts over several months, we were unable to reach an agreement with the Vietnamese government. I learned that senior Vietnamese officials, while very cordial, are superb negotiators and, clearly, great poker players. I encouraged them to consult with the Chinese government, given our successful English-language program that had been in place in China since 1993. As it turned out, some Vietnamese government officials did visit China to observe our program in that country. We could not identify, however, nor did they reveal to us at the time, the nature of the obstacles to establishing a Peace Corps program there. Fortunately, my successor as director, Carrie Hessler-Radelet, reached a successful agreement with Vietnam in 2016.[2]

In June 2010, I received an invitation to participate the Special Olympics' Global Congress in Marrakech, Morocco. This was a special honor for the Peace Corps because the Special Olympics was founded by Eunice Kennedy Shriver, a pioneer in the worldwide struggle for rights and acceptance for people with intellectual disabilities. Tim Shriver, the chairman of the Special Olympics, is a respected global leader, and a leading educator who focuses on the social and emotional factors in learning. The organization's mission is to provide year-round sports training and athletic competition in a variety of Olympic-type sports for children and adults with intellectual disabilities, giving them continuing opportunities to develop physical fitness, demonstrate courage, experience joy, and share their gifts and skills with their families, other Special Olympics athletes, and the community.[3] In several countries, PCVs work with Special Olympics programs, and this was an opportunity to illustrate the Peace Corps' support for this organization that has such a magnificent global impact. The 2010 Global Congress, under the patronage of King Mohammed VI of Morocco and led by Princess Lalla Amina, hosted more than six hundred delegates from all over the world. Its goal was to create a four-year plan to integrate more people with intellectual disabilities into their respective societies through sports.[4]

Rosa joined me on this trip, and we were delighted to participate in several events at the congress with Tim and the organization's leadership team and board members, including a panel discussion titled "Bringing Together Agents of Change to Build Stronger Communities for Our Athletes," moderated by Maria Shriver, the acclaimed journalist and then first lady of California.

Before we attended the Global Congress, Rosa and I had an official three-day visit with Peace Corps/Morocco staff and visited with several PCVs at their sites around the country. One of our senior advisers from headquarters, Diana Schmidt, was then the acting country director, and she had arranged a comprehensive tour.

Our travel group included Elisa Montoya, Esther Benjamin, and Jeff West. We flew into Casablanca and traveled by car to the capital of Rabat. In Rabat we met with Samuel Kaplan, the US ambassador to Morocco, and the leaders of the vital counterpart organizations, including community groups, government ministries, and a couple of nongovernmental organizations. That evening the ambassador and his wife graciously held a dinner for our group. Over the next couple of days we met with one group of

PCVs at a Peace Corps retreat center near the Atlas Mountains and another group in a small regional city. I greatly enjoyed learning about their projects in various sectors, which included youth development, environment, and health.

Our last PCV meeting was in a small village with PCV Rachel Maher. Coincidentally, her mother had just arrived from the United States. I have occasionally met visiting parents in my travels, and it's always inspiring to watch proud parents joyously encountering their son or daughter as he or she demonstrates his or her cultural agility and dedication to service in the host country. In this instance we had a lovely lunch at the modest home of the volunteer's host family, a mountain home built in the Berber style into the side of a hill. It was inspiring to see and converse with the two mothers and their "PCV daughter" about her project and life over a delicious meal. It was the perfect Peace Corps moment.

18 Celebrating Fifty Years

Back to My Peace Corps
Beginnings and Beyond

There is no magic to achievement. It's really about hard work, choices,
and persistence.

—MICHELLE OBAMA, *Becoming*

The American Airlines Boeing 727 began its descent from our flight that
began in Miami, passing at a low altitude over the beauty of lush, emerald-
green mountains, aquamarine-colored ocean, and long white beaches. Eventually the sprawling city of Santo Domingo appeared, separated by the Ozama
River as it coursed its way into the Caribbean. This country held special
memories for Rosa and me—it was my second home and where she was
born. We gazed over the country's natural beauty during another landing
in the modern Airport of the Americas, a trip we'd made so many times
since 1969. This arrival felt very different from my first at the old airport in
December 1967 when I was a newly minted PCV.

This return to my beginnings in the Peace Corps highlighted for me
the incredible journey that began as a college graduate's surprising path to
adventure. Here, I met my beautiful wife, seated beside me as we returned
"home," back to where my life was transformed. We were going to celebrate
the fiftieth anniversary of the warm, friendly relationship created between
this nation and the Peace Corps volunteers who had served here throughout its rich history. That unique, historical bond, forged in the white heat of
the Dominican revolution and the US invasion in 1965, had brought about
this seminal moment. During that time of strife and struggle, many of the
PCVs of that era gained the respect of Dominican citizens by vigorously supporting the country's revolutionaries and not following the Johnson administration's official policy during a crucial period in Dominican history.[1]

On this trip, Rosa and I would be participating in a series of events to celebrate, commemorate, and treasure the more than five hundred participants who had worked side by side with the Dominican people in the spirit of friendship and peace. Current and former volunteers and staff would reunite at a three-day conference and share in the success of fifty years of Peace Corps work in the Dominican Republic. This auspicious anniversary also presented us with the chance to engage with Peace Corps volunteers and staff worldwide and observe the scope and impact of the organization's fifty-year global engagement. I experienced firsthand the warm reception that Peace Corps volunteers continue to receive worldwide.

Our gracious hosts for these anniversary events were Raul Yzaguirre, US ambassador to the Dominican Republic, and country director Art Flanagan. Yzaguirre is an icon in the Hispanic American community and a civil rights activist. He served as the president of the National Council of La Raza from 1974 to 2004 and transformed the organization from a regional advocacy group into a potent national voice for Hispanic communities.

Many returned PCVs made site visits to the towns and villages where they had lived and worked, often hosted by the current PCVs; such a site visit was nostalgic for the former volunteer and also an exciting historical experience for the local citizens. Rosa and I were very happy to enjoy once again the company of so many friends who shared this collective experience, especially Dave and Anita Kaufmann, Bill and Paula Miller, and Dan and Alicia Mizroch. The men all served as PCVs in the late 1960s, so the celebration also represented a special homecoming between lifelong friends! Further, we had a joyful reunion with Judy Johnson-Thoms and Victoria Taylor, the PCVs with whom I had served in Monte Plata.

Dominican officials, our former counterparts, and many Dominican friends hosted events for Peace Corps participants in the grand style of a "family" reunion. Major Dominican newspapers and broadcast media provided extensive coverage of the celebration. Like many returned PCVs, I had the great pleasure of holding a mini-reunion with my former colleagues from the University Madre y Maestra, many of whom I had not seen since 1970!

We all felt honored to be joined by a special guest, Senator Chris Dodd, a proud returned PCV who served when I did in the Dominican Republic. During his five terms in the US Senate, Chris had always been a great champion of the Peace Corps. For many years, he served as the chairman of the subcommittee responsible for oversight of the Peace Corps.[2] Because he had presided over my confirmation hearing, it was especially gratifying to participate in this homecoming with him.

The planning for the Peace Corps' fiftieth-anniversary celebrations, both in the United States and overseas, had begun before my appointment, under the previous director Ron Tschetter. Of course, we were enthusiastic about building upon these efforts. We were determined to hold a worldwide celebration that would highlight this significant landmark in the agency's history and celebrate the legacy of this American success story—it would be a celebration to remember!

I have often reflected on the warm relationships between the Peace Corps and our host countries. The relationships that PCVs fostered for fifty years were indicative of the power of the organization in pursuing its mission of world peace and friendship. The outpouring of admiration, affection, and respect was something to behold as we continued preparing for these global celebrations. In each location, the country director and their staff created scheduled events representing the Peace Corps' past and present role in each country, resulting in rich and diverse programs.

Those of us at headquarters planned several special events in Washington, DC, to highlight and honor the Peace Corps legends who had been Shriver's colleagues and to welcome the returned PCVs and other staff community back home. At the same time, returned PCV affinity groups—such as Friends of Kenya, Friends of Paraguay, and so forth—held anniversary activities in every state and in scores of colleges and universities across the United States. The national celebration aimed to demonstrate the organization's continuing role in American life and history.

Overall, our senior staff traveled to fifteen countries, twenty states, and twenty-eight cities to celebrate the fiftieth anniversary. The Peace Corps senior staff worked to ensure broad representation; Carrie Hessler-Radelet, Stacy Rhodes, and I carefully planned our calendars to maximize our participation in major events in each region of the world and across the United States.

Our trips to visit the volunteers in the host countries were a great privilege, and in my visits I stressed the importance of the individual and collective service of our PCVs and my personal connection with the work of the modern PCV. What a sight it was to see volunteers on the front lines, working in microbusiness-support organizations to create new women-owned small businesses, teaching math and science in rural primary schools, or distributing mosquito nets in remote villages to fight malaria under our Stomp Out Malaria program, working in HIV/AIDS clinics, or helping small farmers improve irrigation systems.

The variety of PCV assignments was truly spectacular, from leading young girl empowerment clubs in rural Jordan, to coaching junior achievement classes in Nicaragua, teaching math in rural Tanzania, teaching internet technology in high schools in the Dominican Republic, teaching English as a second language in a girls' school in rural Thailand, working on improved environmental protection practices in Filipino fishing villages, and helping to advise on improved livestock breeding techniques on farms in Ghana. Though I had once been in similar circumstances as a young PCV, I couldn't help but be impressed by what I saw.

My colleagues and I had the pleasure of participating in several country celebrations during the fiftieth anniversary year, and it typically involved the following scenario. Of course, a meeting with the president of the host country and/or another senior government official would be first on the list for a country anniversary celebration. Many of these leaders had worked with or had been taught by Peace Corps volunteers over decades. We also met with the leaders of the vital counterpart organizations, including community groups, government ministries, and the leading nongovernmental organizations in the country. We visited volunteers at their worksites to observe their activities and attended a dinner or reception hosted by the US ambassador for the PCVs, local dignitaries, and guests.

Another important aspect of my country visits was broad engagement with the national print, radio, and television press through press conferences, individual interviews, or both. In almost every case, returned PCVs who had served in a particular country participated in the events, often in coordination with the returned PCV affinity groups (e.g., in the case of Tanzania, Paraguay, Kenya, or Thailand), along with current PCVs and their guests. A typical visit for an anniversary event would run two days, and Carrie, Stacy, or I attended as the senior Peace Corps representative for a particular celebration.

Ghana is one of the most prominent nations in West Africa, and Sargent Shriver established the first Peace Corps program there in 1961. Its first president was the famous Kwame Nkrumah, who led the country to independence from Great Britain. Known during the colonial era as the Gold Coast, Ghana was also the location of some of the principal slave-trading forts in West Africa.[3] Stacy Rhodes, Jeff West, and I traveled together to Ghana, where we spent three days in a series of events to celebrate the fiftieth anniversary in this historic Peace Corps country.

After our first day of courtesy meetings with government officials, local counterpart organizations, volunteers, and staff, we decided to visit a famous fort. It was a heart-wrenching experience for Stacy and me, brothers in service, to stand before the fortress, built as a trading post with slaves as the primary commodity. We could only look out on the vast Atlantic Ocean through the "door of no return" in the bottom of that castle with sadness, knowing that those poor souls had been ripped from their native land. We felt it was necessary to witness the dungeons where they were held captive and the path they were forced to walk as they boarded the ships in the harbor that would take them to the West Indies or the American colonies, separating them forever from their homeland.

These are experiences not easily comprehended from afar, but they represent a crucial part of the human story that needs to be retold and remembered. Ideally, they set the stage for improving the human condition in the future.

One of the highlights of the trip was our participation in the country's annual teacher day. I joined the vice president of Ghana, John Mahama, for this special event in an upcountry district capital. Stacy, the country director, Mike Koffman, and I were driven two hours from the capital city of Accra to the district capital. Mike had had a tremendous public service career, first as a Marine Corps officer, then as a founder of a nonprofit organization that provided legal services to the homeless in Boston, and then as an assistant district attorney in Massachusetts. After his stint as assistant district attorney, he served as a PCV in the Pacific region, and now we were fortunate to have him as our Ghana country director.

In Ghana, the top teachers were selected each year for special recognition. One of the ten teachers chosen that year was a PCV whose parents were both returned PCVs who had served in Latin America. This national ceremony honors outstanding teachers for their exemplary leadership and work that affected and transformed the lives of the students in their care and the community around them. The overall best teacher receives Ghana's Most Outstanding Teacher Award and a three-bedroom house. The first runner-up receives a four-by-four pickup truck, and the second runner-up receives a sedan; indeed, a very different approach from how we honor teachers in America. I looked forward to participating in this important ceremony, during which the vice president and I would deliver speeches.

When we arrived at the government house in the district capital, I planned to discuss with the vice president a few points regarding the future of the Peace Corps program in Ghana. However, Vice President Mahama, who subsequently was elected president of Ghana in 2012, was more interested in talking about his experience with a PCV during his youth, and I listened to what he had to say with great interest.

He described how, as a young boy, he had attended a small primary school in rural northern Ghana. There were fifty to sixty boys in a very crowded classroom with very few desks and textbooks. They heard one day that a white American was coming to teach them, and they were anxious about this. They had never seen a white man before in their village, and they didn't even know if they would be able to understand his language.

When the young American PCV came into the classroom, he looked around the class and said that he was going to teach them science. He then asked them, "Do any of you know how far the sun is from the earth?" The boys all stared at the floor; they didn't understand why he asked this question or why it was important, but either way, they didn't know the answer.

The PCV walked up to the front of the classroom, took out a piece of chalk, and wrote down on the blackboard the number ninety-three; he put a comma behind it and then proceeded to write zeros on the front blackboard until he quickly ran out of room, and then he continued to put zeros on the walls of that small room, returning to the ninety-three on the blackboard. Then he exclaimed, in a loud voice, "It's ninety-three million miles from the earth! Don't ever forget that!" That day, for future Vice President Mahama, was a turning point in his life when he saw the possibilities of another world. He also told us about several of his friends from his village school in that same class who had gone on to become scientists or engineers.

From the government house, we went on to the stadium to participate in the teacher day festivities. Marching bands and students from all around the area welcomed us and an audience of thousands on the impressive parade grounds of the city. The vice president and I shook hands with and gave the awards to each of the winners, and we had a chance to meet the young PCV who had been selected as one of the winners. It was a long but satisfying day, and I'll always remember my visit to this historic Peace Corps country.

I have equally vivid memories of traveling to a small village in Ghana, where we visited a young PCV from Kansas, Derek Burke. As I recall, he grew up on a farm, and now, in this remote and arid region of the country, he worked with the local farmers on a tree planting project, helping them to plant thousands of acacia trees. As we slowly walked into the village, we were welcomed by the hypnotic sounds of ceremonial drumming and greeted by more than two hundred villagers. I loved seeing the smiling children as we met the village elders and local government officials. We then held a town hall meeting under an enormous baobab tree—a tree large enough to provide shade for all assembled.

As we departed, I was asked to visit with the patriarch of the village, who hadn't been able to join us due to his failing health. He lived in a small hut on the outskirts of the village. The PCV and I went to his bedside. I can still feel the firm grip of the frail-looking gentleman, who appeared to be in his late eighties. He held my hand as he thanked me through a translator for visiting his village and for the "gift" of the young American PCV whom everyone loved. As I drove away, I thought about the symbolic importance of sending one volunteer to serve in a remote village in Ghana and how he walked in the steps of those who came fifty years before him, in service to the country and the building of friendship in the name of the United States.

On a spectacularly beautiful day in June 2011, our plane landed in Dar es Salaam, the largest city in Tanzania, after a short stop in Arusha, near Mt. Kilimanjaro, where the majestic mountains loomed large from the airplane window. Esther Benjamin, Elisa Montoya, and Jeff West accompanied me. Dar es Salaam is a name that conjures up visions of Zanzibar and the ancient trading routes between Africa and the Arabian Peninsula. This nation, formed by the union of Tanganyika (colonial name) and the island of Zanzibar, has some fifty-five million citizens and is 60 percent Christian and over 30 percent Muslim, with two official languages: Swahili and English.

Tanzania was led into historic independence by the legendary Julius Nyerere, known as the "father of the nation," who campaigned for Tanganyikan independence from the British Empire.[4] Influenced by the Indian independence leader Mahatma Gandhi, Nyerere preached nonviolent protest to achieve this aim. His administration pursued decolonization and the "Africanization" of the civil service while promoting unity between indigenous Africans and Asian and European minorities.

The outstanding country program was led by one of our most experienced country directors, Andrea Wojna-Diagne, who received strong support from Alfonso Lenhardt, the US ambassador to Tanzania.

We started our visit by meeting with President Kikwete and his senior officials. It was a pleasure to learn that the president, as a young elementary school student, had been taught by a Peace Corps volunteer. He had a very positive view of the Peace Corps, and he recognized its importance to the relationship between the United States and his country.

We went upcountry to visit a volunteer who was a high school math teacher in a very remote part of Tanzania. In many places in the developing world, it's challenging to find and hire science and math teachers for rural communities, who are desperately needed, as without these subjects, the students in this region would not be able to complete the coursework required to take the qualifying exams for university applications. The school principal and our PCV were very proud of the role he played in this school and of the astronomy program he created to introduce his students to this area of science.

Upon our return to Dar, we had the pleasure of attending a lovely dinner hosted by the ambassador and participating in a fiftieth-anniversary gala, organized by Peace Corps staff and the PCVs. Due to a touch of serendipity, there happened to be several Peace Corps volunteers in Tanzania who were graduates of performing arts programs in universities and colleges across the United States. They created, planned, rehearsed, and staged a magnificent performance about the history of the Peace Corps in Tanzania. The audience included current PCVs, returned volunteers, Tanzanian government officials, Peace Corps partners, and special guests. From my humble viewpoint, it was a Broadway-caliber stage performance. It included concert singing, highly skilled theatrical performances, original music scores by soloist performers, and poetry readings as odes to Tanzanian-US friendship. There we were, on the beautiful lawn and garden grounds of the US Embassy, being entertained by this incredibly talented group of volunteers who expressed their love for Tanzania in the most heartfelt, dramatic fashion possible.

In November of 2011, my team and I traveled to the Philippines to celebrate the joint fiftieth anniversary of USAID and the Peace Corps. My colleagues Elisa Montoya, Esther Benjamin, and Jeff West accompanied me on this trip. As in Thailand, Ghana, and Tanzania, the Peace Corps program in the Philippines was legendary, again launched by Sargent Shriver nearly fifty years earlier.

Benigno Aquino III was the son of prominent political leaders Benigno Aquino Jr. and Corazon Aquino, the former president of the Philippines.[5] President Aquino was a strong supporter of the Peace Corps. In his youth, he had become friends with several PCVs in his hometown and had met many PCVs during his mother's presidency.

Our ambassador, Harry Thomas, a distinguished veteran diplomat, had served as the head of the Foreign Service as director-general. USAID mission director Gloria Steele was also a veteran USAID officer and former colleague who had held several senior positions at headquarters. She had the honor of being the first Filipina American to serve in this position. Needless to say, Gloria was well known throughout the country and highly regarded across the Philippines. Our terrific country director, Denny Robertson, represented the Peace Corps.

The president graciously hosted a luncheon for our group in the historic Malacañang Palace, his official residence and principal workplace— the White House of the Philippines. Many meetings between Filipino and US government officials have taken place there over the years of the countries' bilateral relationship. We had a delightful, wide-ranging conversation with the president and his staff in which he made clear his great appreciation for PCVs' years of service. He was pleased that we were there to celebrate the fiftieth-anniversary celebration of this highly respected American organization.

During our trip, we held a town hall meeting with the PCVs. We received a warm welcome from the cabinet ministers under whose auspices PCVs worked on various projects, such as social welfare, education, and the youth commission. We visited a few volunteers at their sites around the main island of Luzon. We witnessed their marvelous work teaching in schools, working with village fisheries to improve the restoration and protection of marine habitats, and youth development programs through which they coached sports and mentored young people. We also visited a volunteer working with the community of nomadic Samu-Bajau peoples, another unique PCV initiative. These sea nomads are sadly a homeless minority who routinely suffer from racial discrimination, and clearly it was important that they received Peace Corps support. As always, the dedication of our young volunteers, their passion, and the great respect and appreciation expressed by their local counterparts impressed us.

In every city, town, or village we visited, we were warmly greeted by the local officials, typically with a special lunch or dinner designed to honor the extraordinary relationship between the PCVs and the Filipino people. Upon our return to Manila, we attended the major event of the trip, a joint Peace

Corps/USAID fiftieth-anniversary celebration in one of the city's major multilevel shopping malls.

I was delighted to celebrate these two great agencies, representing fifty years of service and international development, peace, and friendship. There are many synergies and linkages between the Peace Corps and USAID. The Peace Corps has always been a training ground and launching pad for hundreds of USAID officers. During my tenure, we signed agreements for strategic partnerships with USAID that supported PCVs who worked in the program areas of HIV/AIDS, malaria, and agricultural development.

We celebrated this great legacy on two floors of exhibition space, showcasing the various projects that the Peace Corps and USAID worked on with their Filipino partners across the country. Current PCVs, former volunteers, many of whom were residents of the Philippines, a large group of invited Filipino dignitaries, and the general public attended the exhibition. Ambassador Thomas, Director Steele, and I gave speeches that honored the fifty-year partnership between our two countries. Overall, we thanked the Filipino people, government, and local nongovernmental organizations for their support and the opportunity to serve and work with them on their national priorities.

In May 2011, the White House asked me to lead the presidential delegation to Paraguay in celebration of that nation's bicentennial.[6] It was a particularly auspicious moment in this nation's history because after sixty-one years of both the Alfredo Stroessner dictatorship and subsequent one-party rule, former Catholic bishop Fernando Lugo was elected in April 2008.

Paraguay is not well known to most Americans. It is a small country bordered by Argentina to the south and southwest, Brazil to the east and northeast, and Bolivia to the northwest. It is one of only two landlocked countries in South America (the other is Bolivia).

Leading a presidential delegation is quite an honor, and I was delighted because Paraguay has been a welcoming host for the Peace Corps for decades. A few of my friends and former colleagues have served as PCVs in Paraguay, and they always had a special relationship with this country. Typically, a presidential delegation is led by a cabinet secretary or head of an independent agency and includes three or four other senior officials in the administration. The members of this delegation were Liliana Ayalde, US ambassador to Paraguay, and Arturo Valenzuela, assistant secretary of state for Western Hemisphere Affairs, an academic expert on Latin America. Elisa

Montoya and Grace Garcia from the protocol office of the State Department also accompanied us.

I was especially pleased because Ambassador Ayalde was a longtime friend and USAID colleague and a strong advocate for the Peace Corps and the work of our volunteers. I have traveled to many countries, but I rarely saw an ambassador as warmly received and admired as Liliana Ayalde. I will never forget the day we walked down the main avenue of Asunción, the capital city, on our way to the high mass at the National Cathedral during the bicentennial celebration. Usually, during this era of tight security, an ambassador will travel in a bulletproof limousine with bodyguards and advance and trailing cars. In this case, Liliana was so popular that she felt completely comfortable walking down the street for public events. Hundreds of people cheered us as we walked down the main avenue in downtown Asunción; many reached out to shake her hand, and many more people called out her name, cheering the United States of America. Quite a gratifying thing to see, and I give all the credit to Liliana for superb leadership of the embassy and her ability to reach out and connect with the greater Paraguayan society.

Representing the Peace Corps was Don Clark, a returned PCV who had served in Bolivia, one of our most experienced country directors. He and his superb staff had created a program that allowed us to meet with PCVs despite our tight schedule of official government events. Paraguay had more than two hundred PCVs at the time working on projects in agriculture, environment, education, health, and community economic development. Ambassador Ayalde and I visited a working-class neighborhood in the suburbs of Asunción to see the environmental and young girls empowerment projects supported by PCVs. Following that visit, I held a town hall meeting at the Peace Corps' office and had a wide-ranging question-and-answer session with the PCVs and Peace Corps staff. The ambassador hosted a special Peace Corps anniversary celebration at her residence. It was a lovely evening filled with presentations and remarks on the historical relationship. The guests included PCVs, Peace Corps staff, senior Paraguayan officials, and local counterparts.

During my visit to Paraguay, we did find ourselves in one awkward situation owing to the presence of a delegation from Iran for the bicentennial. United States–Iranian relationships have been tense for decades, and we tried to keep our distance from them during all of the festivities. The traditional receiving line was set up in the government palace so that each delegation could offer official congratulations to President Lugo, and the US delegation was placed right behind the Iranian delegation, which meant we had to spend about forty-five minutes moving slowly toward the presidential box, much closer to the Iranian delegation than we desired. So we decided to spend our time in polite conversation with the Guatemalan delegation immediately behind us. Fortunately, all of us were fluent in Spanish, so it was quite easy to converse with our Guatemalan colleagues, thereby avoiding the necessity to engage in even idle conversations with the Iranian delegation.

From Ghana to Tanzania to Paraguay, it was gratifying to see the scope of the world's embrace of this amazing American institution as we celebrated fifty years of promoting world peace and friendship by a corps of dedicated Americans.

19 The Impact and Contribution of the Peace Corps

Bringing the World to America

With each village that now has access to clean water, each young woman who has received an education, and each family empowered to prevent disease because of the service of a Peace Corps volunteer, President Kennedy's noble vision lives on.

—BARACK OBAMA, on the fiftieth anniversary of the Peace Corps

Through the Peace Corps' efforts to bring the world back home, Sargent Shriver hoped Americans would gain a better understanding of other people. In one of his many now-famous quotes, Shriver said, "Peace requires the simple but powerful recognition that what we have in common as human beings is more important and crucial than what divides us."

Over the past sixty years, about a quarter of a million young Americans have now served in the Peace Corps, in about 150 less-developed countries. To a person, these volunteers return home with broad and rich experiences that they share with their families and friends—in the workplace and in clubs and associations across our nation. They come home as informed citizens who better understand our global connections and America's role in the world, and this makes a difference in our society.

Returned PCVs continue to have an inner drive to serve, and they look upward and outward for those opportunities that exist in every sector of America, in every walk of life. Some become cabinet members, senators, congresspeople, or local government officials. Others move into business roles as corporate executives and small business owners. One may find them teaching in schools and universities or serving public health as scientists, while others have even adventured into space as astronauts. They are famous authors, journalists, and news reporters. Some have chosen to entertain us as television celebrities, Hollywood movie stars, and directors. Without a doubt, there are many avenues through which one can serve humanity, and returned PCVs have taken many of them.

Like many inspirational leaders, Sargent Shriver saw the potential of this new agency, and he created a grand canvas in launching and leading the Peace Corps. At its founding, he said, "I recommend that we remember the beginning of the Peace Corps. We risked everything at our beginning in a leap of faith that the Peace Corps would succeed. . . . We were a corps, a band of brothers and sisters united in the conviction that if we worked hard enough to eradicate our fears, and increase the outreach of our love, we truly could avoid war and achieve peace within ourselves, within our nation, and around the world."[1] Shriver—who worked on the legislation establishing the Peace Corps in 1961, created its organizational structure, recruited the first volunteers, and placed those volunteers in countries around the world—built an American institution driven by "citizen ambassadors" who were dedicated to service and to creating stronger relationships with foreign nations.

Across the United States in 2011, we saw and enjoyed a tremendous outpouring of excitement about and support for celebrating the fiftieth anniversary of the organization. Throughout the existence of the Peace Corps, universities and colleges have played a significant role in the creation, development, and operations of the agency. Universities have always been the primary recruitment ground for PCVs, and for the first few decades, they served as the training centers for each departing country group, as was the case with San Diego State College for me. Hundreds of these institutions planned fiftieth-anniversary celebrations, and it was important for our team to participate in as many major events as possible across the United States. Just an unbelievable array of opportunities was offered to us to spread the word about the agency's past and present contributions to America and the world.[2]

Each of these university events were unique because of the special history and linkages that each institution had with the Peace Corps, but I must admit that the University of Wisconsin's celebrations, which featured its special expertise and long-term relationships with Africa, were special to me. It was very gratifying to be back on campus, and I gave the closing keynote speech on the Peace Corps' legacy of service in Africa, in which

I praised the university's long-standing position as a top-ranked Peace Corps volunteer-producing university.

One of the events that our recruitment staff often used for campus engagement was a family and friends session. At these meetings, we invited the parents of former PCVs and returned PCVs themselves as well as prospective volunteers and their parents to learn more about the Peace Corps and to hear firsthand accounts about serving in the agency. I was occasionally the featured speaker at these events, accompanied by the returned PCVs. I was often asked the same question: "Why should my son or daughter waste two years in a foreign country after graduation, instead of pursuing medical school, law school, graduate school, or beginning their career in their first job?" My response reflected my view of the inherent value in two years of PCV service, which I saw as an *investment* in their child's career rather than a waste of time. Therefore, I would preface my answer with, "I'll take off my director's hat and consider this question from the perspective of an executive at a global organization like RTI International."

When I review prospective candidates' résumés for junior positions at our organization and see that a candidate has served in the Peace Corps, I want to make sure that we interview that individual. Besides just enjoying meeting and speaking with returned PCVs because I admire them, I have another reason why I want to meet with them. Their PCV experience alone suggests they will have desirable character traits and potential for success that set them apart.

First and foremost, I know they will be resilient and have overcome challenges as a PCV. Second, I know they will speak one or two foreign languages. Third, I know they will be both superb team players and team leaders and will possess what I like to call "cultural agility." PCVs appreciate the differences in others and have the ability to communicate and reach understandings with people of widely varying backgrounds. Therefore, as an executive in a global organization, it was imperative that we interview these individuals, and this is why I believe that service in the Peace Corps is an investment in a person's future career.

In all of these events, our leadership team benefited greatly from the superb preparation and hard work of our regional offices across the United States. I participated as a keynote speaker or panelist at over twenty university or college events, and I thoroughly enjoyed every event. This included being honored by several universities as their graduation speaker during my tenure.[3] My staff and colleagues in headquarters and across the United States deserve great credit for their superb planning and execution of the university events and related heavy travel schedules. In essence, all of us recognized the importance of the historical and contemporary relationship the Peace Corps has with institutions of higher education, and it also presented me with an opportunity to personally deliver our appeal to interested students.

Another valuable initiative was my idea of extending an invitation to all the former Peace Corps directors to attend a special one-day briefing on an annual basis. The goal was to create a dialogue with our former leaders, brief them on the highlights of the current organization, and wrap it up with a wide-ranging panel discussion during an all-hands meeting with the Peace Corps staff.

Former directors are a special club; we all share a common experience of leading our beloved agency. Our coming together showcased the bipartisan support that I wanted to highlight during the Obama administration. Every former director—five Democratic and five Republican appointees—accepted my invitation to attend, and we started an annual tradition that has continued under my successor directors.

The Peace Corps saga began one cold and rainy morning on October 14, 1960, in Ann Arbor, Michigan, on the steps of the Student Union, during the presidential campaign of then-Senator Kennedy. The senator arrived in Michigan on a very late flight after one of the first televised presidential debates against Vice President Nixon. Exhausted, he nevertheless agreed to speak to an estimated ten thousand students who had waited patiently in the cold to hear from the candidate.

It was at this auspicious campaign stop when Senator Kennedy delivered his now famous speech. "How many of you who are going to be doctors, are willing to spend your days in Ghana? Technicians or engineers, how many of you are willing to work in the Foreign Service and spend your lives traveling around the world? On your willingness to do that, not merely to serve one year or two years in the service, but on your willingness to contribute part of your life to this country, I think will depend the answer whether a free society can compete."[4] Thousands of Michigan students responded to the future president's challenge in the following days by signing a petition pledging their readiness to serve.

The University of Michigan leaders decided to replicate this famous event on October 14, 2010, exactly fifty years later, and I was pleased by their

invitation to me to speak at it. However, I assumed it would take place during the workday. But no, they wanted an *exact* replication—at two o'clock in
the morning! (Yes, 2:00 a.m.) Although I would have preferred the reenact-
ment to have happened during regular working hours, my staff and the
university outvoted me, so I eventually agreed. However, I must confess
that my surrender came after I learned that my friend and mentor, Senator Wofford, at age eighty-four, was thrilled to speak at 2:00 a.m. in honor
of President Kennedy and the University of Michigan. After finding that
out, I quickly acquiesced: "Well, if Harris Wofford is prepared to show up
at two o'clock in the morning, I'm certainly going to join him." And, yes, it
was a wonderful event, and well attended by thousands of students, faculty,
returned PCVs, and national, state, and local leaders, including the legendary congressman John Dingell, the longest-serving member of Congress,
who began his career during the Eisenhower administration!

Overall, the University of Michigan hosted a fabulous Peace Corps weekend. Many of the early leaders of the organizations joined us for this auspicious weekend. The distinguished Jack (H.) Vaughn, for example, the second
director after Shriver, attended. Personally, that was very significant for me,
because Jack had sworn my PCV group into the Peace Corps at San Diego
State College in 1967. Life full circle once again.

As one would expect of such a prestigious global research university as
the University of Michigan, literally thousands of its graduates have served
in the Peace Corps. Attendees enjoyed learning about this rich history
through a series of workshops and seminars on a wide range of international development topics led by Michigan faculty, global experts, and returned PCVs.

It was enjoyable to hear from many of the agency's legends and Shriver-
era colleagues, such as Wofford, Vaughn, and Bill Josephson (first general
counsel and conceptual architect of the organization). Carrie Hessler-Radelet
and I spoke about our experiences and views on the Peace Corps of today.

I closed my remarks at the University of Michigan, as in many other
speeches, with one of Shriver's famous quotes: "This bold experiment, the
Peace Corps, still calls us to action. . . . Now let's see what we can build
together in the years to come!" I will always remember that cold morning
in Ann Arbor, sitting next to Harris Wofford and Jack Vaughn, imagining
that I was there, listening to Kennedy's short remarks that night in 1960.
Who could have thought that fifty years later, we would be celebrating the
magnificent institution that he first proposed on this very spot?[5]

During that week, Mary Sue Coleman, president of the University of Michigan, and John Hieftje, mayor of Ann Arbor, graciously unveiled a new memorial, across the street from the student union, honoring the Peace Corps' "founding" in October 1960. They also presented me with a key to the city of Ann Arbor in honor of the fiftieth anniversary.

Several major California universities, including UCLA and UC Berkeley, were among the first to undertake the training of PCVs in 1961. UCLA's work with the Peace Corps began when the first group of volunteers heading for service in Nigeria received training at the university in that country's history, language, and culture. In March 2011, Chris Matthews, a longtime MSNBC anchor, agreed to serve as the master of ceremonies for our special program at UCLA. Chris, who served as a PCV in Swaziland, has always been an enthusiastic and proud advocate of the Peace Corps.

We were at UCLA for a panel discussion titled "Peace Corps: The Next Fifty Years," in which we examined the fifty-year legacy of the agency and its future. The discussion, moderated by Matthews, ranged from the heartfelt to the humorous and drew about a thousand people. In my comments during the panel discussion, I described my PCV experience and offered observations about the Peace Corps of today.[6]

My fellow panelists were UCLA alumni Maureen Orth, a journalist and author and founder of the Marina Orth Foundation as well as a returned PCV who had served in Colombia; Frank Mankiewicz, former regional Peace Corps director for Latin America, former president of National Public Radio, and press secretary for Robert F. Kennedy at the time he was senator in the mid-1960s; and Haskell Sears Ward, a returned PCV who had served in Ethiopia and was now a senior vice president in government relations for SEACOM, an international telecommunications company.

The UCLA event was magical due to the enthusiasm and personal stories of the returned PCVs, and I was honored to receive an invitation to return in June 2011 to deliver UCLA's main commencement address. Stacy Rhodes and I also delivered the commencement address at five other universities with strong ties to the Peace Corps. I spoke at American University, the Monterey Institute of International Studies, and North Central College. Sam Farr, the leader of the Peace Corps Caucus in Congress, represented the Monterey Peninsula region in Northern California, and I was pleased to oblige when he asked if I would be willing to speak at the graduation ceremony for the Monterey Institute of International Studies (now known as the Middlebury Institute of International Studies at Monterey).[7] Esther

Benjamin was a proud alumna of North Central College, and when she informed the school of my interest in speaking at smaller colleges, it quickly extended me an invitation to speak at its commencement in June 2012. It was a wonderful day, and I was pleased to be accompanied by Esther. She graciously set the stage for a lovely day of immersion in the school.[8] Stacy was the proud alumnus speaker at Duke University's Sanford School of Public Policy. In our remarks, we challenged graduates to answer President Obama's call to service and consider Peace Corps service after graduation.

I also was delighted when I was invited by the distinguished Dr. Lou Goodman, dean of American University's School for International Service, to be the commencement speaker in May 2011. SIS was well known for its mission to "prepare students of international affairs to 'wage peace.' We do so because we believe the world needs leaders who are ready to serve." American University continues to be among the top five medium-size colleges with the most alumni volunteers serving in the Peace Corps.

In all these joyful experiences, I had a chance to engage in a lively dialogue with students, faculty, and staff. I hope I delivered an inspirational message, inspired young people to volunteer for the Peace Corps, and offered a respectful tribute to those colleges for their contributions to the Peace Corps over the past fifty years.

Another very special event was the John F. Kennedy Service Awards ceremony held on a bright sunny March 5, 2011, at the John F. Kennedy Library on the campus of the University of Massachusetts–Boston alongside Boston Harbor.[9] Awarded every five years, the John F. Kennedy Service Award recognizes two current Peace Corps volunteers, two Peace Corps staff members, one returned Peace Corps response volunteer, and one returned Peace Corps volunteer for contributions beyond their duties to the agency and the nation.[10]

We were extremely honored because the keynote speaker was Caroline Kennedy, John and Jacqueline Kennedy's daughter, an attorney, author, and the honorary president of the John F. Kennedy Library Foundation. Two years later she would be appointed by President Obama as ambassador to Japan. Further, we were very grateful that Juliet Sorensen, a returned PCV who had served in Morocco, was the master of ceremonies. Juliet, a prominent attorney and law professor, is a member of the Peace Corps "family"; her father was John F. Kennedy's renowned speechwriter, Ted Sorenson, a distinguished lawyer, writer, and presidential adviser.

One could not imagine a more appropriate place or time to host a fiftieth-anniversary event than the JFK Library in Boston. I had visited the library only once before while visiting my son Michael when he was a student at Harvard Medical School. The Peace Corps community in Boston, a very large and active group of PCV alums, was absolutely ecstatic about the opportunity to hear from Caroline Kennedy and to express their admiration for her father and his legacy. It was a day for volunteers to celebrate his legacy of the Peace Corps and their service.

The event was planned and organized in conjunction with Mrs. Kennedy's staff, and the Peace Corps' lead person was Erin Mone, the dynamic director of the Peace Corps' regional office in Boston. The auditorium at the library had a standing-room-only audience.

The fiftieth anniversary was an ideal time to rally the Peace Corps community and all of America by showcasing the organization's impact on the world and its past and present contributions to America. A tremendous outpouring of support and appreciation was evident by all. I was continually impressed by the scope and the sheer number of events that the Peace Corps community created for the special anniversary. Our communications team developed a unique online calendar to capture and highlight the broad spectrum of anniversary activities during 2011.[11]

In an exciting fiftieth-anniversary development, the Smithsonian chose to recognize the accomplishments of the Peace Corps in June 2011 by celebrating its volunteers and the people they serve during the Smithsonian Folklife Festival. This free event is held annually with a different theme every year on the National Mall in Washington, DC. It's an international exhibition of living cultural heritage that encourages cultural exchange. The two-week-long celebration is the largest annual cultural event in our capital, attracting more than one million visitors yearly. The festival generally includes daily and evening programs of music, song, dance, celebratory performances, crafts and cooking demonstrations, storytelling, illustrations of workers' culture, and narrative sessions for discussing cultural issues. Visitors participate by learning, singing, dancing, eating traditional foods, and conversing with people that the festival program presents.

In 2011, the festival ran for ten days, through the July Fourth holiday, and also featured the nation of Colombia, which greatly pleased us at Peace Corps, since we had reopened this historical program in 2010. During the festival, my colleagues and I were the featured speakers, and we participated in several special events featuring returned PCV affinity groups from several countries. We were honored at the festival by being asked to participate in a special panel presentation on the global impact of the Peace Corps that featured Lonnie Bunch, now Secretary of the Smithsonian Institution, who was at that time the founding director of the Smithsonian's National Museum of African American History and Culture. I found it particularly interesting but not surprising that many visitors to the festival commented that they were not aware that the Peace Corps was still operating across the globe.

In September of that year in a special ceremony and on behalf of the Peace Corps, I donated objects from PCVs to the political history collections at the Smithsonian's National Museum of American History.[12] The Peace Corps gathered this collection by reaching out to its returned PCV community for objects representing the experiences of volunteers stationed around the world. The donation includes documents, brochures, posters (such as the sign that hung at the original Peace Corps office in Ghana, the first country to host PCVs), and correspondence, including a congratulatory letter from the White House signed by President Kennedy.

We held numerous major events in Washington, DC, that provided a platform to honor the founders who had worked directly with Sargent Shriver at the beginning of this incredible journey. All of us thought it was important to honor them as legends of the Peace Corps. The events were intended to feature the earliest "influencers" in the creation of the Peace Corps, including stalwarts like Senator Wofford, who was steadfast in his support and participation in every significant event in DC during the anniversary period. We also invited Bill Moyers, the PBS luminary, journalist extraordinaire, and the first deputy director of the Peace Corps, to join us for several events and were extraordinarily grateful to him for accepting. I'll always recall the delightful, animated conversation that Stacy Rhodes, Elisa Montoya, and I had with him, his wife, Judith, and his senior staff at the New York PBS station. The wide-ranging discussion covered his memories and amazing stories about the early days of the Peace Corps and working with Shriver, his history with Lyndon B. Johnson and the Kennedys, and, of course, his legendary career as a journalist and political commentator. Moyers is often called the "soul of America," and those few hours we spent with him provided a fascinating walk through fifty years of an important part of American history.

Stacy Rhodes had a special connection to Shriver in that upon his graduation from law school, after his Peace Corps service, Shriver hired him as a young lawyer at Shriver's law firm. So he took the lead in organizing the participation of the other Peace Corps "giants," as wonderfully described by

him in his oral history in the archives of the Association for Diplomatic
Studies and Training:

> Sarge (as he liked us all to call him) not only founded and directed the Peace
> Corps but went on to direct the "War on Poverty" and establish many of the
> key federal programs and agencies working to this day on behalf of poverty-
> stricken Americans. Sarge regrettably passed away in early 2011, just as we
> were finalizing the preparations for the anniversary. But we all felt it was sig-
> nificant that he'd held on to the year Peace Corps turned fifty years old. . . .
> This gave us the occasion to pay a great tribute to him at fiftieth-anniversary
> events in March 2011, just weeks after he died. I was in charge of putting
> together the historical retrospectives and pulling together some of the amaz-
> ing people from Sarge's early days, including Bill Moyers from PBS, who was
> the first deputy director of Peace Corps under Sarge. Also C. Payne Lucas was
> a very dynamic early staffer and Africa expert [who ran the first programs in
> Africa and later founded AFRICARE]. Bill Josephson was Sarge's first General
> Counsel and the cowriter of the famous "Towering Task" memo, which gave
> Sarge the strategic concepts he needed to get the agency started up in a hurry
> in the earliest days of the JFK administration. And Sarge's "gal Friday," as he
> called Maryann Orlando back in the early 1960s—he likely wouldn't call her
> that today, I imagine, but she was a mover and shaker for him and his exceed-
> ingly capable office administrator in the earliest days. And Charles Peters, the
> journalist, author, and founder of the *Washington Monthly* magazine, who
> was Sarge's field program evaluator and roving troubleshooter, another key
> figure in the earliest days of the Peace Corps. These "founders" made for a
> great series of panel discussions on the establishment of the Peace Corps,
> along with Sarge's sons Tim and Mark, who also came to speak movingly
> about their memories of their father.[13]

We, of course, invited the five returned PCVs who were then serving in
the Congress to join us in as many of the events as they could; given their
busy schedules, they gave generously of their time throughout the year.

Shriver died on January 18, 2011. His many accomplishments beyond
the Peace Corps were described in his obituary by the *New York Times*.

> R. Sargent Shriver, the Kennedy in-law who became the founding director of
> the Peace Corps, the architect of President Lyndon B. Johnson's war on pov-
> erty, a United States ambassador to France, and the Democratic candidate for

vice president in 1972, died on Tuesday in Bethesda, Md. He was 95. . . .
"Sarge came to embody the idea of public service," President Obama said in
a statement. Mr. Shriver's impact on American life was significant. On the
stage of social change for decades, he brought President Kennedy's proposal
for the Peace Corps to fruition in 1961 and served as the organization's director until 1966. He tapped into a spirit of volunteerism, and within a few years
thousands of young Americans were teaching and working on public health
and development projects in poorer countries around the world.[14]

The entire Peace Corps family mourned the loss of this great man, and a
few days later I joined the thousands of mourners at his two funeral services
in the Washington, DC, area. I also invited Gaddi Vasquez, former Peace
Corps director in the George W. Bush administration, to accompany me to
the Shriver funeral service at Our Lady of Mercy Parish, the Shriver family's
church, in Potomac, Maryland.

As described by ABC News, "Family, friends and other mourners gath-
ered today for the funeral of former Democratic vice presidential candidate
and Peace Corps founder Robert Sargent Shriver Jr., who died Tuesday.
Former president Bill Clinton, first lady Michelle Obama, U2 front man
Bono, and singer Wyclef Jean, along with members of the Kennedy and
Shriver families, were among those in attendance at Our Lady of Mercy
Parish, the Shriver family's church, in Potomac, Md. During the ceremony,
Shriver's nineteen grandchildren read passages recalling their grandfather's love of philanthropy, warm hugs, and baseball."[15] One year later, we
were extremely pleased when Mark Shriver accepted our invitation to be
the Loret Ruppe speaker and honored us with a remembrance speech on
the legacy of his father.[16]

As Stacy Rhodes and I reflected on the Peace Corps legacy of the giants
and the amazing PCVs who had served our nation, he reminded me of the
State Department's memorial wall plaque in the main entrance to the State
Department building. This plaque, erected in 1972, lists the names of the
department's fallen officers and is inscribed with the following: "Erected by
the American Foreign Service Association in honor of those Americans
who have lost their lives abroad under heroic or other inspirational circumstances while serving the country abroad in foreign affairs." He recommended we erect a similar memorial in the Peace Corps building entrance
to honor our fallen PCVs. I thought it was a brilliant idea and long over-
due. Stacy led the project team that designed and built the Peace Corps

memorial. This memorial was installed shortly before the fiftieth anniversary events got under way and lists the names of our fallen volunteers, recognizing all PCVs who died during their Peace Corps service overseas.

On September 25, 2011, the Returned Peace Corps Volunteers of Washington, DC, hosted a commemoration of the organization's fiftieth anniversary event at Arlington National Cemetery, honoring Peace Corps volunteers who lost their lives during Peace Corps service. This was a unique event in the commemorative year that was described by the organization as one that "specifically addressed and honored the fallen Volunteers."[17]

The ceremony was held in the amphitheater at Arlington National Cemetery. I joined a distinguished array of speakers that day: Maureen Orth (who served as the master of ceremonies); Senator Chris Dodd; Representative Joe Kennedy III (a returned PCV who had served in the Dominican Republic and a congressman from Massachusetts); representatives of the families of fallen volunteers; the vice president of Liberia, Joseph Boakai; and the heads of the two major returned PCV associations, Kevin Quigley (National Peace Corps Association) and Chris Austin (Returned Peace Corps Volunteers of Washington, DC). The amphitheater is hallowed ground, and many consider the services there on Memorial Day to be the nation's official ceremony honoring American service members. It was a stirring and emotional day of remembrance and celebration of the service of our fallen volunteers who served our nation as PCVs. I was very proud of the Washington organization's superb leadership and organizational planning and also very grateful for the thousands of people from the Peace Corps community who were in attendance on this memorable day.

As the grand finale of this commemorative program, the returned PCV leaders, members of my team, and I led a walk of the flags (representing the flags of each of the countries where PCVs have served over fifty years), with returned PCV groups carrying the flags and representing the nations where they served. We led the procession from Arlington Cemetery, over Memorial Bridge, and into the District of Columbia. It was a beautiful "memorial" day, with much camaraderie and goodwill demonstrated by the crowd that day—a true Peace Corps event!

20 My Peace Corps Legacy
Challenges and Accomplishments

You don't need to protect the truth; you need to live in the truth, and
the truth will protect you.

—THOMAS MERTON

Serving as the director of the Peace Corps had been the high point of my
public service career, and I felt that it was a privilege to lead this iconic
American agency. However, both Rosa and I were now facing some significant health issues that required our full attention. These personal and family considerations led me to resign in September of 2012.

I thanked President Obama for the distinct honor of serving in his administration and for having had the opportunity to lead such an inspiring
and significant mission. I further said in my letter of resignation that "the
Peace Corps is a stronger and more vibrant agency because of your global
leadership and support of the ideals envisioned by our founder, Sargent
Shriver. I had the pleasure of working with an outstanding team of colleagues who support our remarkable volunteers. They make America proud
every day."

I was proud of what my team and I had accomplished since I became
director in 2009. We led a global celebration of the fiftieth anniversary of
the Peace Corps, provided comprehensive and compassionate support to
our volunteers around the world, and addressed some extraordinary challenges in doing so.

As I reflected on my years at the Peace Corps, I spent a significant
amount of time thinking about the volunteer safety and security challenges
that we confronted in a world that was far less secure than the one I encountered during my service as a Peace Corps volunteer.

The safety and security of our volunteers is always a top priority for the
Peace Corps. When I arrived at the agency, I knew it was imperative to do

everything possible to enhance the health, safety, and security of these dedicated Americans serving our country overseas. This was the most important and most difficult job we faced.

Chief of staff Stacy Rhodes eloquently described the challenges associated with that priority in his entry in the Association for Diplomatic Studies
and Training's oral history project: "With seven thousand to eight thousand volunteers spread around sixty-five to seventy developing countries,
you're going to have problems with accidents, diseases, assaults, etc. As
much as we try to assure the safety of the volunteers, and indeed put volunteer safety as our highest priority, you can't eliminate risks out in the real
world. Peace Corps' mission is not and cannot be highly risk averse. As
much as you work to reduce the risks, and train volunteers to be as safe as
they can be, things do happen. So in addition to having to conduct a number of 'medical evacuations' to bring volunteers back to the US for advanced
medical treatment, we did experience two or three volunteer deaths each
year I was there."[1]

Our entire senior management was engaged with monitoring and responding to safety and security issues. The key teams at headquarters
included the regional offices, the security office, the office of health services,
and the general counsel. When faced with the loss of a volunteer, all staff,
both overseas and in headquarters, participated extensively in our response.
In cases of volunteer deaths, I especially relied on the wisdom and support
of Carl Sosebee, our general counsel, and Tim Lawler, the head of the Peace
Corps' counseling and outreach office. As director, returned PCV, and parent I was heartbroken when any volunteer died. We supported the griev-
ing family, and I always strived to ensure that we continued the important
Peace Corps tradition of honoring the volunteer with the respect she or he
deserved for her or his dedication and service to our nation.

I was fully committed to supporting all volunteers who were victims of
sexual assault. I saw each volunteer as a valued member of the Peace Corps
family, and I believed that every victim of sexual assault deserved the utmost
compassion and support. These were difficult and heartbreaking situations
that we faced. As Stacy further describes in his oral history, the country
directors and overseas staff were the "first responders." The security, legal,
and the medical services staff in Washington supported the in-country staff
that were responsible for responding to and addressing any sexual assaults
that occurred. We worked continuously to enhance the safety of volunteers,

especially women, who now constitute over 60 percent of volunteers. Every step of the way, the country directors, medical team, and counseling colleagues tried to do their best to provide compassionate support.

In early 2011, volunteer safety became a national news story after the broadcast of an extremely disturbing report on the ABC news program *20/20*. Six courageous women who had served as PCVs at different periods over several years in Asia, Africa, and Latin America stepped forward and shared their heart-wrenching stories of sexual attacks and the aftermath with an ABC News team. They felt they had not been treated compassionately by the Peace Corps and portrayed the agency as unwilling to address what they believed to be a systemic problem of blaming the victim.

The newscast also examined the circumstances surrounding the death of Kate Puzey, a volunteer in the West African country of Benin, who was murdered after reporting sexual assaults of female students by a Beninese teacher hired by the Peace Corps. Kate Puzey was an outstanding Peace Corps volunteer who represented the best that America has to offer. She had a passion for service and a commitment to making the world a better place, and her murder was a tragedy for the entire Peace Corps community. Her tragic death occurred several months before I became the director at the Peace Corps, and the case was still under investigation when I first met with the bereaved Puzey family. Kate's parents rightfully demanded justice for their daughter. Her murder raised serious concerns with the agency's handling of volunteer safety, security, and the confidentiality of volunteer complaints. Understandably, this issue received considerable media attention and generated several stories in various print and broadcast media over a few months.

Congress was very concerned and wanted in-depth information on this case. With the able and tireless assistance of my congressional affairs team, Paul Weinberger and Suzie Carroll, I briefed the chair of the House Foreign Affairs committee Ileana Ros-Lehtinen (R-FL), the ranking member Howard Berman (D-CA), and the majority of the other committee members and their staff on the issues and on the reforms we were putting into place.

As I recall, it took about twelve meetings over a few weeks to complete this process. This briefing led to a congressional hearing of the full committee. In my testimony, on May 11, 2011, I indicated that the Peace Corps had not done enough to protect its volunteers and that we would make it a priority to make changes immediately. I stated, "There is no doubt that these courageous women have opened our eyes to what we need to correct now. Rest assured, blaming the victim will not continue in the Peace Corps of today."[2]

We quickly worked with Congress to institute reforms, such as heightened security, training, and support for victims. We also briefed the relevant officials in the White House, including Gayle Smith, the senior director of the National Security Council, and Chris Lu, Cabinet Secretary, who were extraordinarily helpful throughout this process.

I was determined to be as open and transparent as possible in representing the agency. In this vein, I tapped the wise counsel of two Clinton administration foreign policy and communications experts, Lauri Fitz-Pegado and Jill Schuker, and they introduced me to Chris Black, a distinguished journalist and experienced media consultant. Chris had covered the White House, Capitol Hill, and the 2000 presidential campaign for CNN and had spent twenty years as a political reporter for the *Boston Globe*. During this period, I was fortunate to be able to draw on her expertise every step of the way.

I immediately recognized that we would need external expertise regarding sexual assault issues to carry out the reform process. I was extraordinarily fortunate to have the wisdom, advice, and support from US Army General Barrye Price. He was a former White House Fellow who had been introduced to me by my stellar colleague Esther Benjamin, a former fellow in the same White House Fellows class. General Price had served thirty-one years in the army, including as commander of various posts in the United States and abroad. At that time, he was serving at the Pentagon, as the army's director of human resources policy, and his portfolio included major policy issues such as "don't ask, don't tell," expanded roles for women in the army, sexual harassment and sexual assault, equal employment opportunity policy, religious accommodation, and suicide.

Given that the US Army had been at the forefront in addressing sexual assault, the general's vast experience was of great assistance to the Peace Corps in shaping our new policy and programs. He enthusiastically and most graciously shared with us the army's experience in addressing sexual assaults. Although the military's situation and types of attacks were quite different from what we faced in the Peace Corps, his knowledge and staff resources proved invaluable to my team and me. Thanks to him, we received advice and guidance from his senior advisers that led to connections with key organizations and experts on this topic across the United States.

I am particularly proud of the rapid steps we took to address sexual assault on an agency-wide basis. We established an advisory panel of nationally recognized experts and sexual assault victims, hired the Peace Corps' first victim's advocate, and signed a memorandum of understanding with the Rape, Abuse, and Incest National Network, the nation's largest organization dedicate to eradicating sexual violence. These actions helped us to establish new practices and safeguards to better protect volunteers and to ensure that victims of crime received compassionate and effective support.

My one-hour testimony before the House Foreign Affairs Committee was of course a complicated and challenging experience, and I spent many hours going over my statement and background information to ensure that I would be as transparent and forthcoming in the hearing as possible.

In Benin, James Knight, the US ambassador and an experienced diplomat, was very cooperative in keeping us apprised of the status of the Puzey investigation. Preparing for a congressional hearing requires a team effort, and I relied heavily on the advice of Paul and Suzie, Stacy Rhodes, Esther Benjamin, Elisa Montoya, and Carrie Hessler-Radelet. I will always be grateful for their steadfast support during our tenure together at the Peace Corps. I also received useful advice from Lynn Rosenthal, White House adviser on violence against women in the Office of the Vice President.

Leading up to the hearing, I received excellent advice and strong support from many congressional leaders, including Senator Leahy (D-VT), Senator Isakson (R-GA), Representative Berman (D-CA), Representative Lowey (D-NY), Representative Bass (D-CA), Representative Connolly (D-VA), Representative Tsongas (D-MA), and Representative Poe (R-TX). Further, several of them provided critical leadership, as they worked diligently to pass the legislation following the hearing. I welcomed the committee's bipartisan support of the agency's efforts, as reflected in ranking member Berman's statement in drafting the new legislation:

At the hearing, I suggested that what we needed to do was some good old-fashioned oversight: gathering the facts, asking the tough questions, and developing a responsible, bipartisan approach to fix any problems we find. And I believe that's exactly what we've done with our work on these Peace Corps bills. We've gotten valuable input from NGOs, advocacy groups, our partners in the Senate, and the Peace Corps. The result is a comprehensive, balanced bill that will make the Peace Corps a better organization for all of its volunteers and its partner countries. Madam Chairman, this is a model for how the legislative process is supposed to work.

Throughout this journey to reform the Peace Corps' approach to volunteer safety, I was determined to pursue the most modern and effective programs available. With the tremendous help of my senior team and nationally recognized external experts, we made remarkable progress and set the standard for future Peace Corps operations. Again, I was grateful to see this reflected in Congressman Berman's statement: "To his credit, the Peace Corps Director Aaron Williams detailed the steps the agency is already taking to improve support for victims of sexual assault and other crimes, and what he told us was very encouraging. The Peace Corps has already hired a Victim's Advocate, established a confidentiality policy, and started the process of re-writing and updating their sexual assault risk-reduction and response policies and training. These bills codify some of the important measures that Director Williams has put in place, to ensure that they are retained by future Directors."[3]

On November 21, 2011, President Obama signed into law the Kate Puzey Peace Corps Volunteer Protection Act, honoring Kate and her service.[4] I remain gratified that President Obama commented in the Oval Office that day that the new law codified a number of the reforms the Peace Corps had put into place over the previous two years to better protect and support volunteers. The new law took those reforms a step further and created a lasting tribute to the legacy of Kate Puzey. I am grateful to the Puzey family and all returned PCVs who have worked with us to ensure that volunteers will continue to receive the highest level of support and protection during their service. The overall issue of volunteer safety and the courageous journey of the Puzey family is presented in a very sensitive and respectful manner in Alana DeJoseph's Peace Corps documentary *A Towering Task: The Story of the Peace Corps.*

Other types of security issues erupted in Kyrgyzstan that required our rapid response. I first met General Blaine Holt in 2010, when he was the colonel and commander of the US Air Force base in Manas, Kyrgyzstan. My first window into this officer's influence in Central Asia came in the wake of a horrific car accident in the winter of 2010 that nearly killed one of our female volunteers near a remote border village in the adjacent country of Kazakhstan. Blaine's decisive leadership and coordination with the Peace Corps doctors in both countries, the embassy team, and Kyrgyz defense forces expedited her transport to US military hospitals at Manas, at the US Air Force base in Bagram, Afghanistan, and at the Landstuhl Medical Center in Germany, as well as her eventual evacuation to the United States. The emergency treatment she received at each airbase saved her life and was a heartwarming ending to what could have been a tragic story. It was a great pleasure to welcome her back to Washington, DC, and visit with her and her father at the George Washington University hospital. Thankfully, she fully recovered.

This type of critical emergency response was only possible due to the strong relationships that our country directors typically establish with embassy staff and national governments. Our relationship with Colonel Holt illustrated his support and deep understanding of our mission and the role that PCVs play in Kyrgyzstan. The importance of that relationship became even more relevant during a violent political insurrection in that country over several months in 2010.

Colonel Holt worked with Kyrgyz defense forces and Claudia Kuric, our country director, to carry out the rescue of fifteen PCVs who got trapped in an urban apartment building in the midst of rising violence in Osh, in southern Kyrgyzstan. This successful effort, plus a special extraction of a single PCV in a remote area, was possible due to swift action by the colonel and his staff as they removed the volunteers from the line of fire, avoiding a possible catastrophic escalation of this dangerous situation. In both of these situations in the Kyrgyz Republic, we were fortunate that Stacy Rhodes, Claudia Kuric, and David Burgess, our regional director, led our rescue efforts and skillfully secured the cooperation and support of the National Security Council and State Department. Colonel Holt's extraordinary support of the Peace Corps volunteers and staff, evidenced in both its scope and creative problem solving, prevented disasters in potential life-or-death situations in two instances. In recognition of his tremendous assistance to the Peace Corps, we gave him the Director's Service Award, the Peace Corps' highest honor, for his distinguished service to our volunteers, and I was delighted to present it to him at a special ceremony upon his return to the United States.

In 2011, the Sahel region of West Africa was rapidly becoming a target for Al Qaeda incursions. The Peace Corps and the US embassies in the region had been carefully monitoring the safety of our PCVs posted there.

In January 2011, I was attending the annual Africa Region Country Directors Conference in Accra, Ghana, when we learned that the ongoing political instability in the nation of Niger had exacerbated the threat posed by Al Qaeda in that country. We received reports of a kidnapping and murder of two young French nongovernmental organization workers and an increased threat of attacks and kidnappings of Westerners. My senior staff and I decided we needed to evacuate the PCVs quickly.

We had to triangulate our consultations between Accra, DC headquarters, and Niamey, the capital of Niger. The main airport in the capital was open, but the availability of future flights depended on the overall security situation. I consulted with Valerie Staats, Niger country director; Bisa Williams, US ambassador to Niger; and Johnnie Carson, the assistant secretary of state for Africa.

Once the plan was confirmed, it was necessary to relocate the more than one hundred PCVs to the capital or other safe sites and arrange flights back to the United States. However, due to the political instability, the few daily flights out of Niamey were full, and it appeared we would have to wait up to a week or more to evacuate the PCVs. I considered that scenario to be dangerously unacceptable and so decided to charter a Royal Air Maroc jet for our team to fly the PCVs to safety in Casablanca, Morocco.

In March 2012, another dangerous situation arose from a military coup in Mali. It became even more unstable and precarious when it was reported that the coup gave the jihadists who were operating in the north an opening to move south from the historic city of Timbuktu toward the capital city of Bamako.

My senior team and I decided that the growing threat was far too dangerous for PCVs to continue to serve there. Thus, in consultations with Mike Simsik, the country director; Mary Beth Leonard, the US ambassador in Mali; and Johnnie Carson, we decided to evacuate all PCVs. However, as was the case in Niger, flights were limited, and so we were forced to charter an Ethiopian airplane. On Easter Sunday, we flew the PCVs to Accra, Ghana.

Further, consistent with our standard practice, the Peace Corps attempted to place the PCVs in other assignments. More than thirty were transferred from Niger to other countries to complete their service, and in the case of Mali more than forty out of two hundred received other assignments. Overall, we effectively managed the crises in the Sahel region, thanks to the superb work of our country directors, Dick Day, the Africa regional director; and Esther Benjamin, the head of global operations; and their respective staffs.

Thanks to our experienced and determined PC senior staff and our courageous frontline country directors, we successfully faced several challenges that threatened volunteer safety during my tenure as director of the Peace Corps. From our productive partnership with the US military in carrying out the rescue of our volunteers during a siege in Kyrgyzstan, to the Al Qaeda threat to foreigners that led to the emergency evacuation of the PCVs, we overcame all threats. Our volunteers remained safe due to well-planned and secure operations. The types of critical emergency responses needed to reduce threats against volunteers called for us to exercise quick judgment and decision making. That was made possible due to the caliber of my senior team and the strong relationships that our country directors formed in each country. Once again, these challenges emphasized the importance of the rigorous hiring process I put in place upon my arrival at the Peace Corps. My goal was to select the most qualified and experienced country directors. They displayed the leadership that became instrumental in guiding our operations and accepted the utmost responsibility for the safety and security of our volunteers. Further, I was very grateful for and continually expressed my gratitude to the other US government agencies and the US military that consistently supported the Peace Corps' operations around the world.

As I wrapped up my final months at the Peace Corps, I felt some sadness at the prospect of leaving my team. As I considered the overall experiences of our leadership team during our first few years, I was proud of several major accomplishments. One was the assessment of the agency's operations under the brilliant direction of Carlos Torres that resulted in a blueprint for the Peace Corps in the twenty-first century. The report described core functions—portfolio review, enhanced training and medical care for PCVs, and new recruitment initiatives—that would prepare for expansion and shape future operations across the agency. The team provided Congress with a summary of findings, recommendations, and a strategy for implementing the assessment report.

Another was the fiftieth-anniversary activities that showcased our strong partnership with colleges and universities, crucial to recruiting outstanding volunteers. Our terrific recruitment and communications staff was able to create a successful campaign that highlighted and honored the top-ranked recruitment schools and their PCV alumni.

Yet another was considerable progress we achieved with our global agenda, thanks to the tremendous and innovative work of my leadership team and their colleagues. With the approval of our historic budget increase by Congress, we increased the number of volunteers and, in the process, offered hundreds of young Americans the opportunity to serve their country and assist the needy and disadvantaged across the globe.

The Peace Corps grew under my leadership as we reopened programs in Colombia, Sierra Leone, Indonesia, Tunisia, and Nepal. Each country had its own treasured Peace Corps history and folklore. I was proud that we were a key component of the Obama administration's engagement with Tunisia by reopening Peace Corps there, in the wake of the Arab Spring.[5] I will always have fond memories of speaking to the large audience in Tunis, at a reception hosted by our ambassador, Gordon Gray, himself a returned PCV who had served in Morocco. While celebrating our return to that nation, I received a warm greeting from one of the original Peace Corps staff members. Placing in my hand her keychain with her ID badge from 1996, she said, "I've been waiting decades to greet the director at the return of the Peace Corps to my country."

Another highlight of our trip to Tunisia was our visit to the North Africa American Cemetery, located on the shores of the Mediterranean, just outside of the city of Tunis. Most of the more than twenty-eight hundred Americans buried here lost their lives in the landings and occupation of Morocco, Algeria, and Tunisia during World War II.[6] On the walls there I saw the engraved names of two Tuskegee Airmen who had died in this war theater. As my colleagues and I walked quietly through the cemetery I recalled meeting a group of Tuskegee Airmen in Barack Obama's office when he was a US senator. These heroic pilots, now elderly military veterans, were making a courtesy visit to the senator soon after his election. I was there that day for a separate special briefing on Africa, and overall this was truly a glorious moment for me.

During my tenure, the Peace Corps also expanded and created new programs in Africa through partnerships with the President's Emergency Plan for AIDS Relief, the President's Malaria Initiative, Feed the Future Initiative, and Saving Mothers, Giving Life. Due to these programs, PCVs were able to help combat AIDS and malaria epidemics and reduce hunger among mothers and children in towns and villages across Africa.

I'm particularly proud that we created a new type of volunteer by join-ing forces with the President's Emergency Plan for AIDS Relief and the Global Health Service Corps (now called Seed Global Heath), a unique public-private partnership. Through this joint operation, we placed experienced

American doctors, nurses, and midwives as faculty in medical and nursing schools and teaching hospitals facing "brain drain" in sub-Saharan Africa. We were inspired to pursue this program thanks to the visionary Dr. Vanessa Bradford Kerry, the cofounder and CEO of the organization who saw the urgency of this situation. Due to her intellect, public health expertise, passionate leadership, and determination, this innovative program is training hundreds of African doctors and nurses who provide critical prevention and health care to remote communities. Seed Global Health's mission is to "educate a rising generation of health professionals and health educators, bolstering the pipeline of healthcare providers who have local knowledge and deep ties to the region."[7] It was a great pleasure to work with my distinguished colleague Eric Goosby, the leader of the President's Emergency Plan for AIDS Relief, in this venture. I will always be grateful for his vision and support of this pioneering program. However, the shortage of health professionals in this region remains profound, and sadly, the global burden of diseases there is the highest.

In accomplishing these achievements, we were the beneficiary of superb support from President Obama's foreign policy team and steadfast, bipartisan support from Congress. One historic event illustrates this support: the trip I made with a delegation of five senators and representatives on a trip to the Dominican Republic in 2011 in honor of the Peace Corps' fiftieth anniversary. The distinguished senator Patrick Leahy led this special Peace Corps–focused congressional delegation. I was privileged to have the wise counsel and support of the legendary Senator Leahy and his highly respected senior foreign policy adviser Tim Rieser throughout my years as director. This trip highlighted the role of the Peace Corps in the Dominican Republic and the US government's important bilateral relationship on a wide range of issues.

During my tenure, I also greatly appreciated and valued my relationship with Representative Sam Farr, a distinguished returned PCV. On Thursday, September 13, 2012, he graciously honored the Peace Corps and me in the *Congressional Record*, writing, "Director Williams has significantly enhanced Peace Corps' capacity to meet twenty-first-century development challenges."

As I reflected on our accomplishments at our beloved Peace Corps, I recall how Congressman Farr described them in the *Congressional Record*. We "understood the importance of a Peace Corps that draws from the full strength of America's citizens," and we worked diligently to expand the diversity of the volunteer ranks. We did this by forming a partnership with

AARP, strengthening recruitment at historically black colleges and universities, Hispanic-serving institutions, and tribal colleges, and establishing new partnerships with minority-serving institutions. As a result, 20 percent of volunteers were minorities during that period.

We knew that the Peace Corps of today faces a world of increasingly complex global challenges that cannot be solved by one single entity. So we pursued and strengthened partnerships with important global institutions, including the World Food Program, Food and Agriculture Organization, and the Special Olympics to promote best practices, leverage resources, and maximize impact. We rolled out safety and security reforms, many of which were codified into law, to ensure that PCVs, particularly women, have the support they need and deserve. We worked shoulder to shoulder with presidents and prime ministers, world and thought leaders, and current and former volunteers to help the Peace Corps fulfill President Kennedy's vision of world peace and friendship.

I remain humbled that Congressman Farr believed that the Peace Corps, under my leadership, showed "the world a hopeful, uplifting side of America that reflects our fundamental values of peace, prosperity, and progress."[8]

Epilogue

All of us share this world for but a brief moment in time. The question is whether we spend that time focused on what pushes us apart, or whether we commit ourselves to an effort—a sustained effort—to find common ground, to focus on the future we seek for our children, and to respect the dignity of all human beings.

—BARACK OBAMA

It's often been said that PCVs represent the best America has to offer. They live and work in host communities thousands of miles away from family and friends, and they are driven by their common desire to make a sustainable difference. Our volunteers are grassroots ambassadors for the United States; they represent America's values, generosity, and hope.

This is the history and framework that one inherits as the director of the Peace Corps. I always regarded it as a position of trust, and it was a privilege to serve in this position in the Obama administration.[1] It was quite a journey, first of all, to have been part of the historic Obama campaign, and subsequently to serve on the transition team, and then to lead my beloved Peace Corps. There is truly no higher calling than to serve our great nation, and I was pleased that I was able to share this experience with my family.

Throughout my career I have relied on four lessons for leading organizations, and I believe they have broad application for young people who seek to improve the human condition and solve the complex challenges of the twenty-first century. I had the unique opportunity to discuss my views on leadership with the legendary Julian Bond, the famed civil rights leader and social activist. He interviewed me as part of his series on leadership, and I shared some of my thoughts.[2]

The first lesson is that we grow most by challenging ourselves, by stepping out of our comfort zone; one should take calculated risks because tremendous personal growth and resilience will come from such an effort.

The second is that some of the most important things in life are positive relationships. Whether it is in the realm of politics, diplomacy, or business, real change comes in the very personal interactions between real people. Related to this is that one should always hire talented people; you can never have too many smart people on your team, and such teams make better decisions. The third is I have always believed that America's multiracial and multiethnic diversity is one of our great strengths, and so it is crucial that we seek ways to pursue diversity across all organizations. I have always tried to be proactive in such efforts throughout my multisector career. And the fourth is that service isn't just about a moment in time. Service is a mindset for life. Whatever field you choose, whatever line of work, you can always find ways to help others. And when you start your career with a service mindset, it becomes an integral part of your approach to life.

March 22, 2011, was a bright sunny day in San Salvador, the capital of El Salvador, and my team and I had assembled ten PCVs at the residence of the Mari Carmen Aponte, US ambassador. We were there to meet with President Obama, who was on an official visit to that nation. Needless to say, participating in a presidential visit is always an honor and a momentous experience, and I was delighted to introduce our PCVs to the president. I tried to relax the visibly nervous PCVs as we waited, and I counseled them about the importance of thinking about what they would like to say to the president during the meet and greet. I wanted to put them at ease and also pointedly told them that after this meeting their parents would ask them what they had said to the president. Certainly, they did not want to disappoint their parents! When he arrived, I introduced each one to the president as he shook hands with or hugged them, and as always, he was gracious and engaging. As for the PCVs, despite their excitement and joy, they managed to converse with him without any personal meltdowns. On the flight back on Air Force One, I took great pleasure in reflecting on how each volunteer handled that big moment in their young lives.

One of the joys of being Peace Corps director was having the opportunity to observe this wonderful millennial generation who served in the Peace Corps, both overseas and then subsequently as staff in headquarters and in the regional offices. They are doing outstanding work, and I have great faith in their ability to take the baton of leadership in the future and make important contributions to our nation in all facets of our society. It's always gratifying when returned PCVs introduce themselves to me in airports or in the streets of Washington, DC, or at global events in the United States and overseas. They often tell me that serving in the Peace Corps transformed their lives, and I always respond that it also transformed mine, and that we share this common experience. We all belong to quite an amazing family.

As I departed the Peace Corps, I was confident the new director, Carrie Hessler-Radelet, and the executive team of Stacy Rhodes, Elisa Montoya, Esther Benjamin, Carlos Torres, and Carl Sosebee, my superb colleagues, would continue to provide inspired and strong leadership that would lead the Peace Corps to even greater success in the second term of the Obama administration.[3]

Rosa and I flew into Managua in July 2012 for my final visit to Nicaragua. There we would participate and celebrate with our son Steven's PCV cohort (Nicaragua group number 53), in their celebration of their completion of two years of service. This group had served as small business development advisers across the country, primarily in remote areas. Steven and I had made history, in that it was the first time a director's son or daughter had been a PCV during their tenure. Rosa and I were very proud of Steven's service and very happy that he had met his future wife, Nga Trang, who was a PCV in the same group. Serendipitously, I later learned that I had first met Nga at a Peace Corps event at the LBJ School of Public Affairs at the University of Texas, a year before she and Steven arrived in Nicaragua. Now, she's our daughter-in-law and mother of three of our grandchildren! It must be karma, for we are truly a Peace Corps family in every sense of the word.

As I approached the end of the first term of the Obama administration, I reflected on the next stage of my life and our family. Our sons were both born overseas, in Honduras and the Dominican Republic. As children of the Foreign Service, they spent half of their lives overseas, and their perspective on the world had been shaped by this experience. Rosa and I like to think that their view of the world and their empathy for people, no matter who they are or what they do, are results of this exposure and our family's ethos of respect for all. Our sons are now fathers, well into their respective careers in medicine and US government service. Further, our family had expanded, and now we have two lovely daughters-in-law, Angela and Nga, who are terrific mothers to our five amazing grandsons: Gabriel and Ronin; and Joseph, Lucas, and Eliot. Now, we would transition together to the next phase of our lives.

I have been a "historian" since my days of practically living in the Chatham branch of the Chicago Public Library on the South Side of Chicago. In another life, I perhaps would have obtained a PhD and taught history in a college or university. Instead, I became *part of* history, thanks to the Peace Corps.

The time I spent serving the organization that had once been only a "fantastic idea" in the mind of a young black college student from Chicago turned out to be one of the greatest honors of my life and career.

Acknowledgments

I had the opportunity to pursue my dreams in corporate business, government service, and in the nonprofit world. This was only possible because of the support and love of my dear wife, Rosa Maria, who began this journey with me more than fifty years ago in the Dominican Republic.

My dear friend Harry Simmons, who has known me since the eighth grade in Chicago, had often suggested and repeatedly urged me to write a book about my life and career in the Foreign Service. Finally, disappointed with my lack of action, he introduced me to an experienced writer, Deborah Childs. As I discussed my goal and approach to the memoir with her, she was enthusiastic about the book. I then saw a path forward through collaboration with her. This project has been a journey of two years in the making, and I have tested Deb's patience with my multiple activities in my busy retirement life. Thankfully, she stayed the course and played a key role in my ability to complete this book.

I also want to express my gratitude to the International Division of the University of Wisconsin–Madison, publisher of this work. The International Division leadership was intrigued about this book project, saw the synergy between my Peace Corps and University of Wisconsin roots, and is proud of the University of Wisconsin's historic connection to the Peace Corps.

I am also indebted to my copyeditor, MJ Devaney, for her skillful work that greatly improved the manuscript. I am thankful for the expertise and creativity of the tremendous team at the University of Wisconsin Press, where managing editor Adam Mehring and his colleagues Jennifer Conn and Kaitlin Svabek did superb work in producing this book.

During my career I have been blessed by warm and supportive friend-ships, some extraordinary bosses, amazing mentors, and tremendous col-leagues. There are several friends and colleagues that I want to recognize for their superb assistance in this book project.

First of all, I want to thank Carol Peasley, my friend and former USAID colleague, for the amazing and patient work she did in interviewing me over a period of several months, as she recorded my oral history for the Association for Diplomatic Studies and Training. This provided an impor-tant core framework for this book and a vision for how I could pursue an autobiography.

Stacy Rhodes's eloquent oral history for the Association for Diplomatic Studies and Training was a valuable source of information and fact check-ing that he graciously shared with me. We have walked down many paths together in our careers, and I value his perspective.

Special thanks to my friend and former colleague Helene Gayle for her gracious foreword to this book. I'm honored that this extraordinary and visionary leader graced me with these much-appreciated thoughts.

I want to thank those great leaders who generously offered their testimo-nials on the book: Ambassador James Joseph, Mr. Jack Leslie, and Governor Deval Patrick.

I sincerely appreciate those friends and colleagues who took time out from their busy lives to read chapters of the book to help me ensure I was accurate concerning the experiences that we shared. I'm grateful for their efforts, and I am solely responsible for any inaccuracies or omissions of fact in the book. My valiant readers/reviewers included: my sister Hilda Jones, my brother Philip Williams, former USAID administrator Brian Atwood, Esther Benjamin, Linda Biehl, Tony and Rosy Cauterucci, Philip Gary, Vasu Guden, Ron and Sally Johnson, Ambassador James Joseph and Mary Braxton Joseph, Dennis Kroeger, Ambassador James Michel, General Barrye Price, Henry Reynolds, Stacy Rhodes, Harry Simmons, Joe Thomas, and Carlos Torres. I want to give a special thanks to Elisa Montoya, who provided invaluable records of my Peace Corps travel and speeches.

I also want to thank my Peace Corps colleagues, who I consulted with to ensure accuracy regarding the events that I wrote about and the experi-ences that we shared: Helen Lowman, David Burgess, and Mike Simsik.

I was privileged to have a career in three sectors, and throughout this journey I have worked with many, many superb colleagues.

We had an outstanding staff at the regional Caribbean mission in Barbados. My partner in Bridgetown, Barbados, Larry Armstrong and I were fortunate to work with our impressive local staff members, including our dynamic front office duo, executive assistants Jan Harding and Bernice Wolcott; our sage senior adviser, Darwin Clarke; our tireless regional engineer, Wilfred Brimley; and our amazing administrative officer, the indefatigable Albert Caldera, and his innovative assistant, Sheila Samson. In terms of our US FSO staff, we had on our team talented officers such as Drew Luten, our brilliant lawyer, and Tom Fallon, our stellar controller, along with Bob Posner, Bob Wilson, Chuck Patalive, and of course John Wooten—he of Hurricane Hugo fame.

Building and being a part of strong teams has been an essential part of my career, and my team in South Africa rose to the occasion at this historic moment when the US government supported the democratic transformation of that nation under President Mandela. We led and managed one of USAID's largest foreign assistance portfolios and developed outstanding working relationships across all sectors in South Africa. It was an honor to serve with these outstanding officers, and I am pleased that we have continued our strong friendships over the decades since that historic moment in our careers.

The deputy mission director, my former boss at the Peace Corps in the Dominican Republic, and a long-time friend, Henry Reynolds, was renowned as the top education officer in the Latin America and Caribbean region for many years. Steve Brent, director of the democracy and governance office—formerly on Senator Nancy Kassebaum's staff—had senior positions in both USAID in Washington, DC, and overseas. He led the largest technical office, both in terms of staff and partner organizations, representing a broad spectrum of South African civil society from which came key leaders in the antiapartheid movement. Following his USAID career, he became a professor at the National Defense University and is currently the chair of the Economics Department. Carleene Dei, director of the housing office, became mission director in several posts, including Haiti, where she lived through the 2010 earthquake and led the relief and recovery effort. Margot Ellis, director of the small and medium business development office, served as a mission director, senior UN official, and senior official at USAID in Washington, DC; she is currently senior deputy assistant administrator of the Bureau for Europe and Eurasia bureau. Patrick Fine, director of the education office, served as mission director in several countries and wrapped up his federal career as a principal executive at the Millennium Challenge Corporation; he is now the CEO of FHI/360. Susan Fine, deputy program officer, served as a mission director and senior official at USAID in Washington, DC, and is currently senior deputy assistant administrator in USAID's Bureau for Policy, Planning and Learning. Karen Freeman, director, program office, served as mission director in several countries and as a senior official at USAID in Washington, DC, and is currently assistant to the administrator for the office of Afghanistan and Pakistan Affairs. Jacob Gayle, on secondment from the Centers for Disease Control, was a key partner and technical leader in addressing the HIV/AIDS epidemic and crafting our strategic response at a crucial period in South Africa; Jacob has had a stellar career, serving with distinction at the Ford Foundation, the Centers for Disease Control, USAID, the UN, the World Bank, and the Carter Center. He is now the vice president of social impact at Medtronic, globalizing Medtronic's public health philanthropy and working to increase access to health care for underserved populations around the world. Rick Harber, mission economist, led our key economic analysis team and played an important role as liaison and manager of our key project with the future president's team in the office of deputy president Thabo Mbeki. Paul Weisenfeld, regional legal adviser for southern Africa, served as mission director in Zimbabwe and Peru during his career at USAID. He also held senior positions at USAID in Washington, DC, including assistant administrator of the Bureau for Latin America and the Caribbean, and head of the Haiti task team charged with coordinating relief and reconstruction planning following the devastating earthquake in 2010. He wrapped up his USAID career as assistant administrator at the Bureau for Food Security at USAID, where he led President Obama's Feed the Future Initiative. In 2015, it was my pleasure to reconnect with him when I recruited him to join RTI as a senior executive, and he is currently the executive vice president of RTI's International Development Group. Pam White, executive officer, led the largest staff office in the mission and went on to have an amazing career as a mission director and ambassador in several posts, culminating as ambassador to Haiti, where she led the US government's reconstruction program after the devastating earthquake in that nation.

During my wonderful years at the International Youth Foundation, as we built an amazing global network of corporate partners, I enjoyed the collegiality and brilliant work of Christina Abraham, Samantha Barbee, Esther Benjamin, Jack Boyson, Hildegard Fino, Sravani Ghosh-Robinson, Jean-Pierre Isbendjian, Charlotte Kea, Sheila Kincade, Patricia Langan, Christy Macy, Don Mohanlal, Carol Michaels O'Laughlin, Susan Pezullo, Bill Reese, Ashok Regmi, Clara Restrepo, Petra Reyes, Mitul Shah, Mary Stelletello, and Eliana Vera. We had several outstanding corporate and multilateral organization leaders who believed in us and were superb partners; especially noteworthy are David Ford, president of the Lucent Technologies Foundation; the dynamic team of global corporate executives at Nokia, Martin Sandelin, Kimmo Lipponen, Veronica Schubel, and Laurel Colless; and Amanda Blakeley at the World Bank.

At RTI, I had the distinct pleasure of working with superb colleagues who were instrumental in the successful implementation of the Iraq local government project. Due to the size of this project, scores of individuals played important roles, and our leadership team greatly benefited from the expertise and dogged determination of our colleagues in the areas of project management, finance, contracting, logistics, IT, HR, staff recruitment, communications and public relations, security and risk management, and procurement. This would include, among many others, Suhair Al-Mosully, Cameron Berkuti, Major Bowen, Derick Brinkerhoff, Lamar Cravens, Gordon Cressman, Jon Davis, Amy Doherty, Howard Edwards, Lisa Gilliland, Al Haines, Katrina Jackson, Renee Knight, Bill Marsden, Maria Powers, Amal Rassam, Ban Saraf, Don Seufert, Sam Taddesse, Jill Tenace, and Ross Wherry.

As Peace Corps director I received terrific support from the front office staff, who managed my whirlwind life (my schedule, events, and travel). First and foremost was the amazing Claudia Calderon, my executive assistant at RTI and the Peace Corps. Jeff West and Conor Sanchez were terrific in planning and managing my travel, both foreign and domestic under the wise counsel and direction of Elisa Montoya. Jim Cuffe, our erudite executive secretary, led and managed our massive correspondence like no other.

And finally, I would like to acknowledge those leaders who I have long admired and who frequently were a source of wisdom during my career journey. I have the pleasure of being friends and colleagues with distinguished leaders such as Ambassador Johnnie Carson, America's leading expert on Africa. Johnnie and I attended the same boys' high school in

Chicago, and he also served as a PCV—a bit of serendipity that we joyfully discovered several years ago. On this journey, I have also been fortunate to witness the brilliance and determination of other giants of American diplomacy, individuals such as Ambassador Edward Perkins, Ambassador Harry Thomas, and Ambassador Linda Thomas-Greenfield, who are truly role models for future generations.

Notes

Chapter 1. Life on the South Side of Chicago

1. Devon Jerome Crawford, *Huff Post*, "Martin Luther King Jr.'s Failure and America's Future: A Reflection on the 50 Year Anniversary of the Chicago Freedom Movement," May 31, 2016, updated December 6, 2017, https://www.huffpost.com/entry/martin-luther-king-jrs-fa_b_10212922.

2. Barack Obama, *The Audacity of Hope: Thoughts on Reclaiming the American Dream* (New York: Crown, 2006).

3. Isabel Wilkerson, *The Warmth of Other Suns: The Epic Story of America's Great Migration* (New York: Vintage, 2010).

Chapter 4. Returning Home to a New Unknown

1. John A. Byrne, "Revisiting Harvard's Most Successful MBA Class," *Fortune*, March 26, 2012, https://fortune.com/2012/03/26/revisiting-harvards-most-successful-mba-class. *Fortune* magazine initially brought notice to the members of the highly accomplished class in a 1974 article on the twenty-fifth anniversary of their graduation. By then, the power and influence of its members was nothing short of extraordinary: nearly half of the class had already become chairman, CEO, or COO and one in five were millionaires or better.

Chapter 5. My Call to Foreign Service

1. The American Embassy in Tegucigalpa, Honduras, had a rather large staff in 1976, considering that Honduras was a small country. The USAID office was the largest US agency on the embassy country team. An ambassador (chief of mission) and the deputy chief of mission, or DCM, led the country team. The USAID office was also called a mission, and the leadership team consisted of the mission director and the deputy mission director. The USAID mission was made up of two types of offices: staff offices (which included the program office, the controller's office, the executive office, and the project development office) and the technical offices (which included the agricultural and rural development office, the multisector office, the

public health office, and the housing and urban development office). Office directors led each office, reporting to the leadership team in the mission. There were three types of personnel categories: US FSOs, local staff or Foreign Service Nationals, and contractors who could be either US citizens or third-country nationals.

2. John F. Berry, "Food Company Guilty of Conspiracy," *Washington Post*, July 20, 1978, https://www.washingtonpost.com/archive/business/1978/07/20/food-co-guil ty-of-conspiracy/90161b4b-1eca-430c-97a8-3c9b728005a0/?utm_term=.1e66f379 6157.

Chapter 6. High Hopes for Haiti

1. By 1800, Saint-Domingue, the most prosperous French slave colony of the time, had become the first free colonial society to have explicitly rejected race as the basis of social ranking ("Toussaint Louverture," https://en.wikipedia.org/wiki/ Toussaint_Louverture).

2. "Although its vocabulary is mostly taken from phonetic 18th-century French, its grammar and sentence structure is that of a West African language, particularly the Fon language and Igbo language. It also has influences from Spanish, English, Portuguese, Taino, and other West African" ("Haitian-Creole," https://en.wikipedia .org/wiki/Haitian_Creole).

3. Howard French, "Haiti Justice Minister Slain in Defiance of U.S. Warning to Military to Keep Peace," *New York Times*, October 15, 1993, https://www.nytimes.com/ 1993/10/15/world/haiti-justice-minister-slain-in-defiance-of-us-warning-to-military -to-keep-peace.html.

4. Ward Sinclair, "Haitian Boat People: Flotsam in an American Sea of Plenty," *Washington Post*, April 19, 1980, https://www.washingtonpost.com/archive/politics/ 1980/04/19/haitian-boat-people-flotsam-in-an-american-sea-of-plenty/30b0503f -4012-4afa-8912-b8c130e62fb2/?utm_term=.a0a20b43d3e7.

5. "Haiti's History," *Frontline/World*, https://www.pbs.org/frontlineworld/rough/ 2007/12/haiti_belos_sonlinks.html.

6. Lines 806.30 and 807.00 of the US tariff schedule permit goods that have been sent abroad for processing or assembly to be admitted subject to duty only on the value-added abroad.

7. Robert Pastor, "Sinking in the Caribbean Basin," *Foreign Affairs* 60.5 (1982): 1038–58, available online at https://www.foreignaffairs.com/articles/central-america -caribbean/1982-06-01/sinking-caribbean-basin.Chapter 7. Success Breeds Success.

Chapter 7. Success Breeds Success

1. "The last time Central America received much play in the American news media was during the 1980s, when the region, one of the Cold War's hot zones, was plagued by civil war. For much of the decade, Soviet and Cuban-backed Marxist insurgencies (and, in one case, a Soviet-backed government) fought long, bloody battles against American-supported right-wing forces. When the Cold War ended, the superpowers withdrew much of their support from the region. The civil wars sputtered out in a series of peace accords: Nicaragua in 1990; El Salvador in 1992; Guatemala

in 1996" (Ana Arana, "The New Battle for Central America," *Foreign Affairs* 80.6 [2001]: 88–101, available online at https://www.foreignaffairs.com/articles/central-america-caribbean/2001-11-01/new-battle-central-america).

2. Stephen Kinzer, "Costa Rica Gets Tougher on Contras," *New York Times*, September 10, 1986.

3. "Costa Rica: An Unlikely Success Story," https://www.abc.net.au/radionational/programs/rearvision/costa-rica-an-unlikely-success-story-in-an-unstable-region/7335234.

4. Attorney General Edwin Meese discovered that only $12 million of the $30 million paid to the United States from the "arms for hostages" deal with the Iranians had reached government accounts. Lieutenant Colonel Oliver North of the National Security Council explained he had been diverting received funds from the Iranians to the Nicaraguan rebels (Contras). He did so with the full knowledge of Admiral John Poindexter, the National Security adviser, who had assumed he had the unspoken blessing of President Reagan ("The Iran-Contra Affair," *American Experience*, https://www.pbs.org/wgbh/americanexperience/features/reagan-iran).

5. Costa Rica's president Oscar Arias Sánchez received the Nobel Peace Prize in 1987. "Oscar Arias Sánchez," https://www.nobelprize.org/prizes/peace/1987/arias/facts.

6. "'Lucky' Industrial Pioneer Jack Harris Dies," *Tico Times*, August 8, 2008, https://ticotimes.5e.cr/2008/08/08/lucky-industrial-pioneer-jack-harris-dies.

Chapter 8. The Washington Game

1. Bureau for Latin America and Caribbean office directors and deputy directors included Terry Brown (development resources), Bill Wheeler (development planning), Craig Buck (South America), Chuck Costello (Central America), John Heard and Marilyn Zak (Caribbean), Norma Parker (democracy and governance), Tom Geiger, Garber Davidson, and Kathleen Hansen (general counsel).

2. "The Enterprise for the Americas Initiative (EAI) was launched in 1990, in order to expand investment in and provide some debt relief to countries in Latin America and the Caribbean. The three components of the EAI are: the development of free-trade agreements, including the North American Free Trade Agreement (NAFTA); a US $1.5 billion grant fund to support the implementation of investment reform programs; and a program of official debt relief" (USAID, "Enterprise for the Americas Initiative," https://www.usaid.gov/biodiversity/TFCA/enterprise-for-the-americas-initiative).

3. John Norris, "The Cold War and Its Aftermath," part 2 of 5 in the series "USAID: A History of US Foreign Aid," *Devex*, July 23, 2014, https://www.devex.com/news/the-cold-war-and-its-aftermath-83340.

Chapter 9. Storm-Tested Leadership

1. Andrew Glass, "United States Invades Grenada, October 25, 1983," *Politico*, October 25, 2017, https://www.politico.com/story/2017/10/25/united-states-invades-grenada-oct-25-1983-244072.

2. "Hurricane Hugo," https://en.wikipedia.org/wiki/Hurricane_Hugo.

3. Chris Patten went on to have a distinguished career in the British Foreign Service. His final assignment was serving as Hong Kong's last British governor, and in 1997 he managed the return of the island to Chinese sovereignty, ending more than 150 years of British colonial rule.

Chapter 10. A New Opportunity at USAID Headquarters

1. These included Alfredo Cristiani of El Salvador, Rafael Leonardo Callejas of Honduras, Rafael Angel Calderon of Costa Rica, and Violeta Chamorro of Nicaragua.

2. Einar Berntzen, "Democratic Consolidation in Central America: A Qualitative Comparative Approach," *Third World Quarterly* 14.3 (1993): 589.

3. Elena M. Suárez, "The Caribbean in Economic Transition," in *Choices and Change: Reflections on the Caribbean*, ed. Winston C. Dookeran (Washington, DC: Inter-American Development Bank, 1995), 131.

4. "NAFTA's Impact on the U.S. Economy: What Are the Facts?," *Knowledge@ Wharton*, September 6, 2016, https://knowledge.wharton.upenn.edu/article/naftas -impact-u-s-economy-facts; "Caribbean Basin Initiative: Impact on Selected Coun- tries," *GAO Report to the Chariman, Subcommittee on Western Hemisphere and Peace Corps Affairs, Committee on Foreign Relations, U.S. Senate*, July 1988, https://www.gao .gov/assets/150/146640.pdf.

5. The FLMN was a leftist insurgent movement in El Salvador that became a national political party after the peace accords.

6. Steven Greenhouse, "It's a Hard Job Saving Foreign Aid (but the Job Is Still There)," *New York Times*, February 19, 1995, https://www.nytimes.com/1995/02/19/ world/it-s-a-hard-job-saving-foreign-aid-but-the-job-is-still-there.html.

7. "Engaging Customer Participation: USAID's Organizational Change Experi- ence," November 1998, http://citeseerx.ist.psu.edu/viewdoc/download?doi=10.1.1.5 75.2779&rep=rep1&type=pdf, p. 5.

8. Jessica Mathews, "The Assault on Aid," *Washington Post*, February 28, 1995, https://www.washingtonpost.com/archive/opinions/1995/02/28/the-assault-on -aid/7bf7bba9-e01d-4165-b0af-5967e89e8a61/?utm_term=.f1971c862b91.

9. Jim Hoagland, "A Tale of 2 Departures," *Chicago Tribune*, July 9, 1999, https:// www.chicagotribune.com/news/ct-xpm-1999-07-09-9907090093-story.html.

Chapter 11. Mandela Magic

1. "South Africa," CIA World Fact Book, March 15, 2021, https://www.cia.gov/ the-world-factbook/countries/south-africa/#people-and-society.

2. "Thabo Mbeki," https://en.wikipedia.org/wiki/Thabo_Mbeki.

3. Congressional Research Service, "South Africa: Current Issues, Economy, and U.S. Relations," updated September 17, 2020, https://fas.org/sgp/crs/row/R45687.pdf.

4. "Sandton Convention Centre is South Africa's leading event venue, offering prestigious multi-use event spaces and venues in the financial hub of Johannes- burg" (https://www.tsogosun.com/sandton-convention-centre-scc).

5. "Mahatma Gandhi," https://en.wikipedia.org/wiki/Mahatma_Gandhi.

6. "Hillary Clinton Arrives in South Africa," UPI Archives, March 18, 1997, https://www.upi.com/Archives/1997/03/18/Hillary-Clinton-arrives-in-South-Africa/7769858661200.

7. James A. Joseph, *Saved for a Purpose: A Journey from Private Virtues to Public Values* (Durham, NC: Duke University Press, 2015), 1–9.

8. The US cabinet members of the Gore-Mbeki Commission included William Daly (Commerce), Richard Riley (Education), Andrew Cuomo (Housing and Urban Development), Dan Glickman (Agriculture), Bruce Babbitt (Interior), Donna Shalala (Health and Human Services), Rodney Slater (Transportation), and Federico Pena (Energy).

9. Paul Lewis, "Leon Sullivan, 78, Dies; Fought Apartheid," *New York Times*, April 26, 2001, C17.

10. "Leon Sullivan—Civil Rights Leader (October 16, 1922–April 24, 2001)," *Philadelphia Citizen*, February 2016, https://thephiladelphiacitizen.org/leon-sullivan-biography.

11. Matt Schudel, "William H. Gray III, Congressman for Pa., Dies at 71," *Washington Post*, July 2, 2013.

12. R. W. Apple Jr., "Clinton's Motley Entourage Plays to Different Audiences," *New York Times*, March 27, 1998, https://archive.nytimes.com/www.nytimes.com/library/world/032798clinton-africa-tour.html.

13. Lynne Duke, "In South Africa, Clinton Confronts a Complex Success Story," *Washington Post*, March 26, 1998, https://www.washingtonpost.com/archive/politics/1998/03/26/in-south-africa-clinton-confronts-a-complex-success-story/fa2b07bd-4d36-4910-b3a4-5d4b438f9ab8.

14. Associated Press, "Two Presidents, Two Strong Commitments to Africa," *New York Times*, March 28, 1998, https://archive.nytimes.com/www.nytimes.com/library/world/032898clinton-africa-text.html.

Chapter 12. South Africa's Miracle

1. Mary Kay Magistad, "South Africa's Imperfect Progress, 20 Years after the Truth and Reconciliation Commission," *The World*, April 6, 2017, https://www.pri.org/stories/2017-04-06/south-africas-imperfect-progress-20-years-after-truth-reconciliation-commission.

2. Bill Keller, "How American 'Sister' Died in a Township," *New York Times*, August 27, 1993, https://www.nytimes.com/1993/08/27/world/how-american-sister-died-in-a-township.html.

3. Scott Kraft, "South African Killers Now Work on Behalf of Their Victim," *Los Angeles Times*, October 21, 2008, https://www.latimes.com/world/la-fg-amy21-2008oct21-story.html.

4. The African Centre for the Constructive Resolution of Disputes (ACCORD), https://www.accord.org.za/about.

5. Ibid.

Chapter 13. Recruited by the International Youth Foundation

1. "Rick Little's Quest," *Chicken Soup for the Soul*, https://www.chickensoup.com/book-story/36232/rick-littles-quest.

2. I worked closely with the following dedicated IYF board members: Jaime Ayala, Philippines, president of Ayala Corporation; Sari Baldauf, Finland, named by the *Wall Street Journal* as one of Europe's most influential female business leaders; Maria Cattaui, Switzerland, secretary general of the International Chamber of Commerce; Arnie Langbo, United States, CEO of Kellogg Corporation; Dick Schubert, United States, president of the Points of Light Foundation and former deputy secretary of labor and president of the American Red Cross; and Pär Stenbäck, Finland, former minister of education and minister of foreign affairs who had previously served as general secretary for the International Federation of the Red Cross and Red Crescent Societies.

3. Sheila Kinkade, "Nokia: Connecting Youth to Positive Futures," *YOUth*, Summer 2010, https://www.iyfnet.org/sites/default/files/library/Youth10_InGoodCompany.pdf.

4. Lucent Technologies was one of the "baby Bells" that resulted from the DOJ breakup of AT&T into seven regional phone companies in 1984 ("Lucent Technologies Supports International Youth Foundation's Education, Learning Programs with US$14.9 Million Grant," Lucent Technologies, April 19, 2000, https://www.csrwire.com/press_releases/25261-Lucent-Technologies-supports-International-Youth-Foundation-s-education-learning-programs-with-US-14-9-million-grant).

5. "The Savonlinna Opera Festival is Finland's premier cultural event. World renowned for its high-quality opera performances and concerts, every summer it brings music lovers from across the globe to the charming lakeside city of Savonlinna. The month-long festival is held in Olavinlinna, a towering medieval castle by Finland's largest lake. Savonlinna is located in southeast Finland in the heart of the Finnish Lakeland—a uniquely dramatic ambiance for its 70,000 visitors" (https://operafestival.fi/en/oopperajuhlat).

6. Kinkade, "Nokia."

7. International Youth Foundation (IYF) Nokia Education Fund, https://www.familiesoffreedom.org/subfunds; http://www.globenewswire.com/ru/news-release/2001/09/19/1845052/0/en/Nokia-Establishes-Global-Education-Fund-for-Children-of-Victims-of-Recent-U-S-Tragedies.html.

Chapter 14. Reconstructing Iraq

1. David E. Sanger with John F. Burns, "Threats and Responses: The White House; Bush Orders Start of War on Iraq; Missiles Apparently Miss Hussein," *New York Times*, March 20, 2003, https://www.nytimes.com/2003/03/20/world/threats-responses-white-house-bush-orders-start-war-iraq-missiles-apparently.html.

2. *Learning from Iraq: A Final Report from the Special Inspector General for Iraq Reconstruction*, March 2013, https://apps.dtic.mil/dtic/tr/fulltext/u2/a587236.pdf, ix.

3. Office of the Special Inspector General for Iraq Reconstruction, *Cost, Outcome, and Oversight of Local Governance Program Contracts with Research Triangle Institute*, October 2008, https://apps.dtic.mil/dtic/tr/fulltext/u2/a508655.pdf.

4. *Learning from Iraq*, 105.

5. Special Inspector General for Iraq Reconstruction, *Iraq Reconstruction: Lessons in Program and Project Management*, March 2007, https://permanent.fdlp.gov/lps86 420/Lessons_Learned_March21.pdf.

6. "Under Saddam Hussein, the Iraqi government excavated Babylonian ruins and attempted to reconstruct certain features of the ancient city, including one of Nebuchadnezzar's palaces. After the 2003 invasion of Iraq, the United States forces built a military base on the ruins of Babylon. The United Nations cultural heritage agency UNESCO reported the base caused 'major damage' to the archaeological site. The site was reopened to tourists in 2009" ("Babylonia: Babylon Today," History Channel, August 20, 2019, https://www.history.com/topics/ancient-middle-east/babylonia#section_9).

Chapter 15. The Honor of a Lifetime

1. Gayle served as a special assistant to President Clinton and senior director for African Affairs at the NSC. Earlier, she founded the sustainable security program at the Center for American Progress and cofounded the ENOUGH Project and the Modernizing Foreign Assistance Network. Subsequently, during the Obama presidency, she served as special assistant to the president and senior director for development and democracy at the NSC and continued her distinguished service in the administration as the administrator of USAID in the second term. In 2017, Smith was selected to be the new president and CEO of the One Campaign.

2. Rick Barton served as US representative to the Economic and Social Council of the United Nations and later as the first assistant secretary of the Bureau of Conflict and Stabilization Operations.

3. "President Obama Announces Intent to Nominate Aaron Williams as Director of the Peace Corps," Barack Obama, Presidential Library, https://obamawhitehouse .archives.gov/the-press-office/president-obama-announces-intent-nominate-aaron -williams-director-peace-corps.

4. Stanley Meisler, *When the World Calls: The Inside Story of the Peace Corps and Its First Fifty Years* (Boston: Beacon), 213–17.

5. "Former Senator Harris Wofford, a key architect of the Peace Corps in the days of Sarge Shriver, will introduce Aaron Williams (Dominican Republic 1967–70) to be the next Director of the Peace Corps this Wednesday afternoon in the Dirksen Senate Office Building. The Hearing will be held at 2:30 p.m. in Room 419. Senator Chris Dodd (Dominican Republic 1966–68) will preside over the Hearing" ("Harris Wofford to Introduce Aaron Williams at Senate Hearing on the Next Peace Corps Director," Peace Corps Worldwide, https://peacecorpsworldwide.org/harris-wofford -to-introduce-aaron-williams-at-senate-hearing-on-the-next-peace-corps-director).

6. Robert D. McFadden, "Harris Wofford, 92, Ex-Senator Who Pushed Volunteerism, Is Dead," *New York Times*, January 22, 2019, https://www.nytimes.com/20 19/01/22/us/politics/harris-wofford-dead.html. "Last night, we lost an American hero. On the day we celebrated the life of Martin Luther King Jr., we said goodbye to Harris Wofford. Harris was a tireless champion for national service, a patriot who

loved his country, a beloved friend and mentor to many, and a guiding light who called us to serve and lifted our sights to achieving America's promise for all" ("Official Statement from CEO Barbara Stewart," AmeriCorps, https://www.nationalservice.gov/newsroom/other-news/2019/remembering-harris-wofford).

Chapter 16. My First One Hundred Days

1. "The Peace Corps: A Comprehensive Agency Assessment (Final Report)," June 2010, https://files.peacecorps.gov/multimedia/pdf/opengov/PC_Comprehensive_Agency_Assessment.pdf. The assessment team members (see pages 30–32 of the report for bios) included Carlos Torres (team leader), Megan Blackburn, Ken Goodson, Jean Lujan, MaryAnn Minutillo (agency coordinators), and Diana Schmidt (senior adviser). The agency assessment advisory committee was chaired by the director and included Esther Benjamin (associate director for the Office of Global Operations), Suzie Carroll (deputy director of the Office of Congressional Relations), Elisa Montoya (White House liaison and senior adviser to the director), Stacy Rhodes (chief of staff), Kathy Rulon (senior adviser to the chief of staff), Carl Sosebee (general counsel), and Cathryn Thorup (director of the Office of Strategic Information, Research and Planning). The independent review panel included ambassador James Joseph (former US ambassador to South Africa) and William Lane (vice president of Government Affairs for Caterpillar Corporation).

2. Ibid.

3. John M. Broder, "Edward M. Kennedy, Senate Stalwart, Is Dead at 77," *New York Times*, August 26, 2009, https://www.nytimes.com/2009/08/27/us/politics/27kennedy.html.

4. "Eulogy for a Lion: The President's Full Remarks at Our Lady of Perpetual Help Basilica in Roxbury, Massachusetts," Barack Obama, Presidential Library, August 29, 2009, https://obamawhitehouse.archives.gov/blog/2009/08/29/eulogy-a-lion.

Chapter 17. Raising the Profile of the Peace Corps

1. These superb leaders included Gayle Smith, my transition team partner and then special assistant to the president of the United States and senior director for development and democracy at the NSC; Eric Goosby, global AIDS coordinator, President's Emergency Plan for AIDS Relief; Raj Shah, USAID administrator; Paul Weisenfeld, my former USAID colleague, now the head of USAID's global agricultural development program; and Daniel Yohannes, the CEO of the Millennium Challenge Corporation.

2. Nancy Benac, "Peace Corps Coming to Vietnam for the First Time," *San Diego Union-Tribune*, May 22, 2016, https://www.sandiegouniontribune.com/sdut-peace-corps-coming-to-vietnam-for-first-time-2016may22-story.html. "Peace Corps Director Carrie Hessler-Radelet and the Government of Viet Nam announced today a historic partnership to establish a Peace Corps program for the first time in Viet Nam. The announcement coincides with President Barack Obama's trip to Viet Nam and underscores the United States' broader commitment to supporting the people of Viet Nam through English language learning" ("Viet Nam to Welcome

Peace Corps for First Time," Peace Corps, May 23, 2016, https://www.peacecorps
.gov/news/library/viet-nam-welcome-peace-corps-first-time).

3. "History," Special Olympics, https://www.specialolympics.org/about/history.

4. "Be a Fan of Unity," 2010 Special Olympics Global Congress, Marrakech, June
6–10, 2010, http://media.specialolympics.org/soi/2010-global-congress/Official-20
10-Special-Olympics-Global-Congress-Program.PDF.

Chapter 18. Celebrating Fifty Years

1. Joseph B. Treason, "20 Years after Dominican War, Wounds Linger," *New York
Times*, May 1, 1985, https://www.nytimes.com/1985/05/01/world/20-years-after-dom
inican-war-wounds-linger.html.

2. "Senator Dodd has been a great friend to the Peace Corps, and I'm proud that
his service overseas has helped shape his legacy in Congress, said Director Williams.
Over the course of his thirty-plus years in Congress, Senator Dodd has met with hundreds of volunteers worldwide, and he has been a tremendous advocate for the Peace
Corps. He has consistently fought to increase funding and the number of volunteers who serve in the Peace Corps" ("Peace Corps Hosts Senator Dodd, a Returned
Peace Corps Volunteer," Peace Corps, September 23, 2010, https://www.peacecorps
.gov/news/library/peace-corps-hosts-senator-dodd-a-returned-peace-corps-volun
teer/?_ga=2.180994215.1645312339.1597093003-1433084661.1596389767).

3. Ghana was known as the Gold Coast due to the gold trade. It was also the site
of the infamous Cape Coast Castle, one of about forty "slave castles," or large commercial forts, built on the Gold Coast of West Africa by European traders. "In Cape
Coast Castle, the underground dungeon was a space of terror, death, and blackness.
This stood as a direct juxtaposition to the European living quarters and command-
ing heights of whiteness above, who lived relatively luxuriously. The basement of
this imposing fortress often was the last memory slaves had of their homeland
before being shipped off across the Atlantic, as this signified the beginning of their
journey" ("Cape Coast Castle," https://en.wikipedia.org/wiki/Cape_Coast_Castle).

4. "Nyerere was a controversial figure. Across Africa, he gained widespread respect
as an anti-colonialist and, in power, received praise for ensuring that, unlike many
of its neighbors, Tanzania remained stable and unified in the decades following
independence. His construction of the one-party state and use of detention without
trial led to accusations of dictatorial governance, while he has also been blamed for
economic mismanagement. Held in deep respect within Tanzania, he is often referred to by the Swahili honorific *Mwalimu* ('teacher') and described as the 'Father
of the Nation'" ("Julius Nyerere," https://en.wikipedia.org/wiki/Julius_Nyerere).

5. Benigno "Ninoy" Aquino Jr., a former Filipino senator, was assassinated on
August 21, 1983, at the Manila International Airport. "A longtime political opponent
of President Ferdinand Marcos, Aquino had just landed in his home country after
three years of self-imposed exile in the United States when he was shot in the head
while being escorted from an aircraft to a vehicle that was waiting to transport him
to prison. . . . Aquino's assassination is credited with transforming the opposition
to the Marcos regime from a small, isolated movement into a national crusade."

("Assassination of Benigno Aquino Jr.," https://en.wikipedia.org/wiki/Assassination
_of_Benigno_Aquino_Jr).

6. "President Obama Announces Presidential Delegation to Asuncion, Paraguay
for the Celebration of the Bicentennial of the Independence of the Republic of Paraguay," Barack Obama Presidential Library, May 10, 2011, https://obamawhitehouse
.archives.gov/the-press-office/2011/05/10/president-obama-announces-presidential
-delegation-asuncion-paraguay-cele.

Chapter 19. The Impact and Contribution of the Peace Corps

1. Sargent Shriver, "Speech at the Vigil for the 40th Anniversary of the Peace
Corps," Washington, DC, September 22, 2001, http://www.sargentshriver.org/
speech-article/speech-at-the-vigil-for-the-40th-anniversary-of-the-peace-corps.

2. Some of the universities and colleges that honored the Peace Corps by cele-
brating their historical and present-day roles included American University, the
University of Colorado, Columbia, George Washington University, the University
of Florida, Harvard, Howard, Indiana, Michigan State, the University of Michigan,
Monterey Institute of International Studies, New York University, the University of
North Carolina, North Central College, Ohio State, Stanford, the State University of
New York system (SUNY), UCLA, the University of Washington, and the University
of Wisconsin.

3. I received honorary doctorates from American University, Durham Technical
Community College, the Monterey Institute of International Studies, North Central
College, and St. Mary's College as well as the UCLA Medal, awarded for exception-
ally distinguished academic and professional achievement.

4. "Senator Kennedy's motorcade rolled into Ann Arbor very early on the morning of Friday, October 14, 1960. The election was three and a half weeks away. The
Democratic nominee for president and his staff had just flown into Willow Run
Airport. A few hours earlier, in New York, Kennedy had fought Vice President Nixon,
the Republican nominee, in the third of their four nationally televised debates. The
race was extremely close, and Michigan was up for grabs. Kennedy's schedule called
for a few hours of sleep, then a one-day whistle-stop train tour across the state"
(James Tobin, "JFK at the Union: The Impromptu Campaign Speech That Launched
the Peace Corps," National Peace Corps Association, https://www.peacecorpscon
nect.org/articles/jfk-at-the-union-the-impromptu-campaign-speech-that-launched
-the-peace-corps).

5. "Fifty years ago, then-Senator John F. Kennedy gave a historic campaign speech
at the University of Michigan, which led to the creation of the Peace Corps. Today,
Peace Corps Director Aaron S. Williams joined the University of Michigan President Mary Sue Coleman in Ann Arbor to commemorate the momentous event"
("Peace Corps Director Visits Michigan: Commemorates 50th Anniversary of JFK's
Speech That Inspired the Peace Corps," Peace Corps, October 14, 2010, https://
www.peacecorps.gov/news/library/peace-corps-director-visits-michigan-commem
orates-50th-anniversary-of-jfks-speech-that-inspired-the-peace-corps).

6. The following excerpt from the UCLA Newsroom provides a snapshot of that very warm and heartfelt event: "The event commemorated UCLA's longstanding collaboration with the Peace Corps. More than 1,800 UCLA alumni have served in the Peace Corps, including ninety-two volunteers currently serving in forty-six countries. Many of the former volunteers were in the audience, which also included Maria Shriver [then the First Lady of California] and Bobby Shriver, two of the children of Peace Corps founding director Robert Sargent Shriver" (Judy Lin, "Peace Corps' 50th Anniversary Celebration Ranges from Heartfelt to Humorous," UCLA Newsroom, March 3, 2011, http://newsroom.ucla.edu/stories/peace-corps-panel-193 241).

7. "Peace Corps Chief of Staff Speaks at Duke University," Peace Corps, June 13, 2011, https://www.peacecorps.gov/news/library/peace-corps-director-delivers-com mencement-address-at-ucla-and-monterey-institute-of-international-studies.

8. "Peace Corps Director Williams Delivers Commencement Address at North Central College in Illinois," Peace Corps, June 11, 2012, https://www.peacecorps.gov/news/library/peace-corps-director-williams-delivers-commencement-address-at -north-central-college-in-illinois.

9. "Peace Corps Leaders Honored with Kennedy Service Awards," Peace Corps, March 5, 2011, https://www.peacecorps.gov/news/library/peace-corps-leaders-hon ored-with-kennedy-service-awards. The recipients in 2011 for the Peace Corps volunteers category were Robert Ferguson (Mexico) and Chris Fontanesi (Romania, 2007). The recipients for the Peace Corps staff category were Frances Asturias (Guatemala and HQ, 1968) and Mostafa Lamqaddam (Morocco). The recipients for the returned Peace Corps volunteers category were Kathryn Davies Clark (Sierra Leone, 1968–69, Jamaica, 1984–87) and Joe Carroll Jaycox (Venezuela, 1962–64).

10. https://www.peacecorps.gov/about/history/awards.

11. "Peace Corps' Fiftieth Anniversary Global Calendar," https://peacecorps2010 .sched.com.

12. "National Museum of American History Receives Peace Corps Objects— Smithsonian Focuses on Volunteers during the Peace Corps' Fiftieth Anniversary," Smithsonian Institution, September 20, 2011, https://americanhistory.si.edu/press/ releases/national-museum-american-history-receives-peace-corps-objects.

13. Stacy Rhodes, interviewed by John Pielemeier, December 7, 2016, Association for Diplomatic Studies and Training, Foreign Affairs Oral History Project, Foreign Assistance Series, https://adst.org/wp-content/uploads/2013/12/Rhodes-Wil liam-Stacy-1.pdf.

14. Robert D. McFadden, "R. Sargent Shriver, Peace Corps Leader, Dies at 95," New York Times, January 18, 2011, https://archive.nytimes.com/www.nytimes.com/ 2011/01/19/us/politics/19shriver.html.

15. Kevin Dolak and Bill McGuire, "Sargent Shriver Remembered Fondly at Funeral," ABC News, January 22, 2011, https://abcnews.go.com/US/sargent-shriver -remebered-fondly-funeral-service/story?id=12738791.

16. "Mark Shriver Speaks about His Father at the Peace Corps," Peace Corps Worldwide, January 24, 2012, https://peacecorpsworldwide.org/mark-2/.

17. "50th Anniversary Event at Arlington National Cemetery—Peace Corps," https://www.youtube.com/watch?v=cMpCAV4ieUI.

Chapter 20. My Peace Corps Legacy

1. Stacy Rhodes, interviewed by John Pielemeier, December 7, 2016, Association for Diplomatic Studies and Training, Foreign Affairs Oral History Project, Foreign Assistance Series, https://adst.org/wp-content/uploads/2013/12/Rhodes-William -Stacy-1.pdf.

2. Sheryl Gay Stolberg, "Congress Urged to Increase Oversight of Peace Corps," *New York Times*, May 11, 2011, https://www.nytimes.com/2011/05/12/us/politics/12 corps.html.

3. "Ranking Member Howard L. Berman's Statement at Full Committee Mark-up of H.R. 2337 and H.R. 2699," US House of Representatives, Committee on Foreign Affairs, September 21, 2011, https://foreignaffairs.house.gov/2011/9/ranking-mem ber-howard-l-berman-s-statement-full-committee-mark-hr-2337-and-hr.

4. "Progress in Implementation of the Kate Puzey Peace Corps Volunteer Protection Act of 2011," November 2012, https://files.peacecorps.gov/multimedia/pdf/ media/Progress_on_Implementation_of_Kate_Puzey_Act_Nov_2012.pdf?_ga=2.19 728124.594970598.1597286603–1433084661.1596389767.

5. "Fact Sheet: The President's Framework for Investing in Tunisia," Barack Obama, Presidential Library, October 7, 2011, https://obamawhitehouse.archives.gov/ the-press-office/2011/10/07/fact-sheet-presidents-framework-investing-tunisia.

6. "North Africa American Cemetery," American Battle Monuments Commission, https://www.abmc.gov/North-Africa.

7. https://seedglobalhealth.org/about/#.YKW7GqhKg2w.

8. "In Honor of Peace Corps Director Aaron Williams (Extensions of Remarks— September 13, 2012)," *Congressional Record*, vol. 158, no. 123, https://www.congress .gov/congressional-record/2012/9/13/extensions-of-remarks-section/article/e1522 -3?q=%7B%22search%22%3A%5B%22Aaron+Williams%22%5D%7D&s=10&r=324.

Epilogue

1. "Statement by the President on the Resignation of Peace Corps Director Aaron S. Williams," Barack Obama, Presidential Library, August 21, 212, https:// obamawhitehouse.archives.gov/the-press-office/2012/08/21/statement-president -resignation-peace-corps-director-aaron-s-williams.

2. "Aaron Williams Interviewed by Julian Bond: Explorations in Black Leadership Series," August 5, 2013, https://www.youtube.com/watch?v=eIEu23acfwM.

3. Jenny Lei Ravelo, "Aaron Williams Ends Peace Corps Journey," Devex, August 22, 2012, https://www.devex.com/news/aaron-williams-ends-peace-corps-journey-78 969/amp.